The Norwegian Merchant Fleet in the Second World War

The Norwegian Merchant Fleet in the Second World War

Kenneth L Privratsky

Pen & Sword
MARITIME

First published in Great Britain in 2023 by
Pen & Sword Maritime
An imprint of Pen & Sword Books Limited
Yorkshire – Philadelphia

Copyright © Kenneth L Privratsky 2023

ISBN 978 1 39904 386 1

The right of Kenneth L Privratsky to be identified as
Author of this Work has been asserted by him in accordance
with the Copyright, Designs and Patents Act 1988.

A CIP catalogue record for this book is
available from the British Library

All rights reserved. No part of this book may be reproduced or
transmitted in any form or by any means, electronic or mechanical
including photocopying, recording or by any information storage and
retrieval system, without permission from the Publisher in writing.

Typeset by Mac Style
Printed in the UK by CPI Group (UK) Ltd, Croydon, CR0 4YY.

Pen & Sword Books Limited incorporates the imprints of After
the Battle, Atlas, Archaeology, Aviation, Discovery, Family History,
Fiction, History, Maritime, Military, Military Classics, Politics,
Select, Transport, True Crime, Air World, Frontline Publishing, Leo
Cooper, Remember When, Seaforth Publishing, The Praetorian Press,
Wharncliffe Local History, Wharncliffe Transport, Wharncliffe True
Crime and White Owl.

For a complete list of Pen & Sword titles please contact

PEN & SWORD BOOKS LIMITED
47 Church Street, Barnsley, South Yorkshire, S70 2AS, England
E-mail: enquiries@pen-and-sword.co.uk
Website: www.pen-and-sword.co.uk
or
PEN AND SWORD BOOKS
1950 Lawrence Rd, Havertown, PA 19083, USA
E-mail: Uspen-and-sword@casematepublishers.com
Website: www.penandswordbooks.com

For

Lucile Margaret Rodley
Hilde Rakstang and Jan George Fiske
Mette and Anton Monge
Terje and Astrid Rakstang
Dag and Else-Marie Asprong

And in memory of those in
The Norwegian Shipping and Trade Mission

Contents

Preface		viii
Acknowledgements		xi
Chapter 1	Norway Emerges as a Giant in Shipping	1
Chapter 2	Norway Becomes a Battleground	17
Chapter 3	A National Fleet Develops as Norway Falls	37
Chapter 4	Nortraship Starts Operating in London	58
Chapter 5	A Shipping Crisis Develops for Britain	74
Chapter 6	Nortraship Expands to New York as the Crisis Deepens	87
Chapter 7	Britain Looks for More Help as Nortraship Priorities Differ	104
Chapter 8	Global War Leads to Cooperation and More Ships	122
Chapter 9	The War Ends but Nortraship's Work Continues	139
Chapter 10	The Struggle of Seafarers Tarnishes the Legacy of Nortraship	156
Appendix I: Nortraship Fleet from April 1940 to May 1945		174
Appendix II: Translation of the Provisional Royal Decree issued by King Haakon on 22 April 1940		175
Appendix III: Translation of the Royal Decree issued by King Haakon on 18 May 1940		176
Appendix IV: Evolution of Departments within Nortraship Offices During the War		179
Image Credits		180
Notes		183
Bibliography		190
Index		193

Preface

Norwegian heritage goes back eight centuries in my family. My mother was very proud to be one hundred per cent Norwegian, born of immigrant parents arriving in America in the early 1900s from Kristiansund. She raised me to share her pride. I thought I should mention this disclaimer at the start, because the Ukrainian roots of my paternal surname mask that part of my background! I take pride indeed in being half Norwegian and was especially honoured when, in early 2016, one of my cousins there invited me to participate in National Day festivities in Kristiansund on 17 May. That is the day each year when Norwegians celebrate the signing of their country's constitution in 1814. Specifically, I was asked to march in a parade with him and others that morning, to provide remarks when the parade concluded at a memorial for fallen seafarers, and then to lay a wreath in their memory. That experience eventually became the genesis of this book.

I thought I knew quite a lot about the history of Norway and its sagas of the sea extending back to the time of the Vikings. My many years in the military and study of warfare left me feeling confident that I had gained a pretty good understanding of the Second World War as well, including Germany's invasion of Norway in 1940 and the eventual bombing of Kristiansund. As I researched my remarks for that day, however, I came to discover how much I did not know about the invasion and especially the significant support that Norway provided the Allies with during the war despite losing their country to the Germans. I searched for books about Norway's seafarers in preparation for my remarks. The only one in English I found was by Nora Slocum, published in 1969 and entitled *Saga of the Sea: Norway's Merchant Marine in World War II*. That seemed especially relevant, and I bought a used copy on the internet. I discovered it was a translation with two sources: a book by Lisa Lindbaek entitled *Tusen Norske Skip* ('A Thousand Norwegian Ships') published in 1943, and a manuscript of her other material. Lindbaek, a Norwegian, had been travelling by ship to the United States in the early 1940s when she became stranded in Africa for some unknown reason. While there, she encountered Norwegian seafarers who had been interned. When she eventually reached the States she gained employment as a reporter for the Norwegian-language paper *Nordisk Tidende* in Brooklyn and in that position met other seamen. From her conversations with them Lindbaek compiled notes which later formed the chapters of her book. She referred to it as an anthology of their stories from the seven seas. The gentleman in New York who wrote the foreword for her book was Øivind Lorentzen, the Director of Shipping in the United States for Nortraship, a Norwegian Government organization established in London in the same month that Germany invaded Norway. It managed the largest merchant fleet the world had ever seen. King Haakon VII, as he and others in the Government were fleeing across central Norway from the Germans, personally appointed Lorentzen to head the organization. It proved to be a controversial choice. I had never heard of him or the so-called Nortraship organization he led.

What would compel a woman like Lindbaek to publish a book like this at the height of the war? The answer, I think, is simple. She grasped the enormous contributions that Norwegian shipping and seamen were making at the time. She probably knew what most of us still do not realize, that the small country of Norway, then occupied by the Germans, had become key to the Allied war effort. She wrote as Britain was struggling to protect its ships from German submarines and its homeland from bombers. Ship losses had caused imports to plummet, leading to more and more severe rationing. Her book came out a year after the United States entered the war, as its shipyards were beginning to make up for the losses at sea. Simply put, the merchant fleet from Norway had been helping to keep the Allies in the war until then. Lindbaek saw that. Norway possessed the fourth largest fleet in the world on the eve of the Second World War, and its ships were by far the most modern. A thousand Norwegian ships eventually supported the Allies, starting in 1939 and continuing past the end of the war. There would have been many more had Germany not captured them in Norway. Hundreds of Norwegian ships would sink, and thousands of seamen and women would lose their lives.

I spoke to these losses at the Seafarers' Memorial in Kristiansund before laying a wreath at the monument in their memory. I told the audience that morning that the Battle of Britain could have had a quite different outcome had it not been for those ships and their crews. It is hard to think otherwise. After all, at that time Norwegian tankers were hauling close to half the oil Britain needed. There would have been considerably less fuel for the Spitfires to burn without the support of those tankers in the year leading up to that fight. The British people would have faced even stricter rationing without the cargo on other Norwegian ships too. President Roosevelt, Prime Minister Churchill and officials on both sides of the Atlantic recognized the value of this help. What surprised me that morning in Kristiansund, however, was discovering how little even the Norwegians around me knew of their country's enormous contribution to the Allied victory. Since then, I have found from many other conversations that those of us outside of Norway know even less.

I would like to think my book helps complete the story Lindbaek and others started. Although much has been written about Germany's invasion of Norway and even about merchant shipping in the Second World War, there remains very little published in English about the contribution of Norway's ships and the organization called The Norwegian Shipping and Trade Mission, nicknamed Nortraship, that was formed to manage them. My intent in *Norway's Merchant Fleet in the Second World War* is to share this little-known story so that it does not simply fade away. I try my best to tell it in the context of the war itself. What happened is not without controversy. Some have accused Norwegian shipowners of profiteering during the wars of the twentieth century. There is certainly a basis for such opinions. There can be little doubt, though, that those aboard Norwegian ships remained far removed from any profits made. Norwegian seafarers who survived those perilous years at sea returned home to confront a war of a different nature. That part of the saga might come as a surprise to readers and reminds us all of what can happen when war heroes eventually come home.

Kenneth L. Privratsky
Major General, US Army (Retired)

Acknowledgements

This book would not have been possible without the help of others. Ten years after the end of the Second World War, a Norwegian named Kaare Petersen wrote a book entitled *The Saga of Norwegian Shipping: An Outline of the History, Growth, and Development of a Modern Merchant Marine*, which is available in English and includes chapters on the First and Second World Wars. Nearly forty years later, another book appeared in English edited by Bård Kollveit and entitled *Trade Winds: A History of Norwegian Shipping*. It also included discussion of the involvement of Norway's ships in the wars. Both were very helpful to my research. Without question, the most valuable sources for me were written in Norwegian. The first was Jon Rustung Hegland's two-volume history of his country's shipping during the war entitled *Nortraships Flåte*, published in 1976. It provides details of all ship activity and losses during that war, as well as information on the formation of Nortraship. The second came two decades later in a five-volume study titled *Handelsflåten I Krig 1939–1945*, with books by Atle Thowsen, Bjørn L. Basberg, Guri Hjeltnes and Lauritz Pettersen. These provide an abundance of detail on the formation and inner workings of Nortraship and controversies surrounding the organization, during and after the war, Norway's fleet captured by Germany, and the effects on seamen and their families. These substantive histories have not been translated from Norwegian unfortunately. Therefore, the rest of the world cannot appreciate the full magnitude of what happened. I owe much gratitude to the authors of these sources, which I use extensively in some chapters that follow.

Images used come from a variety of sources. I am particularly indebted to digital collections established by National Archives of Norway and Wikimedia Commons. Use of many images is governed by Creative Commons licences. I have provided an alphanumeric reference for each image in the plate section, and full attributions appear towards the end of the book.

I owe special thanks to my cousin Hilde Rakstang, who located and communicated with Jan Lorentzen, the grandson of Øivind Lorentzen, in Norway. Jan granted me permission to use photographs of his grandfather in this book, and I remain grateful to him.

This book would not be possible without the consideration and assistance of commissioning editor Henry Wilson, a good friend of mine. I appreciate everything he and others at Pen & Sword have done to make publication possible.

Finally, I would like to thank my daughters, Erika and Kylie, and my wife, Kathy, for their support throughout this project. Erika took time out from her busy schedule to develop the maps for this book. Kathy helped me unfailingly, from beginning to end, locating pictures, researching answers to questions, proofreading, and especially tolerating my crankiness for many weeks as I laboured to translate Norwegian! This book is as much hers as mine.

Few books are free of errors, and I expect this one will be no exception. Any mistakes of fact, translation or interpretation are mine alone.

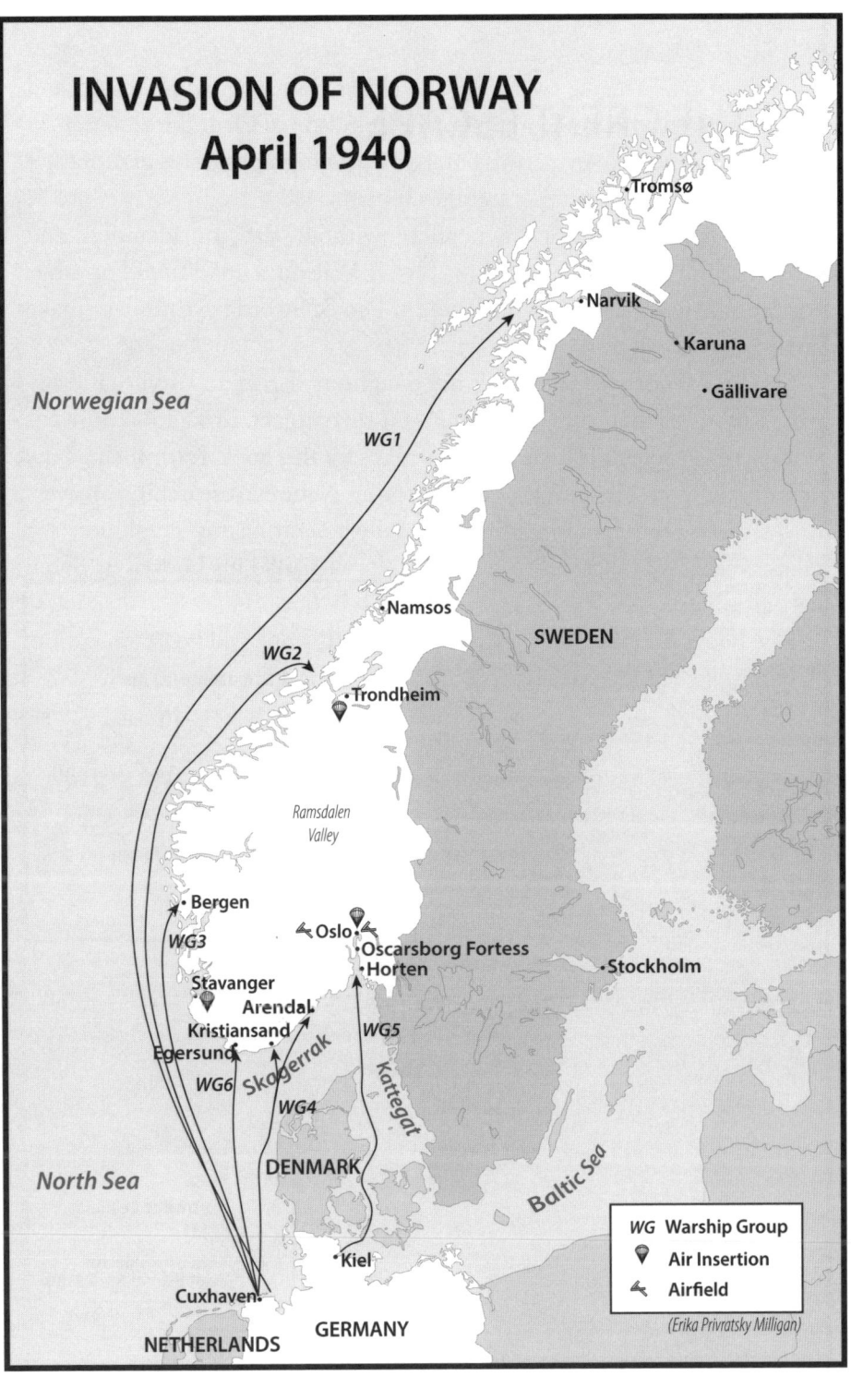

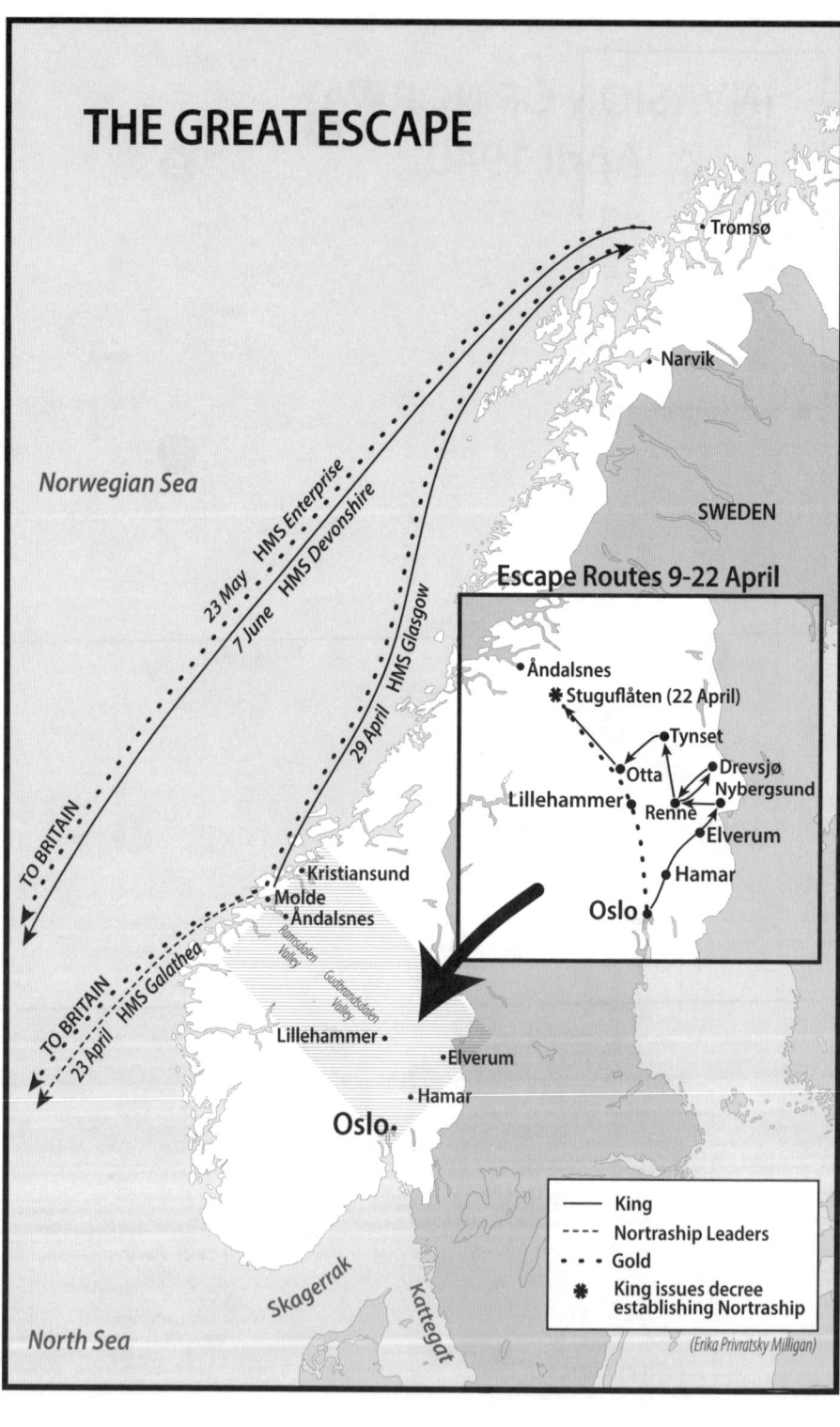

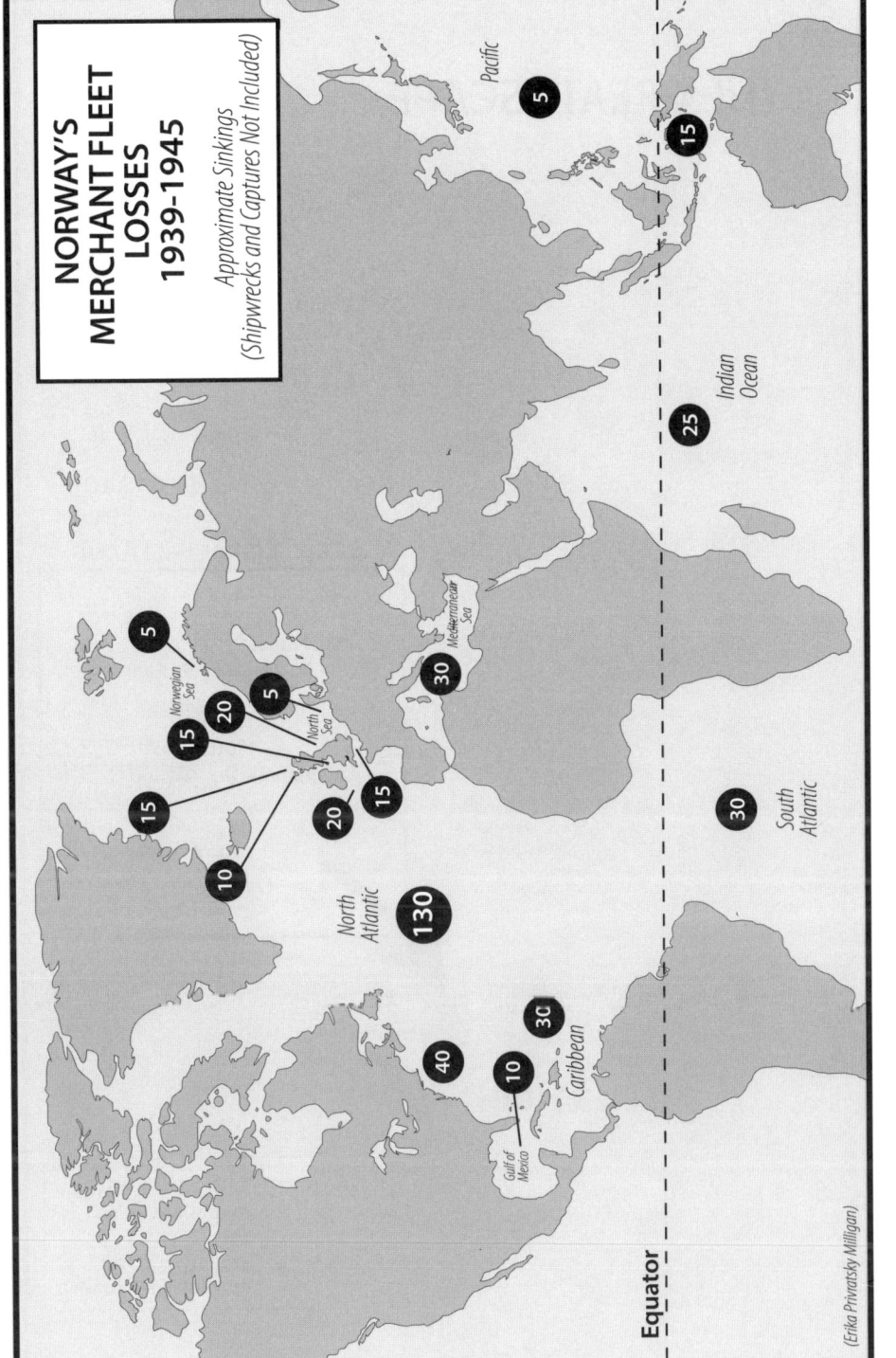

Chapter 1

Norway Emerges as a Giant in Shipping

Seafarers aboard the merchant ship *Ringulv* welcomed the clear skies on the morning of 9 April 1940 as they stood on deck and caught their first glimpses of the Norwegian coastline. Most had been at sea for nearly a year. This recent voyage had started in New York two months earlier. After a brief stop in Canada, they had joined a large convoy crossing the Atlantic with supplies for France and Britain. Army trucks lined the upper deck. A slow, coal-burning steamship, the *Ringulv* had often struggled to keep pace with other ships during rough weather, and when a gale struck during the crossing, she had fallen out of the convoy. It had been particularly frightful for the crew as they steamed onward alone in waters hiding German U-boats. Thankfully, their ship had arrived safely in Le Havre, where she unloaded cargo, and then continued to Swansea to take on Welsh coal for Norway. This would be the last leg of the voyage before the ship returned to New York. Many of the crew were looking forward to seeing families again, if only for a few hours, and sharing gifts purchased in foreign ports. Spirits soared as the coastline neared. Suddenly, without any warning to those on deck, the ship's captain reversed course and took the ship to full power, dashing all hopes of happy homecomings. Those aboard later learned to their dismay that the *Ringulv* was returning to Britain because Germany was in the process of invading Norway. The worst was yet to come for the captain and crew. Days later, with their ship docked in Scotland, they repainted the *Ringulv* and installed an anti-magnetic cable around her hull to protect against magnetic mines. Then they set sail for France with the coal originally intended for Norway. A month later, off the French coast, the Germans boarded the *Ringulv* and took possession of her. They would add the Norwegian merchant ship to their own fleet, and all her crew ended up in concentration camps in Morocco.[1]

Thousands of other Norwegians sailing on ships around the world that day in April would discover to their dismay that Germany had just invaded their homeland. It came as a surprise not only to them but to the entire world. The fate of the *Ringulv* and her crew would be repeated dozens of times in the following months as the invaders tried to gain control of other Norwegian ships. Many would suffer even worse fates. It probably did not register on crews at the time that they would be out of contact with loved ones for the next five years, or that their ships would become the objects of a protracted tug-of-war, first between Britain and Germany and later between Britain and its closest ally, the United States. They certainly did not realize that Norwegian ships like their own would become the backbone strengthening the chances of an Allied victory in the Second World War. Thousands of them, unfortunately, would perish at sea long before the fighting stopped. The story of why the Norwegian ships had become so important was centuries in the making.

Norway owns a long history as a seafaring nation. The geography of the country almost guarantees that most Norwegians would develop an attraction for the sea, since it captivates so much of the landscape. Over 60,000 miles of rugged coastline weave from the Skagerrak Sea in the south, up Norway's western side bordering the North Sea and the Norwegian Sea, past the Arctic Circle to the Arctic Ocean. Archeologists have discovered carvings and artefacts proving that even the first inhabitants of this land relied on the sea for survival. Fascinating sagas tell of Vikings leaving these shores a millennium ago to pillage villages in Britain, around Europe, into Russia and across the Atlantic to North America. Those stories surely inspired their descendants not to fear the sea but to see it as a source of adventure and livelihood. High mountains, steep cliffs and thick forests constrained inland settlement and made living near the sea attractive because it offered a plentiful supply of food. Hundreds of fishing villages eventually dotted the coastline. Some morphed into ports and shipyards, which could rely on abundant timber for shipbuilding from thickly forested mountains nearby, especially after sawmills made timber work easier. Trade into and out of those ports became essential for day-to-day existence, since the short growing season of the north limited what and how much farmers could bring to markets. The sea simply became necessary for survival for many years. At the start of the nineteenth century, it probably would have been difficult to find a Norwegian who knew nothing of the sea. Many had taken to the sea to earn a living.

Long after the years when Vikings sailed the oceans, Norway had developed the reputation of a good trading partner and an excellent provider of ocean-going transport. Trade was carried by ships with sails, and Norwegian captains mastered many of them. They and their crews were renowned as being among the best. Norway's population numbered about a million at the turn of the nineteenth century. Trade across the North Sea to Britain and south to other countries in Europe was becoming a major contributor to the gross national product of the small Scandinavian country, along with fishing, timber and agriculture. The Napoleonic wars of the late eighteenth and early nineteenth century left many economies in ruin. Embargoes at sea during the wars had reduced imports and exports, affecting production, reducing revenues and eventually causing many businesses, merchants and shipowners to go bankrupt. All nations suffered as an international recession set in. The wars left even more lasting marks on Norway, however. At the time, the Kingdoms of Denmark and Norway were united under King Frederick II, who had supported Napoleon. When the fighting finally ended with Napoleon's defeat in 1815, Norway found itself recovering under the rule of Sweden, the King of Denmark having been forced to cede his lands to his Scandinavian neighbour. It was not a good development. Over the next ninety years, Norway would re-establish itself as a giant in ocean shipping, but it would do so without independence.

At the end of the Napoleonic Wars, ships sailing the world continued to be driven by the winds. Some were small, with just a mast or two for trading in coastal waters. Others were much larger, with three or more masts for faster oceanic travel, some known as 'clipper ships' because they could 'clip' time from voyages with speeds of 14 to 18 knots. It was not until twenty years later that the first steam-powered vessels appeared in ocean-going fleets. Norway was not in a strong position to invest in this new development, which rendered ships faster and no longer reliant on the wind. Norwegian shipping companies were small, generally possessing just a few ships, sometimes founded by families, neighbours or friends coming together with a little money to invest. It was quite common for a company to possess just a single ship. Often owners were just the captain and his wife, one to sail the ship and find cargo and the other to keep the books. Captains hired a crew and navigated their vessels from port to port, depending on the winds, to solicit cargo until their holds were full. They exercised complete control over schedules, destinations and cargo. This was the common practice of shipping at the time, not just for Norwegian companies. It became known as 'tramp trade' and ships took on the nickname of 'tramps' because they travelled from place to place without regular schedules. Norway's comparatively smaller ships remained especially suited to such business.

Destinations for Norwegian ships in the first part of the nineteenth century remained restricted to the British Isles and the European continent. Navigation laws over the years prevented countries like Norway from participating in other markets further away. Some governments started loosening protection in the 1820s and 30s, and thereafter Norwegian tramps extended their trading routes into other hemispheres, depending on weather and winds. The large trading opportunities with the British Empire remained closed until Queen Victoria opened these markets to foreign competition when she signed the repeal of the Navigation Act in 1849. Norway then became one of the countries trading to and from the dozens of British colonies. As such protectionist barriers kept falling, more and more countries began participating in global trade. Norwegian ships soon were carrying the country's main exports of fish and timber around Cape Horn and the Cape of Good Hope into completely new markets and returning with a wide range of new imports for their countrymen to enjoy.

Norwegian shipyards were also small at this time, specializing in using the country's abundant timber resources to build wooden ships. Steamships were not only much more expensive; they required materials like iron or steel, both of which Norway lacked, as well as bigger shipyards.[2] These new ships became larger than ships with sails because of the added space needed for their sizeable power plants and additional crew. They also required significant amounts of coal to fire the boilers that propelled the ships, a source of energy that Norway had to import in large quantities just for its homes and businesses. Sailing ships were much cheaper to operate because the wind provided a free source of power; however, contrary winds could also restrict both speed and direction. Thus, with their limited financial resources and less access to government funds, Norwegian shipowners kept increasing their fleets by adding more sailing ships, many of which were older and purchased from Sweden.[3] As the years went by, iron and steel replaced wood in the hulls of some of these ships.

The middle of the century brought other new opportunities for small countries with shipping capabilities. The Crimean War pushed the warring nations to their limits because of the long supply lines into areas where few ports existed. They looked to neutral countries like Norway to help move what they needed, and they paid shippers well. Norwegian shipowners diverted ships from trade elsewhere to take advantage of the lucrative opportunities to haul war cargo, and in the process they continued to expand their fleets with more sailing ships, most of them acquired second-hand from countries investing in the newer steamships. When gold was discovered in the United States, many Europeans caught the gold fever, and Norwegian ships commenced sailing around Cape Horn to take advantage of the gold rush. Then interest in travel abroad spurred the development of ships designed specifically for transporting passengers to distant places. Shipowners sought those opportunities as well. By 1870, Norway's population was approaching two million, double what it had been at the start of the century, and the country's fleet had grown to be the third largest in the world. Several thousand ships were registered to fly the Norwegian flag, and shipping had grown to be the primary source of revenue for the small country. For the first time in its history, many in Norway were prospering, but the prosperity was to be short-lived.[4]

In 1873, shortage of money, speculative investments and cost overruns in high capital projects in Europe and North America led to stock markets crashing. People rushed to withdraw their savings. Banks closed, and numerous bankruptcies followed. A depression persisted for over a decade, pushing millions of workers worldwide out of work. Over the next three decades, hundreds of thousands of Norwegians fled their homeland seeking opportunities elsewhere, mostly in the United States. In Norway, where shipping had grown to be the country's primary source of revenue, shipowners suffered like others as trading opportunities vanished. When conditions eventually improved, they found themselves in no position to invest in the new steam-turbine technology that had inspired investment prior to the depression.

Other countries, especially Great Britain, where industrialization had produced huge advances, had begun by this time to invest hugely in the new steamships. It was not until the end of the century that steamship construction and purchases picked up in Norway. In the 1890s, Norway ranked sixth among all nations in the world in the construction of steamships. In terms of actual tonnage in global trade, that amounted to a mere 2 per cent. The mainstay of steamship building remained Britain; by the end of the nineteenth century its shipyards were building 74 per cent of all steamships sailing the oceans.[5] The British merchant fleet was by far the largest in the world and would remain so for many years.

The overall nature of shipping changed in the latter half of the century as well, and although Norway began to adapt, it did so much more slowly than other countries. The first change had to do with markets. Coal-fired steam engines made ships faster, and because they were no longer dependent on wind their passages became more reliable. Customers learned to like the predictable arrival and departure times of these new ships. It enabled them to order products and plan deliveries to or from ports better. In the years ahead, the potential for regularity in ocean shipping would produce a new service called 'liner trade', whereby shipowners would enter into agreements to provide scheduled deliveries. It was quite different to the tramp trade that had been common for decades with Norwegian ships. Shipbuilders started constructing faster and bigger ships to accommodate the added interest in this new trade. Known as 'liners', the new ships routinely contained on-board cranes to make them self-sufficient in loading and unloading in port. Steamship owners hired networks of agents to market their services, secure cargo and help synchronize its arrival and departure; their captains no longer had to go ashore to tout for cargo to fill their holds. Norwegian shipowners, in contrast, continued to be satisfied with their cheaper, second-hand sailing vessels operating in niche tramp markets.

Another major development that had an extraordinary impact on shipping was the demand for petroleum products spurred by the second phase of the industrial revolution. For centuries, liquids had moved in small quantities in casks and barrels. The discovery of large oil fields in the Americas and later in the Middle East drove a new interest in specialized ships capable of hauling liquids in bulk quantities, measured not in gallons but in thousands of tons. The first sail-driven tankers appeared in the 1860s. Steam-powered tankers followed a decade later. As motorization took hold around the world, demand for such tanker ships would increase exponentially for years to come.

Thus, as the nineteenth century ended, shipping had changed considerably. It had become competitive and global. Steamships now were carrying two-thirds of all cargo worldwide, and 75 per cent of those ships continued to be built in British shipyards.[6] Britain remained the dominant country by far in global shipping. Its merchant ships represented half of the entire world's fleet, and over half of British vessels by this time were steamships. No country depended more on its shipping, though, than Norway. It could claim the world's fourth largest fleet, with 3,325 ships of various sizes and types. Only half of these were suitable for ocean trade, the rest being restricted to coastal shipping. Nonetheless, the ocean-going ships had penetrated markets in many places. On a per capita basis, the fleet carried a whopping 1,227 tons per Norwegian. That might not seem much until it is compared to the three nations with bigger fleets: Britain's carried 667 tons per inhabitant, Germany's 96 tons, and the United States' 63 tons.[7] Unfortunately, however, Norway's fleet was losing its lustre in the marketplace at the turn of the new century. Shippers around the world continued to regard Norwegian ship captains and crews highly, but they now saw Norwegian ships as old and outdated. Despite producing substantial revenue for shipowners and the government, the Norwegian fleet remained largely powered by the prevailing winds. Old ships with sails still monopolized a fleet that was becoming increasingly less competitive.

The big news for Norwegians as their country entered the twentieth century was the return of full independence from Sweden. The relationship between the two Scandinavian countries had been relatively good over the decades since Norway had become subordinated to its neighbour, but in 1905 Norwegian citizens voted overwhelmingly in a referendum to approve a return to the constitutional monarchy that had existed in 1814. They chose Prince Charles of Denmark to be their king. King Haakon VII, as he became named, would never forget that the people had elected him. The will of the people would guide his decision-making during his reign and become very important as the world erupted into wars.

It is also likely that the Norwegians never forgot why they had lost their independence nearly a hundred years before. After the country had found itself on the losing side in the Napoleonic Wars, Norway took no sides in other conflicts, while the country's shipping industry made a great deal of money supporting the war efforts of other nations. A quarter of a century after the end of the 'Long Depression', Norway had progressed from being a poor nation to one that was relatively prosperous, even though its wealth was not shared by all segments of society. Shipping had far outpaced the fishing, timber and agriculture industries over the years and now was responsible for half of the Norwegian economy. Just as many countries in the world had come to depend on Norway's shipping, Norwegians remained dependent on shipments to and from those countries for day-to-day living. Maintaining good relationships with other countries became essential for prosperity to continue. King Haakon and the Norwegian Government would find it much more difficult walking that neutral line when war came closer to home.

As it had for many years, Great Britain remained the dominant nation in global shipping as the twentieth century got underway. Its fleet of over 8,000 ships approaching a capacity of 50 million gross tons was much larger than fleets of other countries, and about half of those ships were suitable for crossing oceans. The British fleet still hauled almost half of all tonnage crossing the oceans anywhere, with the United States' fleet ranking a distant second, followed by Germany's. Combined, those other two fleets reached barely a third of the tonnage capacity of the British fleet.[8] Britain's requirements simply were much greater because it served colonies rooted in every continent. The British Empire spanned the globe from the South Pacific and Asia to the Middle East, Africa and North America, encompassing nearly a quarter of the world's land area with dominion over millions of people who relied on British shipping. The British Isles were totally dependent on many imports, ranging from raw materials to foods and textiles. These included all oil, rubber and cotton, and food staples like sugar, well over half its requirement for wheat, flour and cheese, and nearly half of all the meat and butter consumed in Britain.[9] In 1908, the Government had purchased the controlling share in a massive oil field discovered in the Middle East, in a company that would become known as British Petroleum a half century later. Oil had now become a vital strategic interest requiring even more of the new tanker ships.

Simply put, Britain dominated shipping at the start of the twentieth century because the Empire depended on it hauling products around the world. The sheer size of the Empire meant that ships were often not used as efficiently as possible. Nearly half of the world's fleet was flying

British flags at the time, but those ships were carrying less than a quarter of seaborne trade.[10] It was a price that Britain paid for spanning the globe. The outbreak of the Great War on 28 July 1914 just made matters worse. Many from throughout the Empire joined Britain in the fight, eventually increasing the size of the force to over five million. All would need equipping and sustaining for as long as the war lasted. Less than a year after fighting commenced, shipping requirements had accelerated so significantly that the British Government needed to take extraordinary action to meet the needs of the Empire. It requisitioned a third of the British commercial fleet for military purposes. Acquiring even more ships became imperative, especially after losses mounted at sea.

Germany found itself in a predicament as well, for different reasons. Like Britain, it had a plentiful supply of coal for ships, homes and industry, but it also relied heavily on many imports, including about half of all food calories its population consumed.[11] With a relatively short coastline, Germany's access to the oceans was much more limited than many other countries' despite its large merchant fleet. And as a result, some German ships became trapped in port early in the war as the Royal Navy established blockades. As its ability to sail the oceans safely decreased, Germany became reliant on others. At first, neutral countries like Norway could deliver products directly to German ports as they always had. Later, as embargoes set in, neutral countries like the Netherlands and Denmark, which shared borders with Germany, would discharge cargo at home ports and send them onward overland to Germany.

Norway thus became a crucial partner for two of the primary adversaries at the start of the First World War, but not without problems or controversy. It found itself in a difficult situation. Although Norway mobilized its military, the Norwegian armed forces were small and ill-prepared. They had not fired a shot in anger since the Napoleonic Wars. Norway had no choice other than to remain neutral if it wanted to maintain its shipping industry, the country's economy and the livelihood of its citizens. King Haakon and his counterparts in Denmark and Sweden tried to reinforce their neutrality to the world in a meeting at Malmö, on the southern coast of Sweden, in December 1914.[12] The three Scandinavian countries nonetheless remained caught in the middle of key trading partners.

When two of the biggest fleets in the world became consumed or restricted by the war, neutral countries like Norway stood to benefit. Britain and Germany soon were clamouring for shipping help. Both needed raw materials for their war industries. Norway was a major exporter of pyrite, nicknamed 'fool's gold' because of its lustre and pale, brass-yellow hue. It was used to make sulphuric acid, a key ingredient in the manufacture of explosives. Trade with Britain accounted for 25 per cent of both Norway's exports and imports, and Germany was a large partner as well. Norwegian fish was important to both countries, with Germany alone importing about a million barrels of cured herring annually.[13] The United States remained neutral for the first years of the war and retained the biggest fleet among other neutral countries; however, the thousands of miles separating it from the fighting helped ensure that Norway's role on the world stage would grow once the fighting began. The first diesel-powered ships had appeared in 1904 and although they were becoming popular, less than 10 per cent of Norway's ships were powered by diesel a decade later; many of its ships remained more suited for coastal rather than ocean shipping. Norway's fleet consisted largely of coal-fired steamships and older, much slower sailing ships. The age and speed of ships, however, no longer restricted demand. Ships, regardless of how they were powered, were at a premium, and shipping rates soared.

After war broke out, all shipping countries faced another dilemma. Insurance rates rose to crippling levels because of war risks. Shipowners baulked at sailing into harm's way, yet they could hardly leave their ships idle because they had bills to pay. Ship captains could not risk the safety of their ships and cargo without the protection of insurance, but private insurance companies either refused to offer cover, or restricted cover and demanded much higher premiums. Eventually, the Norwegian Government itself had to step in and pass legislation to mandate insurance to keep its fleet sailing, the cost of which shipping companies inherited. All of this tended to push demand for even higher rates.

Neutral countries continued trying to cooperate with the belligerents as best they could, but neutrality proved an uneven pier for shippers to walk. The Norwegian Government recognized that it needed to support its largest trading partner, and to avoid the appearance of collusion, it asked shipowners to negotiate with Britain on its behalf. Norwegian shipowners agreed to make available to the British Government all ships not in use exclusively in the Norwegian trade. Some were time-chartered for the duration of the war and crewed by British officers and mariners.[14] As the war continued and demand for materials increased, pressure mounted on Norway because of the large size of its fleet, from both Britain and the United States.

The British knew their country played a key role in sustaining Norway. British mines remained the main source of coal for Norwegian steamships and their homeland. By 1916, Britain insisted that Norwegian ships arriving in its ports carry British goods elsewhere in order to receive coal for their empty bunkers. Many of the places Norwegian ships called at in distant oceans were British colonies. And although the Hague Convention of 1907 prevented neutral ports from refusing to bunker ships in need, those countries retained the right to limit quantities of coal to what was needed for ships to reach the next nearest home port. Britain owned most ports on trade routes around the world at the time and therefore held sway over Norwegian ships needing coal or other provisions.

Allied patience eventually wore thin with failures to negotiate shipping deals with neutral countries. As early as December 1914, Britain had threatened to impound any Norwegian ship hauling whale oil to Germany.[15] In 1916 it applied the principle of angary (the right of a country at war to seize or destroy neutral property out of military necessity, provided that compensation is paid) to take control of over a hundred Dutch ships anchored in American and British harbours.[16] In the winter of 1916–17 Britain forbade the issue of export licences for coal to Norway, which led to catastrophic effects as it coincided with an especially cold winter, forcing Norwegians to resort to wood for fuel in homes and factories. Britain did not resume shipments of coal until February 1917, only after Norway agreed to stop pyrite shipments to Germany.[17] When it entered the war two months later, the United States applied additional pressure on Norway by embargoing exports to it and other countries continuing to trade with Germany. Such actions forced the Norwegians to the negotiating table. Eventually, the Norwegian Shipowners Association and the British Government signed an agreement for 130 additional ships in return for 250,000 tons of coal per month.[18] The Norwegian Government did not participate directly, to preserve the appearance of neutrality, but it encouraged the negotiations. It probably would have made little difference to Germany at this point in the war, since it had declared unrestricted warfare on all ships at sea and was no longer in position to threaten Norway as it had been earlier in the war.

Losses at sea had become worse since the beginning of the war. The first Norwegian ship to go down was the *Tysla* on 8 August 1914, just ten days after the war started. She was en route from Australia to Rotterdam with a load of lead and zinc when she struck a mine. By the end of the year, a total of nine ships had been lost. The following year, as German U-boats became more active, Norwegians lost seventy ships totalling over 90,000 gross tons, forty-nine of them hit by torpedoes.[19] When Germany declared any vessel in the North Sea and around the British Isles to be at risk, Norway's older and slower sailing ships became particularly vulnerable. Between 1914 and 1918, U-boats or mines sank 177 Norwegian sailing ships, over half of the country's total ocean-going tonnage under sail.[20] When Germany declared unrestricted warfare on shipping in 1917, losses increased for all countries, neutral or not. Norway lost 432 ships in that year alone, with losses averaging two per day during some months. By the time the Armistice was declared in 1918, Norway's ocean-going fleet had lost a total of 829 ships, reducing its size by 50 per cent since the start of the war. Of those, 336 had been shipping for the Allies and another 115 had been on charter to Britain; 558 were lost around the British Isles, 124 when travelling between Great Britain and France, and 122 while travelling between Great Britain and Norway. Some of the ships had simply disappeared, possibly sabotaged with bombs by German shippers. Another thirty ships had been put out of action but not sunk. The ratio of Norwegian losses far surpassed those of the Allies they were supporting. France lost 40 per cent, and Britain 38 per cent. The United States lost less than 7 per cent of its fleet.[21]

Replacing lost ships remained a costly challenge until late in the war. It simply was not possible to purchase replacement ships as fast as they were being lost. Britain and France were short of construction materials, and the armies' need for men drained available labour from shipyards. Shipping companies purchased whatever used vessels they could find in the marketplace. It was not until the United States entered the war in 1917 that replacement ships from the American shipbuilding programme offset some losses.

Norway's sacrifice during the war was costly. In addition to ship losses, over 2,100 Norwegian seamen lost their lives. Compared to the losses suffered by other countries, this might have seemed insignificant. Britain and France together lost over two million. Some cities in France lost an entire generation of men. All countries included, twenty million military and civilians died. Another twenty million were wounded. Those numbers were too staggering for most people to understand. And before the war ended the Spanish Flu pandemic spread throughout the world and persisted for a year afterwards, leaving at least fifty million more people dead. Populations everywhere suffered. Economies fell into ruin once more.

While some lauded Norway's contributions and touted the country as a great 'neutral ally', others accused it of profiteering during the war. Many criticized the Norwegian shipping industry for being greedy. There was some substance to these allegations. Freight revenues for Norwegian shipowners during the First World War amounted to 3.5 billion Norwegian kroner, a threefold increase over pre-war years. Despite the enormous costs of insurance and bunkering, about 40 per cent of those revenues appeared to be clear profit.[22] There can be no doubt that many of Norway's shipowners and investors became wealthy because of the war. The unease about shipowners' profiteering did not escape ordinary Norwegians at home. Like the citizens of the countries at war, they too had been subjected to rationing of basic products and had experienced other hardships as shipowners were profiting. In January 1918, massive demonstrations broke out in the streets of Norwegian cities because of economic hardship and income disparities.

The war years had disrupted international trade and made shipping a dangerous enterprise around Europe in particular. As oceans became safe and countries were able to begin trading again, shipping continued to remain profitable. Materials for reparations and rebuilding replaced war materiel in cargo holds. Profits continued for many shipowners. In 1920, for example, shipping companies in Norway amassed record earnings of another 1.3 billion kroner. Replacing ships lost during the war years with newly constructed ones had proved expensive, at a cost on average of about three million kroner per ship. After the war, as demand lessened, construction costs plummeted to a quarter of that or less. Such profits and new opportunities enticed speculative investment in ships in Norway and elsewhere, and by the end of 1920 the size of the world fleet had increased by a whopping 40 per cent.[23] The same speculation applied to new 'shareholder societies' and investment groups in Norway seeking profits in international trade, occasionally under accusations of racketeering. Some of those groups approved shareholder dividends of 70 to 80 per cent or more.[24] It is not hard to understand why some people continued to view the Norwegian shipowners as a bunch of profiteers. Such opinions would persist well into the next war.

By the end of 1921, demand for ships dropped, a decline in rates followed, and soon thereafter half of the world's ocean-going fleet sat idle. Norway's revenues, however, perhaps underlining beliefs about profiteering by its shipowners, kept inching upward in the decade following the First World War and continued into the Depression years. Part of this was because the nature of the shipping industry was changing again. And this time, Norwegian shipping companies had the financial wherewithal and the vision to take advantage of new expectations and markets.

Interest in a new type of ship powered by diesel fuel had developed after the first of its type was launched in 1903. Some shipping companies added them to their fleets when they had the money to do so. After the war, demand for these new vessels increased significantly because of the additional benefits they brought. Even though diesel-powered ships were more costly than coal-fired or oil-fired steamships on a per-mile basis, they offered advantages in terms of the ease of bunkering, smaller crews, faster speeds and greater capacities. No longer were coal handlers and stokers needed. Smaller engine rooms became possible, which meant more space for cargo. As a result, internal combustion engines revolutionized transportation on the seas as they had on land. By 1939, Norwegian shipowners had eliminated their sailing ships and replaced many of their steamships with new diesel ships, including about 300 new liners. Over 60 per cent of the entire Norwegian fleet had become diesel-powered, compared to 25 per cent of the British fleet and only 10 per cent of the United States'.[25] With these new diesel power plants came added speeds, from around 10 knots in 1920 to 16–18 knots by the end of the 1930s. Even the newly motorized tramps sailed at speeds of around 14 knots.[26]

Not surprisingly, as oil became more important for powering the world's ships, cars and planes, the demand for tankers accelerated as well. The size of the world's tanker fleet during the First World War had been small, only about 6 per cent of total tonnage, and oil companies in Britain and the United States had controlled 90 per cent of those ships.[27]

After the war, oil companies divested themselves of their tanker assets to concentrate resources on producing oil. As this process began, Norwegian shipowners, flush with cash, proceeded to purchase the tankers on resale markets; they also invested in the construction of others. The conditions for purchase from the oil companies were often favourable: 30 per cent of the cost of the ship as down payment, with the balance mortgaged at the oil company's expense.[28] In 1914 there were only eleven tankers in Norway's fleet, but by 1939 Norway had purchased and built so many more that its fleet of 272 tankers had become the third largest, comprising one-fifth of the total tanker capacity of the world. Only the tanker fleets of Britain and the United States were bigger. Norway's tankers, however, had become the envy of many because 84 per cent of them were diesel-powered.[29] Norwegian diesel-driven tanker tonnage had become the largest and most modern in the world, slightly bigger than Britain's and a million tons larger than that of the United States'.[30] Not unexpectedly, when another war broke out, with warring nations even more reliant on oil fuel for their fighting systems, Norway's tankers would be much in demand.

But Norwegian investment was not limited to ships carrying dry and liquid cargo. Shipowners also invested in diesel-powered ships designed specifically to carry cargo requiring refrigeration in transit, commodities like vegetables, fruit, meat and dairy products. The speed of these ships, when combined with refrigeration, became particularly desirable for trans-ocean shipping and between North and South America.

As the 1930s came to an end, Norwegian merchant ships had become attractive to many countries. Shipowners had replaced losses from the First World War and added many more, to create a diversified fleet of well over a thousand ships. The result was a modern fleet of ships with an average age of a dozen years, the same as twenty years earlier. More than half the ships had been built in the last ten years. Fleets of other countries had aged considerably over that time and remained slower.[31] This meant that Norwegian ships were more reliable, less prone to break down at sea regardless of weather, and more dependable for shippers. Simultaneously, the Norwegian Government had taken other steps to support its shipping industry. New ship types required updated construction, operation and safety standards, as well as new training for engineers and navigators. Key to much of this was a classification society known as *Det Norske Veritas*

('The Norwegian Truth'), which had been formed in the previous century to establish a uniform set of rules and procedures for the shipping industry to keep ships, seafarers and cargo safe. Without approval from this society, ships could not be insured. There was much focus during the inter-war years on strengthening *Det Norske Veritas* to make sure Norwegian ships maintained high standards.

As their fleets modernized, so did the methods in which Norway's shipowners employed their ships to make money. No longer did they concentrate on tramping, sailing from port to port to find freight to fill cargo holds, as ships' captains had done for decades. Advances in communication and weather forecasting enabled them to seize opportunities in the marketplace, advise captains from afar and keep vessels out of harm's way if necessary. Their newer and bigger ships were perfect competitors in the liner trades developing across oceans and in shipping lanes between the Americas. Diesel-powered ships could carry more and were capable of increasing speed to make up for time lost due to conditions at sea. Liner trades required ships that could maintain schedules, and shippers were willing to pay premiums for regularity. Contracts between shipping companies and shippers resulted in detailed schedules, rates and tonnage requirements. Once signed, these contracts eliminated competition for periods of time, often for a year or more. Agreements meant that ships under contract were no longer available to others until contracts expired. This would become a troublesome roadblock for those wanting greater access to Norwegian ships.

On the eve of the Second World War, Norwegian ships were no longer regarded as old and outdated. Ships with sails were long gone, and Norway had become a giant in the world of international shipping. Its entire fleet was highly regarded by shippers around the world. Much had changed by the early morning hours of 9 April 1940, when the shocking news of an invasion surprised those aboard the *Ringulv* and other Norwegian ships throughout the world. The Norwegian Government and shipowners soon found themselves in an entirely new predicament, though, as they fought for survival and for the ships that held the key to their country's future.

Chapter 2

Norway Becomes a Battleground

Norway came away from the First World War with some important lessons about preparing its fleet in case another emergency occurred. Notifying ships' captains scattered around the world about the outbreak of war and the potential dangers at sea had proved almost impossible at that time. Captains were understandably worried about insurance for their ships and cargo, and they were uncertain whether to head to port or continue their scheduled voyages. As tensions started to rise in Europe in the mid-1930s, Norway took action to protect the country's merchant fleet if the threatening rhetoric escalated into actual hostilities. The Norwegian Shipowners Association had established the Norwegian War Insurance Fund to provide cover for ships and cargo until captains could navigate to friendly ports in case of war. That cover was introduced by a Royal Decree, which was amended in May 1939 to protect ships regardless of whether Norway itself became involved in war. The Norwegian Government had established an early warning system in collaboration with the Shipowners Association, the Ministry of Trade and the Ministry of Foreign Affairs to notify captains of emergencies. Initial tests proved disappointing due to differing short wave capabilities, but by the time Germany invaded Poland on 1 September 1939 the notification system had improved markedly. Announcements went out over a national network and through news broadcasts for two days, instructing ships to proceed to neutral ports. Ship captains duly followed these orders, and two days later, when Britain and France declared war on Germany, the Norwegian Shipowners Association and Government then ordered all ships in international waters to proceed quickly to Norwegian or neutral ports. Many of those ships, however, were on their way to Britain, and captains therefore steered away from British (and French) ports after receiving those messages, much to the consternation of these two countries. The Association and Government quickly amended its instructions to clarify that ports in the British Empire and in France were safe havens as well.[1] The notification system had worked.

The Norwegian Government issued another decree on the day that Germany invaded Poland which focused on ship charters and, anticipating that Norway's ships would soon be at risk, on the safety of their crews. The decree required that all contracts between shipowners and foreign charterers be submitted for Government approval. It also mandated that shipowners take immediate action to increase the number of lifeboats on their ships by a third more than was needed to hold the entire crew, in anticipation that some lifeboats might be put out of action if ships were damaged. Additionally, owners were required to stock lifeboats with food and water. To administer these and other requirements, the Government created a new office, the Directorate of Shipping,[2] within the Ministry of Supply (also called the Ministry of Provisioning). Any Norwegian seaman who found himself in the water rather than in a lifeboat had the benefit of lifesaving suits without equal at the time. Invented in Norway, these full-length bodysuits kept the sailor dry and upright in the water until rescue arrived.[3]

There can be no doubt that seafarers aboard Norwegian ships had become concerned for their safety well before some learned it was no longer possible to return home. Seas became perilous just days after the declarations of war. Less than a week into the war, a German submarine torpedoed SS *Athenia*, a British passenger ship built in Scotland and sailing to Montreal with 1,418 passengers and crew. Many of the passengers were Jews fleeing from Germany. She sank off the coast of Ireland on 9 September, and 117 people died, most of the victims being trapped on lower decks and struggling up stairways to try to reach the lifeboats. Four days after that, the first Norwegian ship became a casualty when the cargo vessel *Ronda* struck a mine after departing Antwerp for another stop before heading across the Atlantic to New York. Seventeen of her crew perished including the captain and his wife. Over the next seven months, fifty-seven more Norwegian merchant ships met similar fates, and 377 seamen lost their lives. Germany intended to threaten the lifeline of supplies that sustained Britain, its industries, its war-making capabilities and, by extension, the very morale of the British people and their willingness to fight back. Norway, still an important trading partner of both countries, once again confronted the challenges of maintaining its neutrality. This time, however, Germany was to eliminate neutrality as an option.

Hitler did not have eyes on Norway when his military surprised the Poles with a blitzkrieg attack. Although the Germans had rebuilt their merchant fleet to replace the one dismantled by the Treaty of Versailles after the First World War, Germany remained reliant on foreign shipping. It was acutely aware that the British Royal Navy dwarfed its own Kriegsmarine and could bottle up German ships as it had done before. The German Navy was in no position to break blockades established by the British. Therefore, it was sensitive to any development that indicated either Norway was not going to remain neutral or that an adversary like Britain might take advantage of or infringe upon Norway's neutrality. Germany needed neutral shipping or access to shipping lanes to Sweden and Norway to maintain the flow of raw materials important to its own war industries. Likewise, trade with Germany remained important for Norway. It did not take long for German intelligence to detect that the British were trying to secure Norwegian merchant ships and were perhaps looking to station military forces in Norway.

British planners had been concerned about the size of the British merchant fleet, even though it was larger by far than any other fleet in the world. Before declaring war on Germany, Britain had started requisitioning British merchantmen and arming them for the anticipated conflict at sea. Planners had also been eyeing Norway's ships and its tanker fleet for some time. The Oil Board had estimated in January 1939 that, if Britain ever went to war with both Germany and Japan, its military would require over ten million tons of oil products in the first year of fighting, nearly as much as the consumption of the entire United Kingdom the previous year.[4] An annual consumption of 20 million tons was a particularly sobering prospect, since the deadweight tonnage of the British tanker fleet in September 1939 was just over 5 million, which included a half million tons carried by thirty-eight Norwegian tankers already on charter to British oil companies. The fleet's carrying capacity or gross tonnage at that time was two-thirds of the deadweight tonnage, or about 3.5 million tons;[5] it might have been as high as 4 million tons, given the increased capacity of the Norwegian tankers. Although tankers could make more than one delivery per year, the distances they had to travel were considerable, since the main sources of oil for the British were in the Middle East, the Caribbean and the Americas, a major supplier being Venezuela. There were few refineries in Britain, so most refined fuel, including the crucial 100-octane fuel required by Spitfires, had to come from abroad. As threats developed at sea, planners knew that the need for tankers would increase if the flow of oil was to be maintained.

It did not take long for losses to begin. In the first ten days following Britain's declaration of war, German submarines sank five British tankers. They would sink seventeen more in the next nine months.[6] There were few ways to make up for such a shortfall. Building new tankers took considerable time and money. The only viable choice in the short term was to charter vessels from other countries. Britain attempted to secure ships on long-term charters from the Netherlands, Denmark and Sweden, but these countries declined to negotiate. The British were particularly interested in getting Norwegians to the negotiating table because of the size and high quality of their tanker fleet; they wanted the Norwegians to agree to charter 150 of their tankers. Discussions started between representatives from the two countries in September 1939.

The Norwegian Government, not surprisingly, was again concerned about getting caught between belligerents who were important trading partners and did not want to jeopardize their neutrality by openly taking sides. They were acutely aware that Britain was Norway's largest trading partner in both exports and imports, and once more the Government relied on the Norwegian Shipowners Association to act as a front organization to negotiate the terms of an agreement. The British Foreign Office met with members of the Association in early October and obtained their consent that, in order to keep the Norwegian Government in the background, a committee of shipowners would enter discussions with Britain. Negotiations that commenced on 24 October broke down because of disagreement over several issues, the most important being rates and insurance. The British were not willing to pay more than six shillings per ton, and the Norwegians wanted much more. Also, the cost of insurance as previously decreed by the Norwegian Government was higher than that available on the open market. Premiums were especially high for ships operating in the English Channel and around the British Isles, given the threat of German U-boats. Owners wanted the British to subsidize the difference in cost and to replace any ships lost with like vessels.⁷ Another issue that surely rankled with the owners was the recent British action in impounding Norwegian ships. As part of the Royal Navy's blockade of German ports, it had taken control of twenty-nine Norwegian ships carrying cargoes to Germany, eventually leading to the loss of 368 shipping days for their owners. It is not hard to imagine the frustration suffered by the committee from the Norwegian Shipowners Association at the negotiating table with the British. Those days lost at sea represented millions of Norwegian kroner in revenue. Additional concerns developed when Britain then began requiring advance notification of cargo on board ships to avoid their seizure.⁸ As a consequence, negotiations broke down.

It was not just tankers that were vital to Britain. When Germany invaded Poland, France lost its main source of coal, since it had been relying on shipments from both Germany and Poland to meet its energy requirements. The British could not satisfy the needs of the French in addition to their own, so the two allies established an Anglo-French Shipping Committee before the end of the year to determine and manage requirements. Britain became the formal negotiator for the coal needs of both countries.⁹ Thus, securing more dry-cargo ships to haul coal to France became imperative as well.

Meetings with Norwegian shipowners resumed in London in early November, and negotiators finally reached a tentative agreement, but not before the British threated to cut off imports of Norwegian fish and, once again, to halt exports of coal. Memories ran deep of the catastrophic effects on Norway when Britain had cut off coal shipments during the First World War. What came to be known as the Scheme Agreement started to take effect on 11 November 1939, with handshakes by the negotiators, although issues persisted regarding insurance and the desire of shipowners that tonnage in the agreement be tied to trade opportunities and, in the case of loss, to the construction of comparable replacement ships. The Norwegian Foreign Minister Halvdan Koht became so frustrated at one point in subsequent talks that he ordered the Shipowners Association to slow down ship transfers in the tentative deal. The two sides finally initialled the agreement on 22 February 1940 and signed it in London on 11 March.¹⁰ It was intended to last for the duration of the war, with a review every six months.

The Scheme Agreement, which included about 40 per cent of Norway's trade tonnage, provided a significant addition to the British-controlled fleet. The Norwegian fleet at the time consisted of 1,172 ships totalling 4.4 million gross measurement tons, including 252 tankers comprising 2 million tons and 920 dry-cargo vessels of 2.4 million tons. There was also a whaling fleet of thirteen processors totalling 155,000 gross measurement tons and 107 whaleboats adding an additional 55 tons. Norway itself relied upon a half million tons of dry-cargo capacity and a quarter of a million tons of tanker capacity to meet the country's needs.[11] The agreement provided for rates as high as sixteen shillings per ton depending on the type of ship, much higher than the British wanted, as well as war bonuses for Norwegian seamen sailing in dangerous waters; and most importantly to the British, it provided for the charter as soon as possible of the 150 tankers they had wanted. Many of these were under contract to others at this time, and Britain agreed to wait until these contracts elapsed, but most tankers were transferred to British control within the next few months.

The Government of Norway had tried to keep its distance from negotiations with Britain because it did not want to disturb relations with Germany, its other important trading partner. German intelligence had picked up on the negotiations between the two countries, however, although it did not know the details of the agreement. Any mystery surrounding the British-Norwegian negotiations disappeared on 11 January 1940, however, when a French magazine published details of the Scheme Agreement.[12] This news added to German concerns about Norway's neutrality and Britain's eagerness to intercede.

For years, Germany had been relying on imports of Swedish ore to supply its manufacturing sector, and Norway, and thus Norway's continued neutrality, played an important role in Germany being able to maintain a year-round flow of that ore. When Baltic waters froze in the winter, transportation of ore shipments directly from Sweden to Germany was no longer possible by ship. As a result, during the winter months, ore was carried by rail from Swedish mines in the north to the small industrial port town of Narvik in northern Norway. Located inside the Arctic Circle, the town with its railhead and port was tucked into the end of a winding inlet lined by vertical cliffs a couple thousand feet high overlooking a scattering of islands in the fjord. From the North Atlantic, a channel extended about fifty miles inland, providing hiding places for ships and locations for defence batteries to protect the passage to the town.

A 20-mile single rail line connected Narvik to Sweden, passing through two dozen tunnels carved into rugged mountains. Otherwise, Narvik was only accessible by sea. Although the Germans saw the advantage of possessing airfields on the western side of Norway for bombers to attack Britain and fjords along the coastline to harbour submarines, the foremost strategic interest in Norway had always been Narvik. This remote port was vital to maintaining the uninterrupted flow of ore from the Kiruna and Gällivare mines in Lapland, the northern area of Sweden. Without that ore, Germany would lack much of the steel it needed to wage war. Perhaps not surprisingly, it agreed to purchase 30,000 tons of fish from Norway annually in order to maintain access to Narvik; its ships would then sail south through Norway's neutral waters to its own ports. This meant that it was not unusual to see German merchant ships off the coast of Norway, something which would help hide plans for invasion when the time came.[13]

Narvik had become the focus of British concerns as well, because they too knew the importance of the port and the rail line crossing into Sweden. Some British and French leaders had proposed that troops be stationed in Norway, believing this would encourage Germany to relocate some of its forces from the west to the north, and would impede the flow of ore to German armament factories. Any large deployment, however, had to be weighed against the impact of siphoning away forces from the lines of defence then being prepared in France. The Allies were very concerned about German merchant ships being able to avoid intervention by sailing near the coastline of Norway in the neutral zone. The British had been considering mining areas off the Norwegian coast to force those vessels out into international waters.

When the Soviets invaded Finland in November because the Finns would not cede borderlands to them, Winston Churchill, then the First Lord of the Admiralty, saw an opportunity to insert some British forces into northern Norway to take control of this vital area as well as the rail route to the Swedish mines. Britain proposed to Norway that a British force be allowed to land at Narvik and transit to Sweden and beyond under the pretext of assisting Finland, but the Scandinavians flatly refused. The Norwegians became so concerned about the British landing forces in the north of their country without permission that they mobilized some of its own military in the area.[14] German intelligence had picked up on this proposed encroachment on Norway's neutrality as well. On 7 December German submarines sank three merchant ships, two British and one Greek, off Norway's north coast. Less than a week later, the subject of a possible occupation of the country became a topic of discussion with Hitler himself.

Months before, Vidkun Quisling, the leader of a fascist party in Norway known as *Nasjonal Samling* (National Union), had visited Germany in the hope of promoting interest in a coup to install a fascist government in his country. Quisling was a former Norwegian Army major who had served for a brief time as the Minister of Defence in the early 1930s. He promoted the idea that while the fascist movement in Norway had many followers, Norway's Government maintained a close relationship with Britain, and that it was therefore highly likely that Norway would eventually align with the Allies. Contrary to Quisling's claims, the *Nasjonal Samling* party he touted had never had many sympathizers. In 1933 the party received a mere 27,850 votes from over a million cast. Quisling himself had failed to secure a seat in Parliament representing Oslo, gaining less than a quarter of the required votes. Three years later, support for his party had fallen by 20 per cent.[15]

Quisling's visit eventually caught the attention of senior military leaders in Germany, including Admiral Erich Raeder, the head of the German Navy, and Alfred Rosenberg, a top official of the Nazi Party. Raeder had himself seen the advantage of securing operating bases on the Norwegian coast for action against Britain. In December, Rosenberg advised Hitler about what Quisling had been saying and made an appointment for the Norwegian to share his thoughts directly with the Führer at a conference. Hitler listened but reiterated that Germany had no plans to encroach on Norway's neutrality unless it became clear that Britain was intervening. Only days later, Hitler invited Quisling back to hear more from him. Although nothing further developed from this second meeting with Hitler in December, planning towards an eventual occupation of Norway commenced the following month. Events would soon accelerate those plans.

On 16 February 1940, the German oil tanker and supply ship *Altmark* was returning to Germany with 299 British prisoners captured by the *Admiral Graf Spee*, a German pocket battleship and commerce raider prowling the South Atlantic. *Altmark* had been refuelling at Port Arthur,

Texas on the day that Britain and France declared war on Germany, and her crew was expecting to return to Germany; however, the captain received instructions to proceed south instead and to become the support ship for *Graf Spee*. For the next five months *Altmark* met the raider multiple times, providing her with oil and taking on board captured crew from British merchant ships *Graf Spee* had overpowered. Then she received orders to return to Germany. The Royal Navy had pursued the German ship to no avail and knew of the prisoners incarcerated onboard. When they learned the ship had arrived in the north and entered Norwegian waters on her way back to Germany, the British urged Norway to intervene. The Norwegian Navy stopped the *Altmark* but did not discover the prisoners, and then, as more questions developed about her cargo, the German captain refused to cooperate further. Frustrated at the lack of action by Norway and anxious to free the mariners, Churchill personally ordered the Royal Navy to proceed into Norwegian waters to retrieve the prisoners. The confrontation was swift and successful. British ships cornered the German vessel in a fjord, boarded her and freed all the imprisoned mariners, killing eight of the *Altmark*'s crew and wounding ten others in the process.

Churchill was lauded in the British papers for his forceful intervention to save the sailors, much to Hitler's chagrin. The incident, justified as it might have been, was viewed by Germans as well as by some Norwegians as a clear intrusion into Norway's neutral waters. The *Altmark* affair became the catalyst for Germany's invasion of Norway. It convinced Hitler that Britain simply would not honour Norway's neutrality, and on 1 March he issued an order for German forces to occupy Norway. The invasion, known as Operation *Weserübung*, was planned for 8–10 April 1940.

The Norwegians, even if they had received more notice, would have been ill-prepared to face an invasion. Sweden had watched activity in Germany with much concern in recent years, mobilized its military, increased its defence budget and added hundreds of combat aircraft and other weapons. Norway and Denmark had done little, and by 1939 both were ripe for the picking. At the start of 1940, Norway's only sizeable land force on active duty was situated around Narvik in the far north, because of the mobilization just over a month before to prevent any incursion there by Britain. Except for Oslo, Norway's port areas remained vulnerable, with only limited coastal defences or none at all. The country had no credible air force compared to Germany's powerful Luftwaffe, and only a small navy with outdated warships. Its army numbered 120,000 men at full mobilization and was divided into six divisions, with responsibilities spread over a thousand miles across the entire length of the country. These divisions lacked both tanks and anti-tank weapons. In keeping with its Constitution of 1814, Norway had no standing army. Although citizens served for a few months of military training, much of the Norwegian army remained ill-trained, poorly equipped and, especially when compared to units of the Wehrmacht, lacking in effective leadership. It had even recently eliminated the important leadership position of sergeant from army ranks. Only about 16,000 men were on active duty, most now concentrated in the north, with some others at coastal fortifications near key port areas. King Haakon himself was the nominal head of the military. However hard the Norwegian army might fight, it would prove no match for the Germans, who had demonstrated how well trained and equipped they were when overrunning Poland.

Hitler tagged General Nikolaus von Falkenhorst, an infantry veteran of the Polish campaign and one of the few German army officers with experience in amphibious operations, to lead the planning for Operation *Weserübung*. Falkenhorst reported directly to Hitler, and Hitler himself became actively involved in finalizing the invasion plan. What resulted was the first joint operation in the history of warfare, intricately timed so that attacks would occur together at six key locations across more than a thousand miles from the north to the south of Norway. The intent was to overwhelm the Norwegians quickly and to avoid fighting wherever possible. The ultimate aim was not just to seize the objectives, but also to convince the Norwegians and King Haakon that German occupation was necessary to protect their country from Britain and France. The Germans wanted to encourage a peaceful transition to a pro-German government, and to take control of Norway's large fleet of merchant ships as well as the country's financial resources.

The plan called for six warship groups to seize different objectives simultaneously on the morning of 9 April. Key objectives were the port locations of Narvik, Trondheim, Bergen, Stavanger, Kristiansand and Oslo, as well as some adjacent areas of interest and nearby airfields. Virtually the entire German Navy would be involved, including two battleships, three heavy cruisers, five light cruisers, fifteen destroyers and thirty submarines.

About 9,000 combat troops would board the cruisers and destroyers and move to the objectives for landing. Another 4,000 would travel by plane and be landed at airfields near the objectives as soon as they were secure. Other forces included a battalion of paratroopers, a tank battalion, a company of armoured cars and six companies of motorized artillery.[16] More than a thousand planes would support the operation, including three wings of bombers. About half the planes would be troop transports to drop paratroopers near objectives and to carry follow-on echelons. With airfields secure, the Luftwaffe then would begin landing thousands more troops and positioning fighters and bombers. Supporting the warship groups would be several dozen merchant ships, including tankers, with equipment, supplies and fuel. The plan called for those ships to depart German ports as early as 3 April so as not to arouse suspicion in Norway's neutral waters and to be in position at objectives by 8 April. Fuel would be especially important for the warship group with the objective of Narvik, which was well over a thousand miles from ports in Germany. Destroyers in that group would need to refuel before they could return home.

While the six warship groups invaded Norway, another attacking force led by panzer units would storm across Germany's border and invade neighbouring Denmark. The Danish king was the brother of King Haakon of Norway, but he would confront German aggression quite differently, surrendering his country and turning over its resources to Germany. The invasion of Denmark ended with complete success the same day that it started. The greatest resistance came at sea, but not from guns. To avoid the capture of its fleet, the Danish Navy, in port at the time, scuttled most of its ships to prevent them from falling into German hands.

German operational security proved remarkably effective in both operations. Troops moving to airports and seaports to board planes and ships knew nothing about the plan they would implement to take over Norway. Although the British began detecting some unusual ship movements in the first week in April, as merchant vessels started moving toward objectives, they did not piece together the information and conclude that anything unusual was about to happen. They had debated several plans since the conclusion of the Russo-Finnish War pre-empted their plan to deploy forces to Narvik under the pretext of helping the Finns. Churchill had secured approval for one plan, code-named Wilfred, to mine key waters around Norway in order to restrict German approaches in neutral waters to Narvik and the Norwegian Leads (sheltered sea lanes) south of Trondheim. He hoped to push German ships further out into the North Sea or Norwegian Sea, where the Royal Navy could legitimately attack them. Another plan, called R4, had also received approval. It would see forces deployed to the key port areas of Trondheim, Bergen and Stavanger as needed to prevent German access. Units had been earmarked for deployment.

As Britain was starting to implement Wilfred and mine Norway's neutral waters, Germany was in the process of executing an invasion plan that had the potential to put a great portion of Norway's merchant fleet at risk, especially if it could coerce the Norwegian king or his Government to cooperate. Churchill himself would admit that the Germans totally outwitted him. The British just could not figure out what was about to occur. And then, after it happened, they struggled to decide what to do. Their response would prove indecisive, ineffective and embarrassingly unsuccessful.

Norwegians and Swedes also detected unusual ship movements in the first week of April, but neither sensed the significance of what might be happening. British aerial reconnaissance spotted some of the German ships as well, but no one anticipated that Germany was positioning ships for an invasion. Two formations of Royal Navy ships were then operating in waters off Norway in support of the mine-laying mission detailed in Wilfred.

The first exchange between Britain and Germany happened on the morning of 8 April. German and British warships encountered each other in foggy weather as seas started to grow rough, signalling the arrival of gale-force winds. The British destroyer HMS *Glowworm* exchanged fire with one and then encountered a much bigger ship, the German cruiser *Admiral Hipper*, and when exchanging fire with it, sustained damage. HMS *Glowworm* laid a smokescreen as she tried to break contact, then encountered the *Hipper* again and rammed the German ship before sinking. Little did the Royal Navy know then that the *Hipper* was leading Warship Group 2 toward Trondheim. Warship Group 1, with its ten destroyers led by the battleships *Scharnhorst* and *Gneisenau* for protection, was passing nearby and continuing towards their northernmost objective of Narvik. The encounter left the British further confused about German intentions. Some thought the German ships might be moving out into the Atlantic; others believed they were heading back to Germany. Again, no one contemplated that the ships were in the process of executing a detailed plan for the invasion of Norway.

The gale-force winds slowed the ten destroyers spearheading Warship Group 1 as it headed north. Many of the 2,000 soldiers aboard became seasick, and a few fell overboard in the rough weather. Some of the ships became separated from the group. By midnight, Warship Group 1 had entered the channel leading toward the port village of Narvik. It had anticipated landing soldiers to man shore defences but found none of the shore batteries operable or worthy of manning. Around 0400 hrs, destroyers spotted and sank the Norwegian ship *Eidsvold*, killing 177 of the 185 on board. Soldiers then landed to capture a depot at Elvegardsomen. By 0500 hrs the destroyers had entered the inner harbour and sunk the Norwegian ship *Norge*, killing another 105 men. The loss of these two ships and their crews constituted the single biggest loss of the war for Norway.[17] The small Norwegian garrison ashore proved to be no match for the invaders, and it did not take the Germans long to get their combat troops on the ground and take complete control of the town.

It appeared to the Germans that the attack had succeeded well, notwithstanding the encounter with the Royal Navy and the separation of some ships because of the storm. There were now eleven German merchant ships anchored at Narvik, and four more support ships with fuel were expected. When the warships arrived, only the tanker *Jan Wellem* from that support group was in port; she had arrived from the Arctic under American flag and markings, steered through the channel by a Norwegian pilot not suspecting anything awry.[18] The other four ships had been lost en route, either sunk by the British or scuttled to avoid capture, including the sister tankers *Kattegat* and *Skagerrak*. This meant that refuelling would take much longer from a single tanker, probably eight hours or more for two ships, and that less fuel would be available for all the destroyers. The destroyers in Warship Group 1 now were bottled up at the end of the long channel and badly in need of fuel before they could return to Germany. Little did they know that other British ships from the disrupted Wilfred and R4 operations were heading towards them to impede any escape.

To the south, the seizure of other objectives had gone mostly as planned. After her encounter with HMS *Glowworm* on 8 April, the damaged cruiser *Hipper* led Warship Group 2 into the channel leading to Trondheim just after midnight on 9 April. This group had about 2,000 combat troops aboard. The Germans regarded the city as important for controlling the central and northern parts of the country. It had rail links to both Oslo and Sweden, as well as an airfield nearby that could prove valuable for supplementing and relocating forces. Although the Norwegian commander in Trondheim had received an alert that an invasion appeared to be underway, he had no combat forces to speak of, only staff. Shore batteries fired on the passing vessels but caused no damage, and the German ships discharged troops to neutralize and man posts guarding the channel. They believed the defensive positions would prove helpful if the British decided to respond. Attacks on those coastal batteries later in the day led to nearly two dozen German and only a few Norwegian casualties. Long before that happened, though, German troops had landed a little before 0500 hrs and began occupying Trondheim itself. The Norwegians were in no position to defend the old city. It was a walkover. The next day, the Germans would take control of the adjacent airfield at Værnes. Luftwaffe cargo planes would then land men and equipment to consolidate gains and prepare for a possible Allied response.

Bergen, further south, was reasonably well protected and manned, unlike Trondheim. Warship Group 3 with slightly fewer men than Groups 1 and 2 would have to pass several manned defences with coastal artillery as it skirted the islands dotting the channel leading to the city. The Norwegian commander had about 500 troops at his disposal. After receiving alerts of gunfire around Oslo he ordered coastal lights extinguished and his men to prepare for action. He also called for reinforcements, which would not arrive. Shore defence batteries hit two German ships, killing three dozen men and stalling the advance momentarily. German troops landed to attack shore batteries closer to Bergen and suffered over two dozen more casualties in the fierce fighting that followed, nearly double what they inflicted on the Norwegian defenders. Later, German planes bombed the batteries, and by early morning, German ground troops including a band were marching into the city. Ships then started to mine the approach to Bergen to supplement captured shore battery defences in preparation for a possible British response.

The mission of Warship Group 6 was quite different to that of the other groups. Its naval component consisted of only four minesweepers. The group's mission was to take control of the small port of Egersund, about 100 miles down the coast from the town of Stavanger and the location of a cable station important for communications. The minesweepers would carry troops to capture the port and run the cable station afterwards. Another objective was the airfield at Stola, about 10 miles from Stavanger. It was the closest airfield to Britain and offered opportunities for the Luftwaffe later. The Germans believed the airfield would be a high priority in any British response in Norway. Since Stavanger lacked coastal defences, the Germans had pre-positioned a merchant ship at its port loaded with coastal weapons and ammunition to bolster defences in the area after they took control. Norwegian customs officials, however, had become suspicious and demanded to know what cargo was on board. Rather than disclose that information, the German captain scuttled his ship.

The airdrop on the nearby airfield at Stola proceeded with difficulty. Fog caused the mission to be aborted after eight planes loaded with paratroopers had taken off. Four of the planes returned safely; two of the remaining four collided in mid-air, killing all the paratroopers and crew; only two planes succeeded in dropping paratroopers, about 130 in total. A Norwegian detachment defending the airfield killed several of them before surrendering. After reinforcements arrived by air, German infantrymen marched into Stavanger with a gun to the head of the detachment commander and coerced the residents into surrendering without further resistance. South at Egersund, the men on the minesweepers secured their objective without firing a shot, even though two of the four minesweepers failed to show up.[19]

The southernmost objectives were Kristiansand, Kjevik, a village across the bay from Kristiansand, and Arendal, a small village nearly 50 miles up the coast to the north-east towards Oslo. Kristiansand offered a valuable port close to the German mainland; it also was a naval base with a couple of destroyers, some submarines and patrol vessels. Kjevik was the location of a small airfield, valuable like the ones further north for reinforcements and re-supply. Arendal was important because it was the location of an undersea communications cable connecting Norway to Britain. Several coastal batteries protected Kristiansand. Additionally, the local commander had several hundred men at his disposal, including two companies of infantry. He had received reports that coastal batteries defending approaches to Oslo had fired on ships, and he alerted his forces well before the German ships arrived, since heavy fog had slowed the approach of Warship Group 4. By the time the warships neared the city, it was after daylight, and the fog had started to lift. The Norwegians had launched some reconnaissance planes, which spotted the ships. Coastal batteries were therefore on alert and fired when the ships came into range. Although the fire inflicted no damage on the Germans, the group commander pulled back his ships and called for airstrikes. Then he tried another pass into the port area, but again decided to withdraw his ships as fire from shore batteries continued and fog returned. It was not until shortly before noon that Warship Group 4 finally was able to get troops ashore, seize the coastal batteries and enter the town. They faced no resistance once in Kristiansand, and that afternoon, another German band was playing in the streets. Other forces seized Kjevik and Arendal without incident. As at Stola, reinforcements and equipment began landing at the Kjevik airfield shortly thereafter.

German objectives in seizing control of the capital of Oslo were more complicated and went well beyond overcoming defences and landing troops to secure the city. Hitler's intent all along had been to avoid combat as much as possible. This had proved difficult. At other locations, his units had sustained greater losses than anticipated due to Norwegian resistance and the weather. Avoiding casualties and damage was particularly important in Oslo, though, because Germany wanted the Norwegian Government to accept its intervention as a means of 'protecting' the country against the British, who had been mining Norwegian waters. Hitler wanted the Norwegians to cooperate and permit a peaceful transfer of administration. Thus, securing the blessing of King Haakon became paramount. The Germans knew that any violence in the capital would discourage public support and delay the installation of a fascist government.

Quisling had not been included in the planning of the invasion, and as it unfolded, he remained as unaware as others in Oslo of what was happening. He had assured German leaders that a Fifth Column of supporters was active in the country, ready to welcome and assist Germany in a transition of power. The Germans, without any evidence of the actual influence of Quisling or his acceptance by his fellow citizens, had seen him nonetheless as the potential leader of a new fascist government. On 5 April, just days prior to the invasion, Germany's representative in Norway, Curt Bräuer, hosted a gathering for senior government officials in Oslo with the aim of convincing them of the value of closer, peaceful ties between the two countries. The session took on a different tone when Bräuer showed them a film highlighting the Reich's military power and achievements in the months leading up to the invasion of Poland. It was a not-so-subtle message of intimidation about what might be expected if Norway did not follow Germany's desires. However, the Nazis' plan for Oslo and thus Norway was not to turn out as anticipated.

The difficult task of trying to secure Oslo without alienating Norway's Government fell to Warship Group 5. Like the other groups, it carried a landing force of about 2,000 men. The plan had multiple objectives. Near the entrance of Oslofjord was the main Norwegian naval base at Horten, which had to be neutralized or captured in the early morning of the attack. The Germans also wanted to seize the Fornebu airfield to the west of Oslo and the Kjeller airfield to the east. The plan anticipated four battalions of infantry disembarking at the port of Oslo as hundreds of paratroopers took the airfields to enable the landing of thousands of more troops, supplies and equipment. It is doubtful that many thought these objectives could be seized without resistance, and fighting did indeed erupt at all locations.

The flagship of Group 5 was the large cruiser *Blücher*. In a decision widely criticized later, the commander on board, Rear Admiral Oskar Kummetz, decided to have his flagship lead the others up the fjord to the capital. The *Blücher* was heavily loaded with supplies, including over 30 tons of munitions. Also on board were over a thousand crew and troops as well as two major generals, one the commander of the infantry division spread out across the ships in the group and the other from the Luftwaffe to lead airfield operations around Oslo.

Stations along the fjord started reporting the passage of unidentified ships as Warship Group 5 approached. Shortly before midnight, a Norwegian whaler converted to a patrol boat challenged a German ship, fired warning shots, then collided with the bigger ship and sank. Shortly thereafter, air-raid sirens started going off in Oslo, and the city went into blackout. Lights marking the passage and coastline of Oslofjord were extinguished as well. No one knew what was happening. Colonel Berge Erikson, the commander of Oscarsborg Fortress in the northern part of the fjord known as Drøbok Sound, had mustered his men to their gun positions after hearing reports of unknown ships entering the fjord. The fortress was on an island about 10 miles south of Oslo, creating a bottleneck for any formation of ships passing. So concerned was he about the potential for trouble that he contacted the temporary commander of the torpedo battery, Andréas Anderssen, and asked him to report to his station as well. Anderssen had been at home as the alerts started arriving; he had retired a dozen years before as commander of the battery but had previously agreed to come back on a temporary basis. He returned quickly to ready the three torpedo tubes at the fortress for action. Both these men would receive the War Cross, Norway's highest military honour, after the war. Their actions that morning proved instrumental in delaying the German attack and permitting Government officials to determine a course of action.

As the *Blücher* eased up the fjord in the lead shortly after 0400 hrs, searchlights were scanning for ships. Beacons at Oscarsborg Fortress illuminated the cruiser in the darkness. Erikson, recognizing her as a warship bigger than any in Norway's navy and sensing something horribly wrong, gave the coastal guns the order to commence firing. They fired two rounds, both of which struck the German cruiser, igniting flammable material and setting off munitions. The damaged ship responded with withering gunfire as she coasted further up the fjord. Then Anderssen's battery fired two torpedoes, both striking the ship as well. Just before 0630 hrs, the *Blücher* sank, and about half the men on board died in the flaming waters.

Leading the remaining ships was the pocket battleship *Lützow*. Her commander assumed control of the Warship Group and ordered the other ships to reverse course. Before doing so, the *Lützow* engaged Oscarsborg Fortress and in return took three hits herself. These aggressive Norwegian shore battery attacks made a shambles of this critical part of the German invasion plan, because ships were no longer able to transport ground troops directly to the port of Oslo.

About the same time as the *Blücher* was meeting her fate, other ships had approached and engaged Norwegian ships at Horten Naval Base. There were losses on both sides. The Germans eventually sent an envoy ashore to advise the base commander that if he did not surrender, the ships would shell the base. It was sufficient to convince the admiral in charge to surrender.

The plan for getting troops inside Oslo, though, had to change because of the continued threat from the coastal defences at Drøbak. The German ships landed the ground force miles away from Oslo, and they marched on foot to the capital. Later, the Luftwaffe responded with a withering bombing attack on the Norwegian fortress that had disrupted the attack, although it took a while to neutralize the island completely. As infantry moved toward the capital on land, further setbacks were encountered at the airfield adjacent to Oslo, where the small Norwegian air force had come to full alert. The Germans had hoped that overflights of bombers and fighters would be sufficient to intimidate Norwegian defences protecting the airfields into surrendering, but Norwegian pilots took to the air to counter the German planes. Over eighty planeloads of soldiers had been destined for the Fornebu airfield, first dropping paratroopers and then landing thousands more combat troops. As happened at Stola near Stavanger, however, fog intervened to disrupt the plan, causing most planes to abort and some others to collide in mid-air. It was nearly 0900 hrs, more than three hours past the planned arrival time, when German transports finally were able to land the first forces at Fornebu. Their approach to the Kjeller airfield was much more successful, however; they bombed it and took possession quickly.

Despite successes in many locations, there was ample reason for Hitler to be concerned. Resistance in some places had proved surprisingly strong despite the country's lack of readiness. Hundreds of men had been killed. Half the German fleet remained bottled up at Narvik awaiting re-supply of fuel and ammunition. The next morning would find those ships confronting a flotilla of British warships aimed at destroying them, and by the time these engagements ended, two German destroyers and eight merchant ships would be sunk, and five other destroyers would be badly damaged. German forces remained on land, but in the weeks ahead, as more ships and Allied ground forces arrived, they would evacuate Narvik and try to establish another defence closer to Sweden. The fate of Germany's main strategic interest in Norway remained very much in doubt, because British ground troops were on their way to try to take control of Narvik.

In Oslo, the situation was different but equally concerning. By noon, German forces had managed to enter the capital with a band playing. Despite this ceremonial appearance of troops in the city, the landings around Oslo had proved the least successful and costliest by far. Even though the Germans encountered no resistance in the streets, residents came out of their homes confused and concerned as to what was happening. To make matters worse, King Haakon and the Norwegian Parliament (the *Storting*) were nowhere to be found. Paratroopers who had taken Fornebu earlier in the day were now given the mission of finding and capturing the King. Vidkun Quisling and the Germans took on a mission of their own, too: to gain control of the Norwegian merchant fleet. Both missions would fail.

Chapter 3

A National Fleet Develops as Norway Falls

The mining of Norwegian waters in early April 1940 ended months of debate about how Britain should stifle German interests in Norway. The British hoped that the mines would impede the passage of German ships off the coast of Norway, but they suspected that the Norwegians might react strongly to such a violation of their neutrality, and they were particularly concerned that it could affect the Scheme Agreement the countries had signed just two months earlier to provide access to more ships, especially the chartering of more Norwegian tankers. Consequently, Britain had developed a plan to requisition Norwegian ships in its ports if a backlash resulted.[1] The German invasion happened so quickly after the mine-laying, though, that the British became concerned for the future of the entire Norwegian fleet. As soon as the invasion was launched, a race started between Britain, Germany and Norway to gain control of the country's merchant marine, then distributed all over the world. But no one suspected at the time, least of all government officials in Oslo on the early morning of 9 April, just how important their country's fleet would become. Out of the confusion of the German invasion came the formation of the largest shipping company ever to exist.

The Norwegian Government was in session in Oslo the day before the invasion. Some members were aware of intelligence reports about unusual ship activity off the Norwegian coast. That morning, newspapers had reported on the Royal Navy's mining of neutral waters along the west coast. Other information had arrived that a Polish submarine had attacked a German merchant ship named *Rio de Janeiro* off the country's southern coast and that hundreds of German soldiers had been rescued from the sea. Only one official became sufficiently concerned by these events to urge any action. After seeing the reports of ship sightings as early as 5 April, Colonel Rasmus Hattedal, the Norwegian Army's Chief of Staff, urged Birger Ljungberg, the Minister of Defence, to begin a partial mobilization of the military. Then, after learning that German soldiers had been rescued from the sunken merchant ship, he urged full mobilization on 8 April. Norwegian Government ministers, however, took no action on his recommendation. Before adjournment that evening, they only agreed on the need to lift the mines if the British would not do so themselves, and they drew up a resolution demanding their removal.[2] Apparently, no one except Hattedal sensed anything was awry.

Shortly before midnight, all of them became aware that something was indeed wrong. Messages started arriving from the west coast about strange ships entering ports along the coast and shore batteries firing at them. Then reports were received of encounters between patrol boats and ships entering Oslofjord and heading towards the capital. As a result, officials activated air-raid sirens to alert residents and ordered streetlights turned off to black out the city. King Haakon, like all the legislators then in session in Oslo, had no sense that the country was in danger that morning. As aides woke him at 0130 hrs, the startled king had no idea who could possibly be invading his country. Calls went out for government ministers to reassemble immediately. General Kristian Laake, the Commander-in-Chief of Norway's military, was at his farm outside Oslo when he received a call informing him of what was happening. He thought that it might be reasonable to mobilize a small force, perhaps a brigade-sized unit at the most, but he took no action to do so. Partial mobilization of the armed forces as suggested by Laake would have been useless anyway, since such notifications were issued by mail. Only in the case of a declared emergency necessitating full mobilization would notification be broadcast nationally over the radio.

The Norwegians were not the only ones surprised. The German representative Bräuer, a career diplomat and Nazi Party member, was not expecting any military action either. He opened the door of his home in Oslo the evening of 8 April to discover officers from Falkenhorst's staff with information about what was underway. They had travelled inconspicuously from Germany to Sweden and then on to Oslo. The officers issued him with specific instructions from the Führer and provided him with a document for Norwegian Foreign Minister Halvdan Koht detailing Germany's intention to 'protect' Norway because of Britain's mining of the country's neutral waters. Germany sought the Norwegians' cooperation, and Bräuer now had the difficult task of convincing officials that Germany was a friend not a foe. His specific objectives were to ensure that the Norwegian Government cooperated and that King Haakon remained in Oslo. The Germans knew of Haakon's bond with his people, and if they did not gain his support, much greater resistance would ensue. They hoped, perhaps wishfully, to entice him to cooperate. Bräuer was supposed to present the document to Koht at precisely 0420 hrs on 9 April.[3] This was the time when Warship Group 5 was projected to be nearing Oslo with thousands of soldiers prepared to occupy the capital. The German consul did exactly as he was told.

Koht was on his way home shortly after midnight when the air-raid sirens went off in the city. At first, he thought the sirens were a test. When they did not stop, and the city went into blackout, he knew something was wrong and hurried back to his office in the dark. About the same time, Prime Minister Johan Nygaardsvold became concerned and summoned ministers back into session at 0130 hrs to receive updates on what was happening. Bräuer showed up at Koht's office about three hours later and asked to see the foreign minister. It must have seemed odd to have the German visit his office at such an early hour. They met at precisely the time Bräuer had been instructed, talking in candlelight since Oslo remained in blackout. The German explained the rationale of 'protecting' Norway that his country had concocted to justify its invasion and then handed Koht a document with thirteen measures to be taken. Included were ultimatums: that the Norwegian Government should tell its people not to resist, order its military to cooperate with German forces and turn over their facilities to them, disclose the locations of all mines, make all communications and transportation available to German use, and more. One measure mandated that 'War and merchant ships should be forbidden to leave the country, and no plane should be allowed to take off. But shipping to German ports and neutral Baltic ports might be exempted.'[4] Koht, not surprisingly, was incredulous and told Bräuer he needed to consult with Prime Minister Nygaardsvold and others. He promised a quick response. Koht called Bräuer back within the hour and advised him that the Norwegian Government would neither cooperate with Germany nor relinquish control of the country. By then, fighting had erupted from Kristiansand up the coast to Narvik, and in Oslofjord, where the *Blücher* was beginning to sink. Indeed, the two countries were at war, even though many in Norway did not realize it yet. The only question was what the Norwegian Government would do about it.

The man who took immediate action that morning was Carl Hambro, President of the *Storting*, who also had been recently elected President of the Assembly of the League of Nations. Hambro ranked just below the King of Norway in the hierarchy and set the agenda for the *Storting*. He, too, was unaware of the severity of what was happening until Bräuer made his surprising visit to Koht. After receiving notification of the German demands and reports of what was happening elsewhere in the country, Hambro sensed the danger this would present if the King and Government remained in the city. He called the clerk of the *Storting* and told him to recall staff to pack up archives, necessary protocols and the country's seals for loading onto trucks. He then notified the railway to prepare carriages to leave Oslo immediately and informed Government representatives and aides to King Haakon to get ready to evacuate with the rest of the Royal Family. The train was to be ready just two hours later, at 0700 hrs. Each representative was allowed a single suitcase. Their destination would be the town of Hamar, 80 miles north of Oslo and close to the Swedish border, with good communication facilities. Then Hambro raced forward in a taxi to arrange places for the King and his ministers to reside and for Government meetings to continue. His quick action that morning saved the Government from a complete German takeover. The train departed at 0723 hrs.[5]

Hambro also helped preserve the Norwegian treasury and other resources. After arranging the train and alerting ministers to prepare to depart, he directed Norway's Minister of Finance, Oscar Torp, to proceed immediately to relocate the country's gold reserves. Although much of Norway's gold had been moved to the United States by 1940, 240 million kroner or the approximate equivalent of 55 million US dollars in gold reserves remained in the Bank of Norway in Oslo. Torp and Nicolai Rygg, Director of the Bank of Norway, had already taken preliminary steps to protect what remained of the reserves in the event of an emergency by building a bomb-proof vault at the bank's office in Lillehammer, about 150 miles north of Oslo. Rygg alerted his subordinates at the office in Lillehammer at 0600 hrs that the gold would be heading their way. Packed in 1,500 crates and barrels, the reserves weighed over 50 tons. They began moving the gold in twenty-six guarded trucks just an hour later, shortly before the train carrying the King and Government officials departed.

The last trucks would leave as the first German troops were arriving in Oslo a few hours later.[6]

As Torp and Rygg hurried to protect the gold, Trygve Lie, the Minister of Supply, rushed to relocate supplies stored in Oslo further north and away from the expected arrival of German soldiers. These included reserves of oil, grain and sugar.[7] Some residents probably wondered what was going on with the increased movement of trucks away from the capital that morning. Few were aware that the Royal Family and their elected officials were in flight already. It would take several more hours before the sobering events of that day began to register with the general public.

As the train with the King and Government officials was departing, radio broadcasts were initiating the general mobilization of Norway's military. Officials could see the first sorties of German planes bombing the Kjellar airfield.[8] Although the Norwegian military was poorly trained and equipped, many men were assembling in the capital awaiting instructions as the first German troops started arriving from Fornebu about midday. It must have been a bizarre scene, with paratroopers marching in to occupy the capital and a German band preparing to play in the streets as the Norwegian reservists gathered, undoubtedly wondering what they would be called upon to do. There was no fighting in the city that morning.

The German plan for the occupation of Oslo had, however, quickly fallen apart when the attack on the *Blücher* halted the advance of Warship Group 5. Thousands of German troops were supposed to be offloading in Oslo at daybreak. Had that happened, they might have prevented the Norwegian Government from fleeing as it did, given its lack of awareness of the developing situation. Consequently, as warship groups continued their efforts to seize or consolidate forces on their objectives, the Germans' focus expanded to the capture of the King and the country's gold and to establishing control over Norway's large merchant fleet.

The train with officials arrived at Hamar a little after 1100 hrs, and shortly after noon, the *Storting* convened with about 100 of its 150 members present. Everyone present received the sobering news about what was happening at various locations throughout their country and about the rapid collapse of Denmark. The British Minister to Norway, Cecil Dormer, had joined them at Hamar and, at the behest of the Norwegian Government, sent an urgent request to London for immediate military assistance. He received the reply that the Royal Navy presently had many ships with troops at sea nearby and that help would arrive soon.[9] This assurance that British help was on the way would lead to much disappointment in days ahead as the Norwegian military waited in vain for it to arrive.

Back in Oslo, Vidkun Quisling was elated, believing that his fascist party soon would be in control of the country. He had received no advance notification of the German plan either. Once it occurred to him that an invasion of some sort was underway, he scurried to Government offices to allay fears and to explain the good intentions of Germany. He was surprised to discover that most offices he visited were empty. When Quisling learned that the Government had fled the city he wasted no time in trying to take advantage of the situation. He declared himself the 'Chief of State' and broadcast to Norwegians that there would be no mobilization or resistance and that everyone should welcome the Germans.[10] He then proceeded to announce the members of a new cabinet, most of whom were unknown to anyone who might have been listening. In fact, many of Quisling's appointed cabinet themselves did not know they had been chosen.[11] He later summoned the Shipowners Association, Association of Industrialists, Employers' Association, Council of Trade Unions and others to meet with him to discuss the future. None showed up.[12]

The ministers in Hamar soon received word of Quisling taking to the airwaves back in Oslo and proclaiming himself the head of the Government. Some urged that they should begin talks with the Germans to negotiate a solution. Others, including King Haakon, strongly disagreed. The notion that a fascist like Quisling could be included in any part of the Norwegian Government was distasteful to him and many others. By then, Bräuer had returned to Koht's office to again urge consideration of Germany's terms. Like Quisling, he was surprised to discover government offices vacant. He tried telegraphing Norway's foreign minister to let him know that Denmark had cooperated peacefully and would be occupied by Germany for its own protection. Receiving no response, he sent a message that evening asking to meet with the King the following day.[13]

At 1940 hrs on the day of the invasion, at the village of Hamar, Hambro shocked everyone once more by announcing that German paratroopers were in pursuit and closing in quickly on them. He instructed all to reboard the train and prepare to depart in five minutes for the town of

Elverum, further north.[14] As they were doing so, a group of Norwegian volunteers, many with their own weapons, established hasty defensive positions to stop the German attempt to capture the King. Although they eventually proved to be no match for the well-trained Germans, they put up sufficient resistance to halt the advance momentarily and force the Germans to regroup before taking up the pursuit again. It was the second time that day that quick Norwegian action had enabled Government officials to escape capture. The King and his ministers decided to drive beyond Elverum to the small village of Nybergsund to distance themselves even further from the pursuing Germans. By then, King Haakon had received Bräuer's message and agreed to talk with him.

The following day, in mid-afternoon, Bräuer met King Haakon in a small school back at Elverum. The German had asked to meet with him alone; however, the King insisted that Koht be present for the first part of the discussion. Bräuer announced that the Norwegian Government's independence could be preserved providing that King Haakon approved Quisling as its new head. If he did not agree, then he would have to accept a government fully administered by Germany. The King told him that the Norwegian people had to determine who should head their government and that he would never negotiate away the rights of the people who had elected him. He then conveyed to the German diplomat that he would put his offer to the ministers and allow them to make the final decision. Bräuer headed back to Oslo as the King returned to Nybergsund to meet with his ministers. Although Haakon left the decision up to his Government, he emphasized to them that he remained loyal to the people of Norway who had elected him and if the ministers chose to accept Bräuer's new offer, then he would abdicate. The ministers voted overwhelmingly to reject the offer.

That evening, General Laake finally joined them. He proposed that the Government either negotiate or capitulate, rather than develop any type of military plan to defend the country. It became clear to those present that the 73-year-old general was incapable of providing the leadership needed at such a critical time, and ministers accepted his resignation. His replacement was a respected 58-year-old colonel by the name of Otto Ruge, who had been serving as Inspector General of the Norwegian Army. Ruge was promoted to the rank of major general and took charge immediately of mobilization and employment of the fledgling formations.

Ruge issued his first orders on 11 April, less than twelve hours after his promotion to Commander-in-Chief. He knew the Germans would be rushing reinforcements into the country and that his forces, still building up as word of the mobilization spread, would be overwhelmed quickly if they tried to establish a firm line of defence. His strategy, therefore, was to delay the Germans as much as possible to allow time for mobilization to continue. He would pull back his forces gradually to the north-west in the direction of Trondheim, trading space for time, as he waited for the assistance the British had promised. His entire strategy hinged on the British commitment of decisive reinforcements.[15]

Unfortunately for Ruge, efforts to mobilize Norwegians to active duty became hampered by the rapid German takeover of all communications. Nonetheless, in just a few days as word of the invasion spread, a force of about 40,000 determined volunteers had joined the ranks under Ruge's command. But tens of thousands more German troops had arrived and were now advancing on three fronts across central Norway in the general direction of Trondheim, augmented by paratroopers and supported by heavy weapons and warplanes. Their control of communication links in Norway, and their quick takeover of depots that supplied the Norwegian forces, now made coordination and re-supply difficult for the Norwegians. On 12 April, Ruge contacted an intelligence officer on the staff of Minister Dormer, who had been in touch with officials in London. Sadly, communications indicated that the British War Office had little appreciation of the severity of the situation on the ground in Norway or even of the vast dispersal of forces between Narvik in the north and Trondheim in the centre of Norway. Ruge insisted that urgent help was essential to secure Trondheim and provide him with reinforcements. German paratroopers had dropped into his rear area halfway between Lillehammer and the Norwegian coast by then.[16] He was in danger of being encircled. When the reinforcements arrived, they were hardly what he expected.

During their meetings in December, Hitler had taken Vidkun Quisling at his word that the Norwegian fascist enjoyed a strong following in Norway and underestimated the opposition in Norway to him and his small group of followers. Quisling made one last attempt to appeal to the King on the morning of 11 April by inviting him to meet in Oslo to discuss the future.[17] No one took his entreaties seriously. Neither he nor

Bräuer had succeeded in convincing the Norwegians to negotiate. Bräuer would eventually end up on the Eastern Front for his failure to persuade the King to cooperate. Quisling would be hanged as a traitor after the war ended.

When the Norwegian Government rejected Bräuer's offer on the evening of 10 April, Hitler ordered the German military to dispose of King Haakon and his Government officials. The next day, German bombers targeted the village of Nybergsund where they were located. It was a beautiful spring morning, and people were outside enjoying the day. The planes made several passes, dropping cluster bombs and strafing the town. Amazingly, only one person was injured in the attacks, but the town itself sustained severe damage. Elverum was less fortunate when it was bombed the same day. Several of its residents were killed.

The German attacks left the King and his officials very rattled. Some now urged him and Crown Prince Olav to seek refuge in Sweden. Crown Princess Märtha had already departed for Sweden on the evening of 9 April to stay with her Swedish family. She remained there until 12 April, when she travelled to the United States at the invitation of President Roosevelt. She would remain there until the end of the war, establish a close relationship with Roosevelt and help to promote Norwegian interests. The King, however, insisted that he and his ministers remain in Norway, and he recommended that everyone proceed in the direction of Lillehammer. Over the next several days they would disguise themselves and travel in unmarked vehicles, skirting the fighting that by this time had started under Major General Ruge's leadership, beyond Lillehammer through small towns toward the west coast.

Meanwhile, a war of a different sort had started back in Oslo, in Germany and in Britain. It was not a battle between military formations, though. Rather, it was a fight to gain control of the Norwegian merchant fleet. Securing Norway's ships is never mentioned as an important objective behind Germany's decision to invade Norway. Capturing Narvik because of its importance for ore shipments; gaining access to ice-free fjords for use by ships or submarines; and securing airfields for future strikes against Britain: these are all frequently cited objectives, with Narvik topping the list. But some in Germany were clearly eyeing the fourth largest merchant fleet in the world as their military invaded Norway. Bergen and Oslo each had shortwave transmitters at the time; German troops took control of them quickly after they arrived. Soon thereafter, transmissions were encouraging ship captains to seek certain ports for protection. Quisling himself went on the air on 10 April, the same day that Bräuer was meeting with the King in Elverum, and urged Norwegian captains to return to Norway or proceed towards neutral ports in Italy and Spain, which were friendly to Germany. More messages from Norway and Germany followed the next day as the bombers were attacking Nybergsund.[18]

To counter these broadcasts, British officials in London released messages of their own informing ship captains of what was happening and cautioning them that the other transmissions they were receiving came from Germans not Norwegians. They also tried their best to convince the Norwegian Minister in London, Erik Colban, that Britain should take control of Norwegian ships to prevent them falling into German hands. When the Danish Government capitulated the same day that the Germans invaded, the British had taken control of Danish ships in British waters and ports. They would take control of French ships as well when the government in France fell. There can be no doubt that if the Norwegian Government had fallen to the Germans, the British would have taken control of as many Norwegian ships as possible, too, without regard for Norway's interests.[19] The situation in Norway was not clear, though, and there was no direct contact with the Norwegian Government as it fled from the Germans; but that did not stop the British from offering help to save the Norwegian ships.

On the day of the invasion, Britain's War Cabinet telegraphed British Minister Dormer in Norway asking him to inform the Norwegians that Britain would protect their merchant fleet. The following day, the British Minister of Shipping expressed concern to the War Cabinet that Norwegian tankers were of vital importance and urged their immediate transfer to British control. The Cabinet then sent a second telegram. They received no response from Dormer because by then he was with the Norwegian Government and out of communication as they fled from the Germans. He did not receive the messages until a week later. On 11 April Colban learned of the British messages and responded on behalf of his government that the Norwegian merchant marine remained vital to the future of Norway and that his country would not relinquish control of its fleet. The British asked him to send messages to ship captains to warn of the German transmissions and to encourage them to seek British ports instead. He refused to do that as well without further instructions from his government, knowing that such messages would delay many cargoes and have negative economic consequences for shipowners. After Dormer failed to act, the British then asked the Foreign Office to press its Norwegian counterpart for action, but the Norwegians would not budge to British pressure. Colban, however, did release an inspiring message via the BBC to the people of Norway who were fighting for their country's honour, for which he received much praise from some ship captains.[20]

For those captains at sea the situation proved hopelessly confusing. They were all obliged to get their cargo to customers under various shipping agreements, but when they contacted Norwegian embassies and consulates for guidance they often received frustrating replies such as 'No instruction' or 'Use your own judgement'.[21] Norwegian shipowners were understandably concerned that ships might divert to other ports and thereby delay deliveries. One common concern occupied the minds of ship captains and shipowners alike. Insurance of their ships and cargoes had been tied to a decree issued by the Norwegian Government in the mid-1930s. Now that the Government's location and even its existence were in question, both groups became apprehensive about the continued protection of ships and cargoes, for which ship captains at sea remained personally responsible. No one knew whether the previously established Norwegian War Insurance Fund remained valid. Questions arose as well about continuing cover for ships sailing under the Scheme Agreement, under which the British provided insurance. Norway had signed the Scheme Agreement as a neutral country. Had its neutrality changed because of the invasion? As a result of such concerns, some captains steered to the nearest ports simply for protection, thinking that was the best way to keep their ships safe. Shipowner representatives in London began coordinating with British officials regarding insurance cover.

Norwegian Government officials remained unaware of the actions by Germany and Britain aimed at gaining control of their country's ships, because Germany had taken over all communication facilities. When they neared the border of Sweden on 12 April, Foreign Minister Koht and *Storting* President Hambro hurried across to meet with their Swedish counterparts to discover more about what was happening. Koht returned with additional information, including the sobering news that their Swedish neighbours would not consider harbouring the King or

Norwegian Government at this time for fear of angering Germany and thereby jeopardizing their own neutrality.[22] Hambro stayed in Sweden with the Norwegian consulate in Stockholm as the senior representative of his country, while the King and ministers began fleeing from the Germans across central Norway. The Swedish capital thus became Norway's conduit for communication with the outside world and to Norwegian officials. Hambro's presence there became vital for sharing developments regarding Norway's merchant marine and the steps being taken to keep ships out of German hands.

By this time, a prominent Norwegian shipowner named Ingolf Hysing Olsen had arrived in London to help Colban deal with British pressure to gain access to Norway's ships. Olsen was the permanent representative of the Norwegian Shipowners Association in London. He had an office in the Ministry of Shipping and had established strong relationships with Ministry staff. On 9 April, he was travelling to Bergen when he learned of the invasion and made his way towards London instead, arriving two days later. Olsen had established a close relationship with Colban in the past, when the two men worked together on previous shipping agreements with the British. Both were well respected in London. Like others, they had no idea at this time of the whereabouts and viability of the Norwegian Government. After Colban updated Olsen on British pressure to take over Norway's ships, the two agreed that it was essential for their country to maintain control of the merchant fleet.

That same day, they started meeting with officials in the British Ministry of Shipping to articulate their concerns about efforts to transfer control of Norway's ships to Britain and to discuss the need for insurance for the fleet. Together, they convinced the Ministry that Norway needed to continue flying its flag on the country's ships and that they would help Britain gain more access to Norwegian shipping in the future. British officials wanted them again to broadcast information to counter the flurry of messages the Germans had been transmitting to ship captains. Olsen and Colban, however, wanted British help on insurance for the fleet before they sent any messages and therefore resisted the British demands. On 13 April the two sides finally reached agreement that Britain would indeed temporarily guarantee insurance for Norwegian ships at sea providing they proceeded to ports in the British Empire or to other ports friendly to Britain. The British preferred that instructions direct ship captains to

Canadian ports rather than to American ones, since Canada was a British Dominion, although they eventually agreed that American ports would provide safe refuge as well.[23] Over the following days, instructions were passed through Norwegian and British consulates overseas to inform captains of the British guarantee of insurance, telling them to disregard all messages coming out of Germany and Norway, where Germans were controlling communications, and to follow instructions to proceed to Allied or American ports. The 'war' to gain control of Norway's ships, however, was far from over. It continued for several more months, well into the summer, continuing to create confusion and unrest for crews. German consulates in several countries asked their hosts to take control of Norwegian and Danish ships in port. And in the United States, German embassy and consulate staff left their offices to visit ports at times to coax Norwegian captains to depart. All such efforts made no difference.

Had the Germans been able to capture the King of Norway or his Government, they might have been better able to entice those captains of ships at sea to comply. As it happened, not a single Norwegian ship took the German entreaties seriously. All eventually sailed for Allied ports and awaited further instructions. It would take months for this to happen and for detailed follow-on instructions to the ships to arrive. The enormity of what that now entailed – well over a thousand ships owned by private companies and individuals, many now trapped behind German lines in Norway, and over 30,000 seafarers – would not be lost on the King and ministers as they were fleeing across central Norway trying to avoid the Germans. They grappled with how to manage those ships, knowing that all of them would be important to the Allies and vital for the future of Norway.

During the discussions in London, fierce fighting under Major General Ruge's leadership had continued across central Norway. His strategy to delay the advance of the Germans was working, but the promised reinforcements from Britain had still not arrived. British officials in London had unfortunately been developing their own plans without consulting the Norwegians. Although they shared a common concern for Trondheim in central Norway, officials could come to no agreement as to how to proceed. Eventually, the British War Cabinet shifted ground combat units destined for Narvik southward toward the area of Trondheim. Some units cross-loaded between ships at sea and became separated from their equipment. Other supplies had been loaded on ships without consideration as to what was needed upon arrival. There were neither trucks for onward movement of units nor heavy weapons to support advances. The British did not anticipate coming into immediate contact with the determined and very well-trained Germans. Their plan evolved eventually into a multi-pronged approach to secure Trondheim, involving pincer advances from north and south of the city, followed by a direct naval and ground force assault on the city itself. Brigades would land at Åndalsnes, 100 miles south of Trondheim, and at Namsos, 100 miles north of the city. Another brigade would follow in the south. A well-trained French alpine battalion would assist. Very capable Norwegian units were already to the north and north-east of Trondheim fighting the Germans. The attack from the south would be code-named Sickle and the one from the north, Maurice. As Allied units advanced from these directions, a British naval and ground force would seize Trondheim in a move first code-named Boots, then Hammer. Overall, the plan provided a robust fighting force in terms of numbers, although much of it remained poorly equipped and trained. It was a disastrous strategy, though, since the Norwegians were fighting for their lives not there, but more than 100 miles further east of Trondheim. There was simply no tactical urgency in the British plan, and knowledge of the terrain was sorely lacking.

When units started landing at Åndalsnes on the morning of 18 April, nearly a week after Ruge had requested help, the British commander went forward to meet with his Norwegian opposite number. He agreed, contrary to orders, to move his force quickly eastwards by rail to assist the embattled Norwegians, instead of advancing north toward Trondheim. British and French forces were landing at the same time near Namsos in the north and were preparing to join Norwegian units for an advance south. All units soon bore the brunt of a determined German advance assisted by heavy bombing. German attacks caused heavy casualties in the Allied forces to the south, forcing a retreat toward the coast, with some troops breaking away and fleeing into Sweden for safety. The advance of Allied units from the north stopped well before any approached Trondheim. What was supposed to form a strong reinforcement for the Norwegians turned into a rout on both fronts of the supposed pincer movement. The ground war in central and southern Norway was coming to a quick end.

King Haakon, the Crown Prince and the Norwegian Government had fortunately succeeded in evading this fighting in central Norway as they fled toward the coast. When they arrived in the long valley of Gudbrandsdalen they joined the headquarters of General Ruge near the principal railway line running from Oslo to Trondheim and monitored the fighting.[24] During their escape they had been concerned about the future of the state as well as resistance against the Germans, and they understood that the future of Norway depended on preserving the country's merchant fleet, which now became the only source of revenue. It is doubtful they knew how confusing the situation was becoming for captains of ships at sea, who were unsure whether their country's government would even survive the German invasion. It is clear, however, that King Haakon and his ministers realized that something had to be established to control and manage Norwegian merchant ships, since many shipowners now were trapped behind German lines as well. What they decided would help determine the fate of the Allies in the Second World War as well as the future of Norway.

Travelling with them at the time was Øivind Lorentzen, the 60-year-old Director of Shipping for the Norwegian Government, a man with over forty years' experience in the shipping trade before becoming a politician. His directorate, created seven months before by the decree of 1 September 1939, was one of several in the Ministry of Supply. Lorentzen had grown up in a family with a shipping business and had become a partner in his father's company at the turn of the century. He had been an advocate of motorized shipping before the First World War, when Norway's fleet was still dominated by sailing ships, and eventually he established his own company specializing in trade between South America and the United States. His son, Per, was operating the company currently as chief executive officer. As Director of Shipping, one of Lorentzen's responsibilities was to ensure that shipowners did not overcommit their ships to the detriment of Norway's import needs. Policy at the time prohibited shipowners from dedicating ships exclusively to foreign markets. Each shipping company was required to carry imports as well. The King would appoint Lorentzen to a new position with much greater responsibilities, although his title as Director of Shipping remained the same. His role would be much broader and more challenging than anything he or any other Norwegian shipowner had had before.

The King and others knew that the Norwegian fleet would be key to Norway's future when the war ended. Those ships, over a thousand in total, were now spread throughout the world, most without communication with their owners or managers. No one knew the exact number at the time. The Government needed to establish control of them and ensure they continued to generate revenue for shipowners and the country. On 20 April some ministers gathered near the village of Otta northwest of Lillehammer and began drafting a mandate to nationalize the Norwegian fleet. Two days later, the King and ministers had fled further west and reached a farmhouse at Stuguflåten at the end of the Ramsdalen Valley. There, on 22 April, King Haakon signed a provisional Royal Decree placing all Norwegian-flagged ships of 500 gross measurement tons or more and outside German control under the management of the Norwegian Government. The new organization would take on the name 'The Norwegian Shipping and Trade Mission', to be shortened for telegraphic purposes to 'Nortraship'. On that day, Nortraship became the largest shipping company in the world. Øivind Lorentzen was its designated leader.

The following day, Lorentzen left Åndalsnes on the British cruiser HMS *Galathea* for London to set up an office to manage the fleet. With him were two other Norwegians to assist. Arne Sunde would arrange financing for the new organization. A lawyer, he was well known in political circles, having served as Minister of Justice and for a short period as a Supreme Court Justice. He had also represented Norway on the rifle team in the 1912 Summer Olympics and was a major in the Norwegian Army reserves. On 9 April he had volunteered immediately to serve and distinguished himself in action in central Norway, leading a battalion in fierce fighting against the Germans. But it was his banking background that the newly formed organization needed. Sunde had been on the board of the Bank of Norway, and at the time of the invasion he was the head of Bergens Privatbank in Oslo. A strong-willed leader, Sunde would assume an important role in the Nortraship organization, despite having no background in shipping.

The other important person chosen to assist was Benjamin Vogt. He had been Norway's emissary to Stockholm to negotiate the country's independence from Sweden in 1905. He had served as Minister of Trade and Minister of Auditing in years past and more recently as Norway's

Minister to the United Kingdom until the mid-1930s. He was well connected in London. Vogt would become the General Secretary of Nortraship and develop the administration needed for the large operations soon to commence.²⁵ Loaded on the British cruiser with these men as they pulled away from the shores of Norway was some of the gold that had been trucked from Oslo on the day of the invasion. It had been taken from Lillehammer by train to a railway tunnel near the west coast, and a third of it now accompanied them to London. The Government wanted to move the gold out of country in increments in case of a catastrophic loss of it all, since they suspected the Germans knew about the reserve and were eager to capture it. As the Norwegians awaited another ship, they continued hiding the remaining gold in the basement of a clothing factory in Molde.²⁶

At this time, the Germans still had no idea where the King, ministers or gold were hiding, but they knew the British were trying to advance toward Trondheim. Hitler ordered a massive bombing campaign of coastal towns to stifle British plans and to intimidate those attempting to conceal the King and Government. It commenced on 28 April and continued for several days. By the time it ended, the towns of Åndalsnes, Molde and Kristiansund had been seriously damaged, with most of their buildings destroyed. Thousands of Norwegians were left without shelter.

The situation across central Norway was becoming more precarious every day as efforts failed to halt the German advances. On 28 April, as coastal towns were being bombed, British Minister Dormer approached King Haakon with an urgent invitation from London to board a British ship for a safer location. He and the Norwegian Government, after much discussion, boarded the British cruiser HMS *Glasgow* on the evening of 29 April and sailed north towards the city of Tromsø, watching towns along the coast burning as a result of air attacks. Aboard the cruiser was another large portion of the gold reserves. The ship was headed to a location at the northern tip of Norway where there were no Germans. What Dormer did not share with the King and ministers that evening was that the British brigades around Trondheim would be evacuating a couple days later. It is not hard to imagine Major General Ruge's disappointment when he received word that the British were ordering their units to leave. By 3 May, barely two weeks after they had arrived in central Norway, British and other Allied units had reboarded their ships and departed. Ruge had hoped Britain would bolster his meagre force of volunteers much earlier. Now his army was on the run with nowhere to turn for safety, and the Germans were taking total control of central Norway. That left a single area still in contention, the town of Narvik with its port and railway to Sweden, which had been the primary German objective of the entire invasion.

Following HMS *Glasgow* to Tromsø was the rest of Norway's gold loaded on small vessels and fishing boats. On 23 May in Tromsø, all remaining gold reserves would be loaded on the British cruiser HMS *Enterprise* for England and for onward transfer to the United States. After the ship survived two German air attacks crossing the North Sea, the Norwegians took no risk of losing their gold when it crossed the Atlantic. They packed it inside barrels and strapped other empty barrels around them for buoyancy. Then they loaded the clusters of barrels into small yachts lifted onto the upper decks of five Norwegian merchant ships heading to New York.[27] The gold arrived safely and was deposited in the Federal Reserve Bank in New York.

Meanwhile, in Narvik, the German commander Major General Eduard Dietl, who had arrived with Warship Group 1 on 9 April, was anticipating a tough fight. He was an ideal leader for the operation, with much experience in mountainous terrain. Although his conquest of the town had proved easy, the subsequent loss of destroyers and merchant ships put him in a precarious position without the supplies, heavy weapons and ammunition he wanted. He integrated the seamen who had lost their ships into his land force and a few weeks later received a reinforcement of paratroopers, bringing the total strength of his force to around 6,000. Without the destroyers, though, he lacked significant firepower.

The British began adding reinforcements in the middle of April to augment the Norwegian alpine troops in the area around Narvik. They were ill-prepared to fight, however, because their equipment, like that of brigades landing near Trondheim, had not been combat-loaded onto ships, and it therefore took time to offload essential supplies. Troops also were not trained to fight in the wintry conditions of the extreme north. After highly trained French and Polish units arrived, the Allied ground forces numbered around 25,000, supported by the guns of British warships. Commanders could not initially agree on a plan. Attacks commenced on 29 April but became bogged down as heavy snow made movement difficult. It was not unusual for units to take up to ten days to travel only five miles.²⁸ Fighting continued throughout the next month. On 27 May, British ships bombarded Narvik and ground combat units launched a concerted attack. The following day, Norwegians entered the town, meeting no resistance. It became the first location captured by the Allies in the war. Dietl, on the brink of defeat, had withdrawn his troops earlier back toward Sweden and started establishing new lines of defence. Little did he suspect that the fighting was about to end. Much of Narvik lay in ruins, including the piers which were so important for shipments of iron ore.

King Haakon, Crown Prince Olav and the Norwegian Government had spent over a month in Tromsø as this was happening, trying their best to monitor the developing situation in their country. Whatever hopes they had after the positive developments at Narvik vanished when they learned of more evacuation plans. The situation on the European continent by this time had unfortunately affected the prospects in Norway. By the end of May, Hitler's forces had overrun the Low Countries and were pressing onward into France, encountering little resistance. On 26 May the British began evacuating forces from the French port of Dunkirk as the fall of France appeared imminent. Britain had to choose between continuing to fight in northern Norway and perhaps committing more forces there, or starting to consolidate military capabilities for the eventual defence of the homeland as the Germans cemented their control of Continental Europe. They decided to evacuate Narvik after destroying the port. It was a decision that did not sit well with the Norwegians.

Discussions about the final evacuation from Norway had begun as early as 23 May. The British War Cabinet endorsed the plan on 25 May, two days before the final push to capture Narvik, and the Supreme Allied War Council approved it on 31 May. By then a fleet of two dozen ships, including fifteen large troop transports, was preparing to sail to Norway to evacuate all Allied forces, less Ruge's command. Over that week of decision-making, no one informed the Norwegians what was about to happen. On 1 June Dormer advised Norwegian Minister of Defence Birger Ljungberg of the decision. Surprised, Ljungberg asked Dormer if Britain would be leaving any equipment behind so that the Norwegians could continue defending their country. Dormer had to tell him that everything was leaving.²⁹ Beginning on 4 June, British destroyers and Norwegian fishing vessels ferried the Allied troops to waiting troop transports. Four days later, all the troops and equipment had been loaded and were headed across the North Sea to Britain. The Germans were left in complete control of Narvik.

The British once again offered the King safe passage, this time to England. It was hard on him and members of the Norwegian Government to contemplate leaving their country in such a predicament. However, they agreed that it would be best for the future to do so and that they might be better able to resist from afar. On the afternoon of 7 June, the Norwegian Government held its last meeting on Norwegian soil for five years. Afterwards, Trygve Lie, the Minister of Supply, issued instructions for all remaining Norwegian merchant ships in northern Norway to proceed to Britain. At this time the Germans had taken control of most Norwegian merchant ships in port or in nearby waters in southern Norway, but they had been unable to secure many in the north. The King and Government boarded the cruiser HMS *Devonshire* that evening at Tromsø and headed toward Britain.[30] Steaming with them was the remainder of the country's navy, about a dozen vessels and 400 officers and sailors, as well as some army and air force personnel. Their passage was uneventful.

That was not the case for the Royal Navy. As it was preparing to conduct evacuation operations of the forces around Narvik, a flotilla of German warships had been heading north to render support to the beleaguered and outnumbered German forces there. Hitler had declared that Dietl should receive all the support he needed. So concerned had the Führer become about the possibility of losing Narvik that his headquarters had started directing the action there. Thus the Germans were as surprised as the Norwegians to learn of the evacuation of Allied forces. The port had become so damaged by the fighting, though, that ore shipments to Germany would not be possible before January 1941.[31]

German ships were able to inflict some final damage on the British. They sank two British merchant ships, a troopship not used in the evacuation, a destroyer and an aircraft carrier. If the Allied attempt to come to the aid of Norway had not been embarrassing enough, these losses certainly made it so. It could have been worse, of course. The German warships might have intercepted the cruiser HMS *Devonshire* with the King and Norwegian Government on board had they arrived in the north a little sooner.

The war in Norway formally ended on the evening of 8 June, when Generals Ruge and Falkenhorst agreed a ceasefire. The entire country would remain in German hands for the next five years. Although Hitler had succeeded in securing Norway and the important port of Narvik, the invasion had taken much longer than expected. Losses had far exceeded expectations. More than 3,600 Germans had died, over 250 aircraft had been lost, and the German Navy had nearly been decimated. However, Germany now controlled Norway from north to south, and eventually about 400,000 Germans would occupy the country. Hitler had failed to gain any cooperation from the Norwegians as he had hoped. The fight to take control of the country's merchant fleet ships had become an urgent priority for Germany, but Germany lost that fight, and thus its hopes of defeating Britain quickly would vanish, because the Norwegian fleet became vital in shoring up shipping during the next two years of the war, before the entry of the United States.

King Haakon stood firm in his resolve to fight until his country was liberated, but now he had to do so from Britain. He would arrive in London to discover that the organization he had established forty-five days earlier to take control of Norway's merchant fleet had been hard at work implementing his Royal Decrees. The organization had got off to a rocky start, however. Soon after Øivind Lorentzen arrived in London as the Director of Nortraship, tensions erupted with those who had already been working to re-establish control of the Norwegian merchant fleet. And externally, disagreements had developed about the future direction of the organization, its location, and even its commitment to the war

Chapter 4

Nortraship Starts Operating in London

By the time King Haakon and members of the Norwegian Government left Tromsø for Britain, much had happened in the new organization formed in London to manage Norway's merchant fleet. Consolidating management of some fleet operations was not a new idea at the time. A few years earlier, the Director of the Norwegian Shipowners Association had presented a report to the Government suggesting that the Association should take control of all public freight in a national crisis, to protect the flow of essential goods into Norway.[1] Imports accounted for a quarter of the cargo carried by the Norwegian fleet, a significant volume to be placed under separate management. The proposal was not accepted, but it spurred attention in some circles to the idea that separate, consolidated management of the merchant fleet or the cargo it carried could be a solution in an emergency. The situation that developed in April 1940 was far more complicated, however, especially since the Germans were seeking to take possession of Norway's ships. The Norwegians needed to act quickly to maintain control of their merchant fleet. Unbeknownst to King Haakon and others as they fled from German forces toward the coast, some members of the Norwegian Shipowners Association and officials in London were taking steps to begin doing just that. By the time Øivind Lorentzen arrived there, the organization established as The Norwegian Shipping and Trade Mission or Nortraship had already taken shape, although not quite as envisaged in the founding Decree.

As they negotiated with the British over insurance cover and sailing instructions for Norwegian ships in the immediate aftermath of the German invasion, Erik Colban and Hysing Olsen were considering an even greater problem. Since many shipowners were now trapped behind German lines in Norway, communication with their ships had been lost. A management vacuum existed for hundreds of ships scattered throughout the world. Olsen, the representative of the Norwegian Shipowners

Association in London, was a shipowner himself and could still issue instructions to the small number of ships he owned. Colban, however, as Norway's ambassador in London, had no authority over any ships, and captains could choose not to listen to him without penalty. Both men had close relationships with British Minister of Shipping Ronald Cross and his staff at this point and thought that with their help they could start establishing control over the many ships at sea. The Ministry of Shipping would have welcomed the opportunity to assist, since this would increase the likelihood that it could gain access to more Norwegian ships. It had hoped to take complete control of Norway's fleet, but Colban and Olsen refused to support such a takeover. It was understandable why officials then pressed the two Norwegians to seek more authority over the fleet themselves, since the situation in Norway remained so unclear. On 13 April Colban dispatched a message to the Norwegian consulate in Stockholm requesting authority for him and Olsen to issue orders to Norwegian ships in collaboration with the Ministry of Shipping.[2] This was a week before the establishment of Nortraship. His message did not go so far as to propose the requisitioning of ships, but it would at least put Colban in a position to tell ship captains what to do. Whether they would comply would remain to be seen.

Perhaps not surprisingly, some Norwegian shipowners and others in London with interests in Norwegian shipping held very different views and objected to such an arrangement with the British. They believed that more effective management was simply needed and proposed that a special committee be established instead to review shipping problems, ensure that ships had insurance, provide help in arranging crews, manage finances, and so on. On 16 April, a week after the German invasion, the Norwegian Chamber of Commerce in London chaired a meeting to discuss the future of the Norwegian fleet and suggested a formal organization be established to manage ships and related financial matters. Members of the Chamber volunteered to help staff the organization. There was much discussion, and shipowners liked the idea. Colban and Olsen objected to their proposal at first because they believed a separate entity would not be necessary and would prove difficult to start from scratch, as against operating with the assistance of the British Ministry of Shipping. However, the two men eventually agreed with the Chamber and the shipowners.[3] Everyone remained unclear about what was happening in Norway, including the status of their country's government. They did not know what the future held, but they knew it was important to keep ships away from the Germans and to continue sailing for the benefit of Norway.

The Chamber and others immediately began searching for suitable premises, and on 19 April they located a furnished office of 500 square metres in central London at 144 Leadenhall Street, conveniently located next door to the British War Risks Insurance Office and across the street from Lloyds of London. The committee rented it, with an option to use two additional floors in the building. The next day, a staff of a dozen shipping and insurance experts began moving in, initially as volunteers, to start building up the operation. It is doubtful that any of them understood what they were about to establish and how large and sometimes contentious the organization would become. They intended to use the existing network of shipping agents and representatives of shipowners throughout the world to maintain operations, once they had determined who they were.

The perception of those who had helped establish the initial organization was that Hysing Olsen and Erik Colban would form a team to lead the staff, with Olsen ultimately taking charge as Colban continued to fulfil his official duties. Both brought considerable worldwide expertise to the table, with Olsen providing a wealth of shipping experience and Colban possessing a long list of political contacts. The belief of the Chamber's members was that shipowners would still be able to establish contracts and make money on their own. Some might have thought that Olsen and Colban had been too close to officials in the British Ministry of Shipping at the time. But everyone pulled together to help make the new organization a success.

At about the same time came the first revelation that not everyone was 'singing from the same hymn sheet' as those government officials fleeing from the Germans in Norway. As Colban, Olsen and members of the Norwegian Chamber of Commerce were reaching agreement about the need for a new organization, Colban received a message via Stockholm from Foreign Minister Halvdan Koht stating that the management of any such organization should not be centralized in London, but divided between London and either Washington DC or New York City. At this point, Foreign Minister Koht was not aware of everything that had been discussed over recent days in London. Not surprisingly, his message received a chilly reception in London. Two days later, the British Government dispatched a message via its ambassador in Sweden to *Storting* President Hambro in Stockholm describing what Nortraship had achieved thus far and urging that the new organization not be split between Britain and the United States. Upon receiving the message, the Norwegian and British consuls in Stockholm met and decided to recommend to the Norwegian Government that Colban chair the new organization and that the Norwegian Ministry of Foreign Affairs assume management responsibility for the entire merchant fleet.[4]

It is not known how these proposals eventually influenced decisions by the Norwegian Government or whether ministers even discussed them. King Haakon's provisional Royal Decree of 20 April proved to be something quite different. It appointed Øivind Lorentzen as the new Director reporting to Norway's Minister of Supply, Trygve Lie. When word of this reached London, it confused those who had spent so much time developing a management plan since the invasion. The Decree left unresolved the question of whether the organization would remain in London or be split between that city and another. The future role of Hysing Olsen, who had helped steer the interim solution so effectively, now appeared questionable. What became clearly apparent to all, however, was that a new director would soon be arriving in London with a mandate from the King to lead the new organization.

How many ships would be managed by the newly formed organization remained unknown as well. On the day the Germans invaded, more ships than normal had been in or around Norwegian waters, about 20 per cent of the entire fleet. Most of these, except those in northern Norway, had fallen into German hands. Another forty-two ships were in Swedish waters, and the Germans would try to take control of them as well, but twenty-nine would eventually evade the Germans, sail to England and register with Nortraship. Two weeks later, on 23 April, the day after the provisional Royal Decree established Nortraship, there were an estimated 1,028 ships of all types subject to requisition, including 242 tankers and 646 dry-cargo ships.[5] As German forces pushed through the Low Countries and headed towards France, Norwegian ships and vessels from other countries attempted to move to safer harbours. When France collapsed in June, twenty-six more Norwegian ships fell into German hands.⁶ Still, the management of about a thousand ships spread over the world presented an enormous challenge.

There were other complications. Since most Norwegians who owned and had previously managed those ships now were trapped behind enemy lines in Norway without communication to their ships or to the new Nortraship organization, people in London knew little about the whereabouts of ships, the cargoes they were carrying or their ultimate destinations. Operating procedures, financial arrangements and a host of other matters differed from company to company. Many ships were carrying cargo under contract to customers unaffected by the fighting in Europe and with specific terms of agreement and arrangements for payments, all of which were unknown. Lacking such information, the new organization needed to coordinate with dozens of consulates to learn the locations of ships, then to establish communication with ship captains to discover details of the cargo their ships were carrying, and eventually to disseminate instructions and standard operating procedures for the new government-run fleet. Most importantly, the organization needed to make financial arrangements to pay crews' wages and ships' operating expenses and to receive payments from existing commercial customers. Some ships would probably need repairs; others might be scheduled for dry-docking. Nortraship also had to confirm or re-establish a network of agents around the world to manage ships and cargo, ensure that cargo was delivered properly and, for most ships in the fleet not directly supporting the Scheme Agreement, secure revenue cargo for them to carry. To be sure, customers far away from the war in Europe were expecting their cargo to be delivered according to previous arrangements. For much of the fleet, no one knew who the customers awaiting this cargo or the ship agents managing deliveries were. The task was immense and urgent, because ships needed instructions as soon as possible, and some were carrying perishable cargo. Unfortunately, collecting such information and taking appropriate action proved to be a slow, complicated process. It would take not days but many months. Meanwhile, the Germans were trying as hard as possible to gain control of these ships for their own use.

To make the situation even more urgent, Britain continued to clamour for more tonnage. Before Nortraship could offer any more assistance to the British, though, it needed to figure out when ships would be free from charters or other commitments. Pressures would mount to balance requests for wartime support with commercial opportunities. Complicating everything was the sobering fact that the Germans no longer regarded Norwegian ships as neutral. All Norway's ships had become targets.

Lorentzen arrived in London on 25 April with the provisional Royal Decree establishing Nortraship in his briefcase and a power of attorney stating that the organization was intended to be the Ministry of Supply's Shipping Directorate in London with an advisory committee. A small number of newly hired staff had been working with Hysing Olsen to start locating ships and identifying management needs. All anticipated that Olsen, not Lorentzen, would be leading the new organization. Within two weeks the staff mushroomed in size from a dozen Norwegians to over a hundred, including many Britons. There was a severe lack of qualified people at first. Shipowners and agents in England were logical recruits, but personnel hired to staff the various offices brought widely different backgrounds to their work, although Norwegians held the top management positions. Many of the newly hired staff spoke no Norwegian, complicating communication and coordination. A major British accountancy firm was hired to handle most accounting functions. Departments were soon staffed to focus on tankers, dry-cargo ships, general maritime and whaling vessels, insurance, trade, chartering, crewing, accounting and more, with overall administration overseen by Benjamin Vogt, who had arrived with Lorentzen. All departments needed to develop policies to help guide their people and to manage the fleet. It was not long before more office space was needed, and staff started working in different locations.

There was a multitude of challenges and a true sense of urgency as a rush order was put in to install dozens of phone lines. Every day that the fleet lay idle at sea meant a loss of earning power of more than 3 million Norwegian kroner. Much cargo, some perishable, was en route to Norway on ships like the *Ringulv*, which had been turned away from the Norwegian coast so abruptly on the morning of 9 April. Once those ships were located, their cargo needed disposal or redirection. Norway had a large whaling fleet at sea with thousands of tons of whale oil destined for Norway which now needed to be sold elsewhere. Norwegian shipowners trapped behind enemy lines had contracted for the construction of dozens of ships, with payments falling due. Many ship captains were cut off from their owners and the management services they provided, especially arrangements to fund payrolls, provisions, repairs and a host of other needs. The main office of the classification organization *Det Norske Veritas*, which had become so important in establishing new standards and expectations for Norwegian ships and crews, was also trapped behind enemy lines. Financial credit for the new organization was badly needed as well.[7]

Arne Sunde had arrived with Lorentzen and his mission was to look after all the banking needs of Nortraship. He quickly started working on financial arrangements and establishing credit for the new organization. Sunde went to see an old friend who was the Director of Hambros Bank, explained the situation and received a written guarantee of £100,000. As a result of his efforts, the Norwegian Ministry of Shipping, the British Treasury and the Bank of England reached an agreement whereby ship agents eventually could forward money to Nortraship so that Nortraship could pay bills.[8] Before fleet representatives could be involved in these financial arrangements, however, every ship flying the Norwegian flag had to be located and informed it was now sailing for a new 'owner'.

The mission to locate and advise ships at first became the responsibility of Norwegian consulates around the world. There was little information available about charters, bills of lading, captains or crews. As soon as they located vessels, consulates informed captains that their ships had been requisitioned by the Norwegian Government and required each of them to acknowledge this with a formal statement: 'I hold my ship on behalf of the Royal Norwegian Government.' It was a slow process. Efforts would continue well into the summer, as Germany persisted in its attempts to convince captains to sail their ships elsewhere. Eventually, telegrams arrived from all ship captains acknowledging support. Consulates were soon flooded with other telegrams from anxious ship captains. Some needed sailing orders. All needed money. The consulates, however, did not have the funds to meet their needs. Once Sunde and others arranged for credit and banking, this anxiety was alleviated.[9]

Ship captains grew anxious about insurance, understandably, since they were directly liable for ships and cargo. The insurance provided by Britain the previous month had been a temporary arrangement to get ships into port and away from the Germans. Once Germany occupied Norway, though, that insurance became invalid. Fortunately, the British Ministry of Shipping, Lloyds of London and other insurance companies stepped in to provide cover for the entire fleet outside of Norway.[10] They did so without knowing the whereabouts, condition or cargo of much of the fleet. It was an amazing vote of confidence in the new organization.

At the beginning of May, legal questions arose surrounding ships with owners now confined to German-occupied Norway. Some thought that those ships might no longer be considered Norwegian and could therefore be impounded or even confiscated in certain countries. The Norwegian Government therefore designated Lorentzen as the official 'curator' of the fleet, with authority to act on behalf of shipowners when necessary.

On 18 May the Norwegian Government, then at Tromsø, issued a Royal Decree replacing the provisional one which had established Nortraship the month before. Previously, all Norwegian ships of 500 gross measurement tons or more had come under the management of Nortraship, except those already chartered by the Norwegian, British or French Governments. The revised decree expanded that initial requisition to include all ships registered in Norway or domiciled in the country as well as ships located in areas outside of Norway occupied by hostile powers. This included fishing boats and whalers, hundreds of which had escaped from the Germans and fled to Britain, as well as others in places as far away as Antarctica. Nortraship would eventually make many of these smaller vessels available to the British for use as coastal escorts, minesweepers and tugs. The decree went on to expand the authority of Lorentzen to include ships under construction or in port for repair. Ship agents or operators were instructed to deposit revenues after expenses in a special account with the Bank of England, with subsequent compensation to be determined by Norwegian law. Anyone violating these provisions would be subject to heavy fines and/or imprisonment.[11]

By this time, growing pains had become evident in the organization, not just because of new staff, the need to develop policies or the complicated tasks of trying to determine the whereabouts and contracts for ships at sea. Olsen and Lorentzen proved to be two quite different personalities. Olsen already had gained the respect of everyone who had participated in discussions leading up to the new organization, both Norwegians and British. But instead of taking advantage of Olsen's good relations with others and keeping him close by as a key advocate, Lorentzen relegated him to his former Shipowners Association office in the British Ministry of Shipping to serve as a liaison with the British and a member of the advisory committee for Nortraship. Many within the new organization and in the Ministry now came to view Lorentzen as an intruder who did not appreciate fully the hard work that had preceded his arrival. His leadership style tended to be assertive, and as the weeks went by, he seldom solicited comments or recommendations from the advisory committee. He insisted on being involved in most departmental decisions and personally approving all tonnage charters. It was not long before some started seeing him as a micromanaging dictator with little regard for others or for the committee formed to provide advice. To his credit, Lorentzen did focus quickly on getting things done, but his relationship with others in London, and particularly with Olsen, got off to a rocky start. Just two weeks after arriving, Lorentzen advised the British that Nortraship did not intend to provide them with any more ships than had already been transferred under the Scheme Agreement seven months before. That did not sit well with the Ministry of Shipping, and officials, in consultation with Olsen, continued to press for more help. Lorentzen concluded early on that Olsen had become too deferential to the British instead of focusing on the future interests of Norway. He would later accuse him of being more British than Norwegian, as their views about the commitment of ships differed.[12]

Before its first month of existence had elapsed, Nortraship had made much progress; but it soon confronted challenges that produced profound ramifications for months to come. The first came when the British notified Nortraship that they wished to renegotiate the Scheme Agreement. Although they remained frustrated that some of the 150 tankers in the agreement had not arrived because charters had not expired, the Norwegian tankers and dry-cargo ships they had received had succeeded in bolstering freight capacity. The tankers represented an increase of a third in the British-controlled tanker fleet, and because they were faster than many other tankers, the Norwegian ships helped to improve turnaround times. Over a quarter of all foreign ships arriving in British ports by this time were flying the Norwegian flag. Britain still needed more, however, because ship losses continued to rise. It had confiscated as many Danish ships as it could locate when the Danish king surrendered his country to the Germans; it had also completed some agreements with the governments-in-exile of Belgium and the Netherlands. The British now wanted twenty more tankers from Norway no later than October, as well as dozens more dry-cargo ships and the whalers that the King's revision to the decree had added to the Nortraship fleet.[13] The British were also concerned about the pay of British seamen compared to their Norwegian fellows.

It was an opportune moment for the two partners to reopen discussions, because the Norwegians also desired some changes to the Scheme Agreement. Germany's rapid conquest of Western Europe had trapped dozens of Norwegian ships in ports on the Continent, and they were now under German control. In addition to the loss of their ships, shipping companies had lost revenue from past shipments and from existing contracts as the Germans took over financial control of France. Shipowners needed guarantees that their ships would continue to be insured adequately. They were very concerned about the rates they were receiving for shipping and the method of payment. Market rates by this time were far exceeding the Scheme rates of sixteen shillings per ton. The Norwegians desired an increase of 50 per cent. And they wanted all future payments to be provided in US dollars rather than sterling, since the value of the pound was in steady decline.

Negotiations finally came to an agreement. After much discussion, the British guaranteed to Nortraship the French debt due to Norwegian shippers and agreed to use smaller Norwegian ships previously used in the coal trade to France. They committed to increase rates, payable in dollars for all ships, and to provide insurance. The Norwegians agreed to provide the additional tankers and dry-cargo ships as well as dozens of whalers, provided the British would only use the whalers in risk-free waters, and to better equalize seafarers' pay by adjusting war-risk supplements. On 28 May Lorentzen signed off on a memorandum of understanding with the British Ministry of Shipping, with more Norwegian ships to be delivered no later than October. This was the second agreement between the British and Nortraship.

The thorniest topic in these negotiations had been the reduction in the war-risk supplement that affected all seamen on ships operating on contract to the British. By the end of May German consulates had succeeded in sowing discontent among the crews of Norwegian ships. Some had started to refuse to work because their pay had been disrupted as Nortraship staff worked to sort out the whereabouts of ships and payroll requirements. They were unable to communicate with families and friends in Norway, and by this time, dozens of Norwegian ships had been lost on runs across the North Atlantic. Crewing a merchant ship had become treacherous work, and some seamen had opted for safer employment ashore or with shipping lines sailing in safer waters. The rapid collapse of Norway had made a bad impression on some Americans, who did not realize how valiant the efforts of many Norwegians trying to defend their homeland had been. When the Germans sank ships at sea, and rescued Norwegian sailors arrived in the States, the hapless seafarers often found little sympathy. Without employment and with little or no resources, such survivors struggled for subsistence and found few chances of employment as other Norwegian ships sat idle in port waiting for instructions from Nortraship on how to proceed. Some ended up in jail for various reasons.[14]

The pay of Norwegian seamen sailing under the terms of the Scheme Agreement was higher than that of British sailors. In addition to base pay, Norwegians were also receiving war-risk supplements for operating in dangerous waters. In ships sailing routinely across the North Atlantic, around the British Isles or in the Mediterranean, the impact of these bonuses was significant, often doubling or tripling the normal pay of officers and crew. According to the terms of the Scheme Agreement, Britain as the charterer of the ships was responsible for paying the supplements. The British had tolerated and subsidized this difference in 1939 because of negotiator demands and the urgent need for ships. Now that Norway was no longer a neutral country, they simply refused to do so. The British wanted the supplements reduced and capped at 100 kroner per month for all areas, regardless of risk. Pressure had been increasing for officials to do something about the pay disparity because it was affecting the morale of British seamen, some of whom were serving on Norwegian ships.

During the May negotiations, Lorentzen agreed to a reduction. According to the new agreement, Norwegian seamen sailing on ships chartered to Britain would receive a standard war-risk supplement of 100 kroner per month when sailing in dangerous waters, regardless of the degree of risk. The British were not trying to avoid paying bonuses to Norwegian crews; they simply wanted to avoid mutiny by their own sailors because of the disparity in pay. They agreed to continue paying into a separate account to compensate for what Norwegian seamen stopped receiving in bonuses. Because it would be untenable to track the

Nortraship Starts Operating in London 69

resultant differences in pay by crew and voyages, the British agreed to pay one shilling per deadweight ton per month for ships under contract. This amount changed later in the war, but all money went into an account referred to later as the 'Secret Fund'. How it was to be used remained unclear. Would the money be distributed to all surviving seafarers after the war, and if so, how? What about the contributions of those who had perished at sea? What if a sailor who perished had no family? Answers were not provided in the agreement. Reduction in pay would be a bitter pill for Norwegian seamen to swallow. They would not learn about the fund for several more years, but all soon discovered they were receiving less pay. The agreement took effect on 1 July.

As Lorentzen entered his second month as Director of Shipping for Nortraship, tempers were flaring across the Atlantic as Nortraship began implementing its authority over Norwegian vessels operating in lucrative markets there. Owners in America were reluctant to abide by decrees requiring them to relinquish ships to the Norwegian Government and send revenues to a bank in England. Because Nortraship was focused on revenue, it had started requiring information on available cargo space in order to maximize loads and thereby increase income. Agents did not want to keep Nortraship staff informed of available space, so that additional cargo could perhaps be added. Some were concerned that shipowners trapped behind enemy lines in Norway could demand the profits from their ships after the war eventually ended. And it certainly did not relieve any of their frustrations that the directives dictating all requirements were coming out of London. At the time, British and French consulates were urging Norwegian shipowner representatives in the United States to move their ships north to Canada. None of this sat well with those shipowners and shipping representatives in the States with contracts for Norwegian vessels. It was not long before they were meeting with the Norwegian consulate in New York City to try to chart a better path forward.

Over the years, trade across the Atlantic and Pacific and to South America had grown into profitable commercial markets for the Norwegians, with dozens of their shipping lines operating from the United States, including into the Great Lakes. Many of Norway's newest and fastest ships were now participating in high-revenue liner trade out of ports in the States. American businessmen, their country still a long time from entering the war in Europe, remained intent on keeping Norwegian ships operating there as well, despite what the British wanted. Norwegian shippers on the other side of the Atlantic were far removed from what had been happening in London and had little interest in the organization taking shape there. The war was of far less interest to them than keeping their ships at sea moving cargo for customers. Another contrast was between the attitudes of the British and United States Governments to Norwegian merchant ships. British officials consistently applied pressure on Nortraship to provide more ships to support the war with Germany; American officials did not. In fact, most Americans wanted their country to have nothing to do with the war in Europe.

Shortly after the start of the war, the US Government had provided Britain with dozens of ships totalling about a million tons of cargo capacity, including forty-eight vessels from the nation's reserve fleet. Although most of them were well over twenty years old, Britain welcomed all cargo ships that were seaworthy.[15] The transfer irritated some in the States who thought their country was destined to enter the war eventually and that those ships would then prove to be important assets.

The United States at the time was as dependent on foreign ships for its day-to-day needs as Britain was for its war requirements. Its own merchant marine moved barely 30 per cent of the country's imports and exports. Any change to the country's neutral status could lead to increased requirements for moving strategic materials. Because German advances in Western Europe had reduced the availability of ships for hire, the United States became more interested in retaining ships then operating on its own trade routes. It soon would accelerate its shipbuilding programme, but meanwhile there was no interest in forfeiting the benefits of the several hundred Norwegian ships participating in American trades. British demands for more Norwegian ships had therefore found few sympathetic ears in New York and Washington DC.

Norway's Government, to be sure, was torn in two directions. It was committed to supporting the Allied war effort, but it also was concerned about generating revenues from government and commercial contracts to help restore the economy of the country when it eventually became free of German control. Finally, to gain greater cooperation, Lorentzen proposed the formation of a five-person Norwegian Shipping Committee to collaborate with the Norwegian Consul in New York City to assess and manage shipping needs in the United States. The committee duly became a reality and conducted half a dozen meetings during the month of May. Not all members, however, agreed to follow guidance from London.

By the beginning of June, as Norway surrendered to Germany, and the King and Government fled to London, frustrations with the British developed on both sides of the Atlantic. Many Norwegians simply did not believe their country had received the support it deserved to take on the invaders, particularly after Britain had provoked Germany by intruding on Norway's neutrality. Then, with the British retreat from Dunkirk, concern emerged at Nortraship that Britain itself might be in danger of invasion; if that happened, its operations in London would be in a precarious position. Consequently, Lorentzen proposed relocating the entire headquarters to New York. Not surprisingly, this met with a great deal of opposition in London. British officials argued that any move should not involve the whole organization. As a counter, they proposed Montreal as a more suitable location for a small section of Nortraship, given Canada's wartime alignment with Britain versus the continuing neutrality of the United States. Officials believed that establishing an alternative location in Birmingham would also reduce risks to the organization. Their overriding concern was that, if Nortraship were to move to the United States in its entirety, then Britain would lose its close contacts for coordinating wartime shipping needs.

After much discussion at high levels, the British reluctantly accepted the notion of opening a branch office in North America subordinate to the London headquarters to strengthen the Norwegian Shipping Committee already formed in New York. Once the Ministry of War had directed the evacuation of Narvik, essentially pulling the rug out from under Norwegian military efforts against the Germans, the British saw that tensions were increasing between the two countries and they could no longer prevent part of Nortraship from going to North America. They therefore pressed further for a small office in Montreal, and in early June a Norwegian delegation travelled there to assess options. The British did not envisage, however, that a bigger division of the organization was on the horizon.

Meanwhile, the attitude of shipping interests in the United States toward Nortraship had not improved. The Labour Party, which was in control of Norway's Government at the time of the invasion, had put forward a plan to nationalize the merchant fleet and was distrusted because it had not been pro-business in the past. Some shipowners doubted its commitment to private companies after the war, believing that if it stayed in power the party might try to keep the fleet nationalized. Others clearly were concerned about retaining profits and keeping their ships out of harm's way. They had put much effort into establishing contracts and hiring agents in various places to acquire and manage cargo. Now they were being expected to transfer revenues from those trades to the Nortraship account and to depend on others to reimburse them fairly at some time in the future. Others were probably concerned about discrimination. Not all Norwegian ships operated in liner trades; some still operated as tramps, and their owners suspected they would be the first to lose ships as pressure continued from the British for more vessels. Owners simply felt they could manage their ships on behalf of their government better than Nortraship could.

One such shipowner was Thomas Olsen, who simply refused to relinquish his company's ships and challenged Nortraship to do anything about it. He did not believe that Nortraship had been intended to manage the vessels of Norwegian shipowners who resided outside Norway. Olsen was living in New York at the time and, with his brother, managing the Fred Olsen shipping company founded by their grandfather in the previous century. The family was well known in Norway and had developed an excellent reputation in international shipping. Olsen objected to the new arrangement so much that he refused to comply and wrote a pointed letter to the Norwegian government-in-exile in London, informing ministers that he was far better able than the staff of Nortraship to manage his ships for the benefit of Norway. Fred Olsen Shipping had over four dozen ships in operation before the war started. Many of them were supporting the war effort, and some already had been sunk. Olsen's words so upset Minister of Supply Trygve Lie that he stated Olsen's behaviour 'bordered on high treason'.[16] But Olsen refused to release control of his fleet to Nortraship as required by the Royal Decree, believing firmly that he could manage it better, and he told his ship captains to disregard Nortraship directives. His recalcitrance upset many, but to his credit, he was frank about his objections. He did not hide the fact that he was not adhering to Nortraship rules but he had focused his ships on supporting the war. Others soon proved to be less frank.

There was a reluctance on the part of Lie and others to press matters further with Olsen. Fred Olsen Shipping was a prominent company, and if it decided to bring a suit against the new organization in the States, the legal status of Nortraship itself might be called into question. The Norwegian Government had just fled from Tromsø and hardly had time to deal with that possibility. As a result, to the consternation of many, Nortraship tolerated his obstinacy in the hope that if he was allowed to managed his own ships he would forward their profits. It was something that they trusted all shipowners and agents to do, regardless of who was managing the ships.

Efforts from London to get the Norwegian Shipping Committee and Norwegian shipowners and agents in the States to abide by the Royal Decree failed. Therefore, Lorentzen decided his presence was essential and announced, on 17 June, that he was heading to New York himself to repair relations between the committee and Nortraship. By this time, the war situation had become discouraging, especially for those in Britain concerned with shipping. Losses to the British-controlled fleet, including around a hundred Norwegian ships, were about to top 700.[17] Experts had just started assessing the shipping resources needed to replace the massive amounts of equipment left behind in France after the evacuation from Dunkirk, much of which needed to come across the Atlantic from the States. When Italy declared war on the Allies on 10 June, that essentially closed the Mediterranean to the British-controlled fleet, significantly affecting transit times to the Indian Ocean and the Middle East. British ships escaped relatively unscathed from the Mediterranean at the time, since most of them were outside Italian waters. Norwegian ships, however, did not. The Italians captured three of Norway's ships supporting the British and sank another within a matter of days.[18] Then the fall of France on 22 June complicated matters further. It meant that the Germans, who already had been exceptionally successful in intercepting shipping, could now threaten ships around Britain much more easily. A crisis was developing, and once again British officials would look to the Norwegians for help. By then, however, Nortraship would be dealing with a crisis of its own making

Chapter 5

A Shipping Crisis Develops for Britain

The creation of Nortraship was instrumental in ensuring that Britain received the ships Norway had promised under the Scheme Agreement, as well as additional ships as the months went by. Had the British decided to take control of Norwegian ships in British waters when Germany invaded Norway, this would have jeopardized the possibility of gaining more tonnage later, especially from the Americas, where many of Norway's most modern ships were located at the time. Increasing the size of their merchant fleet remained a constant aim of British officials. At the start of the war, the British fleet consisted of about 3,000 ocean-going ships and 1,000 coastal vessels, some 2,000 vessels fewer than in the First World War; but the average carrying capacity of ocean-going ships had doubled from 2,300 tons to 5,250 tons over the two decades since that time.[1] This meant, however, that whenever a ship went out of service or was lost at sea, twice the amount of cargo left supply channels. During the first months of the war, Britain was fortunate to be able to charter ships from neutral countries like Norway, and it was able to capture others. These additions helped to offset losses to such an extent that the actual size of the British-controlled fleet changed very little at first. It was not long, however, before officials realized that a crisis in shipping was looming on the horizon. This resulted from a variety of causes, some of which were present even before the war began.

The first concern was the shortage of reserve stocks, starting with oil. Petroleum products had become of increasingly vital strategic importance, both for day-to-day life and for the military. Recognizing the increased reliance on oil after the First World War, the War Department had planned on building up sufficient reserves to take care of the military's needs for six months if war broke out again. For the Royal Navy, this amounted to 3.3 million tons of fuel, and by 1936 all but a half a million tons were in place. Two years later, as concerns developed about the inadequacy of reserves and the sources of petroleum, the Oil Board raised the figures.

The Air Ministry, for example, was expected to establish reserves capable of covering an entire year of consumption. At the start of the war, though, none of the services had succeeded in building up reserves to expected levels.[2] There was plenty of oil available on world markets, but the problem was two-fold: there was a shortage of storage tanks at some locations in Britain; and a more persistent challenge was the long distances over which ships had to travel to supply the oil from sources in the Middle East, the Caribbean and the Americas. Round-trip travel from these areas, including loading and discharge of tankers, averaged two months, even under optimum conditions. Increasing reserves by millions of tons took time, and by 1939 time was running out. Then, as the war started and supply lines from overseas sources were cut off, resulting in the loss of both cargo and ships, reliance on reserve stocks increased, creating a need for even more replenishment and thus more tankers. As the country consumed more than it could store, Britain soon found itself close to two million tons below its target for oil reserves.

Without the level of reserve stocks they wanted, the British then became even more dependent on accurate forecasts of anticipated consumption and on timely deliveries. Both greatly affected requirements for tanker ships. There was no international standard for classifying ship capacities until well after the war, but the average tanker capacity of the British-controlled fleet at this time was considerably less than 10,000 tons. Ships were quite small when compared to today's gigantic vessels, which sometimes have fifty times more carrying capacity. An annual increase of five or even ten million more tons of oil to make up for reserve shortfalls and meet higher demand meant a minimum of 500 more tanker sailings, and maybe as many as 1,000, by the British-controlled tanker fleet of various ship sizes. If each tanker could make five or six round trips per year, this meant that over a hundred tankers would be needed just to cover the increase, without any interruption in shipping. Less capacity per tanker meant even more tankers or more voyages would become essential.

Complicating matters further was the process of oil refining. Although Britain had some refineries at the time, most refined fuels, especially the high-octane fuel known as British Air Ministry or BAM 100, came from abroad. BAM 100 gave a major advantage to Britain's Spitfires since it increased speed by about thirty miles per hour, added thrust and improved overall manoeuvrability. About half of BAM 100 shipments came from the United States, some from the Caribbean and some from Abadan in the Middle East, which had one of the world's largest refineries, owned by the Anglo-Iranian Oil Company. Shipping crude oil increased the need for tanker capacity, since it took roughly two tons of crude oil to produce one of refined fuel.

Another factor was the tankers' need for maintenance. Unlike today, when supertankers specialize in specific types of liquid cargo, Second World War ships carried refined or 'clean' fuel interchangeably with crude or 'dirty' oil. Tankers carrying refined fuel like BAM 100 deteriorated more rapidly and required more frequent maintenance. Consequently, the more a ship hauled over greater distances, the sooner she had to be pulled out for service.

At the start of the war, the British merchant fleet, by far the largest in the world, included 500 tankers, close to the number needed to accommodate annual requirements in case of war, depending on distances and disregarding any losses or other complications. There was no flexibility in official estimates, though, and the shortage of reserve stocks and the increased projections of requirements made matters worse.

Therefore, not surprisingly given estimated consumption figures, the British Government moved swiftly to bolster its tanker numbers. They had been given assurances that sufficient tankers would be available in the world marketplace. In 1939 the Sea Transport Department, responsible for estimating the availability of ships, concluded that there would be more than 300 tankers surplus to world trade requirements and available to Britain.[3] That conclusion is difficult to comprehend, since such a surplus would have represented more than half of the tankers in Britain's possession and dozens more than the Norwegians had in their large tanker fleet. Confidence in the availability of tankers might have influenced the lack of construction contracts given to British shipyards. No tankers were built in Britain before 1941.[4] At the start of the war, the Government therefore chartered the entire fleet of ninety-three tankers from the British Tanker Company, the transportation arm of the Anglo-Iranian Oil Company in the Middle East. The Ministry of Shipping wasted no time in procuring more from neutral countries, and the Norwegian tanker fleet became a prime target. That is why the British were so insistent on including 150 Norwegian tankers in the Scheme Agreement negotiations that began in the fall of 1939. Even with Norwegian tankers included, the British were hard pressed to meet their needs.

Once the fighting started, estimates and actual consumption confused projections for tanker requirements even more. The Admiralty, for example, estimated its requirement in 1939 to be about 3,276,000 tons. Actual consumption proved to be over a half a million tons less.[5] Offsetting that were estimates by the Air Ministry doubling the forecast requirement for first-line operational aircraft from 300,000 to 700,000 tons per year.[6] It is not difficult to understand how such fluctuations further exacerbated concern about tanker shortages as the war progressed.

The types of ships sailing the world's oceans at the start of the Second World War added to the challenge of determining requirements. Half of all merchant ships in the world by this time were powered by diesel engines. That meant that bunkering these ships in the British Empire required stocks of fuel and tanker ships dedicated to replenishing these sources of supply. Most of the diesel-powered ships in the British fleet at that time could burn coal as well. The same was not true of ships in other fleets, however, and different types of fuel were therefore needed at ports because of the varied nature of the ships now in the British-controlled fleet. This meant additional distribution networks of tanker and cargo ships focused on bunker supplies, especially as other countries in the British Empire became involved in the war and fighting eventually spread to other theatres.

Projections of dry-cargo and related ship requirements were a little more accurate, but by 1940 problems of a different nature were developing. First was the over-optimistic projection that dry-cargo ships under British control would be sufficient to handle wartime requirements. Raw material needs were estimated to be 32 million tons per year, and food was estimated to add a further 15 million, yielding a total of 47 million tons. The importing capacity of British ships was judged to be 48 million tons at the time, and therefore some concluded that demand could be met. However, by the end of the year, not surprisingly perhaps, imports had dropped noticeably because the capacity and availability of the dry-cargo fleet had been overrated.[7] Estimates simply had not considered the potential impact of ship losses or delays, let alone the likelihood that military requirements might increase. It did not take long for losses to start. In the first nine months of the war 150 dry-cargo ships in the

British-controlled fleet were sunk.[8] Fortunately, the British would be able to replace them over time with various vessels from other countries.

Soon after the war began, imports of wheat dropped dramatically in September and October. By November shortages had become so severe that some mills were running out of supplies for processing, and the Ministry of Food raised concerns. The interruptions in grain supply were caused not by ship shortages, but by an unusually late harvest in the summer of 1939 and occasional bad weather in shipping lanes. The Ministry of Shipping subsequently prioritized wheat shipments over other commodities so that, by the end of the year, concerns about shortages had diminished. Unfortunately, the shift of shipping to carry food led to shortages of other commodities, namely raw materials and timber controlled by the Ministry of Supply, which then led to more complaints.[9] In April 1940, concern about possible shortages of raw materials and timber became particularly alarming when Germany invaded Norway, gaining control of the Baltic and the entire Norwegian coastline up to Narvik. That meant Britain lost nearby sources of ore and timber from both Norway and Sweden. It now had to look to the United States and elsewhere for such cargo, which extended sailing times from weeks to months and meant that more ships were needed to keep up with requirements.

It was not long before concerns developed, due to lack of shipping, about the country's ability to sustain imports. By the beginning of 1940 rationing had commenced in earnest to reduce consumption and maintain reserves. Economists in the War Cabinet office concluded that dry-cargo imports in the second year of the war, from September 1940 to August 1941, would decline by 25 per cent to 35 million tons. As troubling as their projection was, it proved optimistic. Actual imports during that time fell to 31 million tons.[10] Rationing kept tightening.

Britain's responsibilities did not end with the homeland, however. Much of the British Empire had become drawn into the war, and colonies around the world also depended on British shipping for their everyday needs. Economists had not succeeded in taking account of those requirements, and the Empire stood to suffer even more as shipping capacity declined.

The events of June 1940 had an enormous impact on the British requirement for ships and on overall shipping performance, conditions that would persist for quite some time. When Italy declared war on the Allies on 10 June, the Mediterranean became effectively closed to Allied shipping. Although the Royal Navy had a sizeable fleet based in Alexandria at the time, it took the rest of the year before it could re-establish sufficient control of some of the Mediterranean to start safeguarding cargo ships travelling there. This had significant ramifications on ocean shipping in general and on supplying parts of the British Empire in particular. No longer could ships travel just the 3,000 miles from Britain via Suez to reach India, Australasia and the Far East; now they had to travel around Africa, increasing the journey by 10,000 miles or more. That meant a round trip from Britain took over three months, and ships had to stop in African ports to refuel and replenish supplies. Such distances caused huge problems in ship availability, the need for additional escorts, turnaround times, inventories, and a host of other issues. This had an impact on oil deliveries and the turn-times of tankers, because Britain was dependent on oil fields in the Middle East.

As reinforcement of Britain's army in Egypt and a build-up of forces in East Africa became necessary, demand for other types of commercial ships emerged. First was the need for troop transports. Moving units across the North Sea to Norway and the English Channel to France had been relatively easy, but getting them to the Middle East and Africa, particularly with the Mediterranean closed to shipping, was quite a different matter. Complicating matters further, few of the many ocean-going ships Britain controlled could carry passengers. Britain had lost six of its troop transports in the short campaign in Norway. It soon would face the requirement to move around 100,000 troops to these new theatres and thus needed to convert vessels or contract for transports – about 150 merchant ships were needed to transport troops to Africa and the Middle East.[11] Needless to say, these shipping needs were not included in initial estimates; it simply had not been possible to anticipate the expansion of the war into other continents.

Germany's rapid advance across the Low Countries and into France complicated supply and shipping even more. When the British evacuated Dunkirk, for example, they left behind the vast majority of their equipment. Losses included thousands of artillery pieces, tanks, vehicles, hundreds of thousands of rifles and machine guns and millions of rounds of assorted ammunition. Although British industries could replace much of this in time, Britain would still rely on the United States to make up a good portion of the losses, especially the immense quantity of small arms and ammunition. That would require more ships not included in forecasts, and months of sailing time. Additionally, Germany's conquest of Europe cut off the availability of goods that the British had been importing from the continent like wheat, oats, potatoes and other crops, as well as coal and iron. These now had to be supplied from further afield as well.

Most importantly, though, the fall of France meant that the Germans could threaten British merchant ships much more easily in the English Channel and as they were leaving the British coast for the Atlantic. Newly conquered bases and ports in France – at Brest, Lorient, La Pallice, Saint-Nazaire and Bordeaux – were 400 miles closer to England than bases in Germany and the U-boats were now only 25 to 50 miles away from the English coast and adjacent to shipping lanes. That was only part of the problem. Airfields in France brought hundreds of German planes into the hunt for British ships. Hermann Göring, the head of the Luftwaffe, had thousands of planes at his disposal, and many of them could now operate out of French airfields and, upon taking off, spot British ships off the coast of England. By mid-August, even long-range artillery was being employed on the coast of France to fire across the Channel and threaten shipping.

Britain had learned a lot about the effective use of convoys in the First World War and began employing them at about the same time that it declared war on Germany. It was no surprise to anyone that the use of escorts to protect merchant ships significantly affected delivery patterns and times. Ships had to marshal with each other in a particular location to wait for their escorts. For those leaving England from the east coast that generally meant assembling between the Rivers Thames and Forth, and from the west coast, off Land's End. As the war progressed and more cargoes originated from North America, it often meant circuitous routings of merchant ships to reach assembly areas, just to avoid German submarines. Once there, they assembled according to speed, most often in two groups, with one convoy sailing at eight knots and another at twelve. Convoys added protection for ships, but they also slowed down many deliveries, significantly reducing the efficiency of shipping. Ships sailing slower than convoy speeds had to move independently; those sailing faster could either travel independently or lower their speed to remain in convoy. Ships sailing at eighteen knots might be able to avoid convoys because they could normally outrun submarines. Seldom, however, could

During the late nineteenth and early twentieth century, the Norwegian fleet was large but outdated, with many merchant ships under sail. (1A)

A row of sailing ships await cargo in Kristiansund, c. 1910. (1B)

During the First World War, German U-boats sank 177 Norwegian sailing ships, most of which operated in the North Sea. The *Snespurven* ('Snow Sparrow') was torpedoed off the coast of Britain in 1917. (1C)

By 1939, Norway's merchant fleet was the most modern in the world. Here is one of its 'liner' cargo ships capable of speeds up to 17 knots, which made them desirable for commercial markets. Some were refrigerated. Such ships were in high demand during the war. (2A)

Norway's modern passenger ships also were in high demand as troop carriers. This one provided a regular service between Norway and Britain before the war. (2B)

A typical Norwegian tanker ship. The Norwegians provided 150 to the British immediately after the outbreak of war in 1939. By 1941 they were carrying nearly half the oil that Britain needed. (2C)

Whaling was big business before the war, and the Norwegians were the first to build floating factories for processing the catch. Norway had twelve whale factory ships at the start of the war, each with nearly twice the capacity of a normal tanker, and the Allies were eager to use them. By the end of the war, all but three had been lost. (3A)

Crews would pull the captured whales into the stern of the ship for processing. (3B)

Smaller whale boats called 'catchers' would harpoon the whales and bring them to the factory ship. Before the war, Norway had over a hundred whale boats supporting the factory ships, and these also served the Allies in various roles. By the end of the war, 80 per cent had been lost. (3C)

Vidkun Quisling, the leader of the fascist party in Norway, encouraged Hitler to invade and claimed to have many sympathizers in his country. He was wrong; Norwegian resistance in most places was determined, and Quisling was executed as a traitor after the war. (4A)

Immediately after the Germans seized control of Oslo, Quisling announced he was the new leader of Norway and went on the air to encourage Norwegian ship captains to sail to German-friendly ports. None did. (4B)

Hitler appointed General Nikolaus von Falkenhorst (left) to plan the invasion of Norway. He is shown here with Lieutenant General Hjalmar Siilasvuo of Finland. (4C)

Curt Bräuer was Germany's representative in Oslo. The invasion came as a surprise to him. The evening before it happened, a delegation from Falkenhorst gave him specific instructions from Hitler, which included the task of convincing King Haakon VII to surrender. He failed, and was sent to the Eastern Front. (4D)

In the early morning of 9 April 1940, Warship Group 5 entered the fjord leading to Oslo. The Norwegians sank the cruiser *Blücher*, killing a thousand of her crew and stalling the operation. The delay allowed King Haakon and his Government to escape from the capital. (5A)

Narvik was a major German objective because it was the only link in the winter months to the Swedish iron ore mines. The battle for Narvik lasted for two months, after which the town was so damaged that ore could not be moved through the port for nearly a year. (5B)

Kristiansund was one of several coastal towns devastated by bombing as the Germans pursued the King. (5C)

King Haakon VII, Crown Prince Olav and Government ministers evaded German efforts to capture them. The King and Crown Prince are pictured here at Tromsø in northern Norway on 7 June 1940. Their cheerful appearance belies the sadness they must have felt. They boarded a British ship that evening for London and would not return for five years. (6A)

Just after the invasion, Major General Ruge was appointed to lead Norway's military. He is shown here on 7 June 1940, the day the King and government officials left the country. He negotiated the surrender with Falkenhorst the following day. (6B)

In London the King established a government-in-exile. As the years went by, he provided frequent updates and encouragement to his people in occupied Norway. (6C)

C. J. Hambro, President of the Norwegian *Storting*, took charge on the morning of the invasion to relocate the King, the Government and the country's gold. (7A)

Johan Nygaardsvold was Prime Minister throughout the war. (7B)

Trygve Lie was the Minister of Supply at the time of the invasion. He drafted the royal decrees signed by King Haakon and initially had overall responsibility for Nortraship. He eventually became Foreign Minister. (7C)

Halvdan Koht was Minister of Foreign Affairs and a noted scholar. He wrote many books, including a biography of Henrik Ibsen. (7D)

King Haakon appointed Øivind Lorentzen to head the Norwegian Shipping and Trade Mission, known as Nortraship. Shown here in London, Lorentzen later moved to New York to manage operations there. (8A)

Lorentzen introduces banker Arne Sunde (right) to Norwegian Foreign Minister Erik Colban (left) in London. Colban played an important role in helping to preserve the fleet. Sunde became Minister of Supply/Shipping and Lorentzen's boss. They had a testy relationship. (8B)

Ingolf Hysing Olsen worked with Colban and others to set up an office in London to manage the Norwegian ships. He eventually led the London operation when Lorentzen went to New York. (8C)

Per Lorentzen, the son of Øivind, headed the Chartering Department in New York. He and his father became the subjects of several allegations. (9A)

Hilmar Reksten, a smart shipowner and protégé of Arne Sunde, questioned Lorentzen's leadership and made several allegations against him and his son Per. (9B)

Dinner on board a Norwegian ship. From the right: Erling Dekke Næss, Crown Princess Märtha, Lorentzen, Crown Prince Olav, Christian Blom (head of Liner Department), the ship's captain. Naess was instrumental in negotiating the final agreement for Norway's ships. (9C)

The offices on Leadenhall Street in London where Nortraship began operating on 19 April 1940, three days before the King issued the decree formally establishing the organization. (10A)

The offices on Broad Street in Manhattan where Lorentzen opened a second Nortraship office in July 1940. (10B)

The London office began operating in April 1940 with just a dozen employees. (10C)

As the months went by and Nortraship became more and more involved in the war, the workforce expanded both in London and New York. Eventually, Nortraship had branch offices on six continents and about a thousand employees. (10D)

Seafarers take a coffee break while wearing a Norwegian-designed, life-saving body suit. These helped them stay upright in the water so that they had a better chance of survival. (11A)

Over 4,000 merchant seamen on Norwegian ships perished at sea while assisting the Allies during the war. The continual hardship and stress of the war at sea is apparent on the face of this sailor in 1944. (11C)

Crews were always on the alert for threats at sea from warships, armed merchantmen, submarines, planes and mines. (11B)

Not until later in the war were weapons installed on Norwegian ships so that sailor-gunners could attempt to provide some defence. The dog with this seafarer seems to be cooperating with the photographer! (11D)

Norwegian ships carried hundreds if not thousands of planes across the Atlantic to Britain. (12A)

Locomotives and rail cars being loaded on to Norwegian ships in the United States. (12B)

(12C)

Stevedores tried to maximize the space on ships. Here drums of oil line the top deck of a Norwegian ship. Oil and petroleum products were always in high demand. (12D)

Convoys offered protection, but they created much congestion at ports since ships arrived in groups. These ships are anchored at Bedford Basin, Nova Scotia.(13A)

A convoy in the English Channel under attack by German artillery firing from the coast of France. (13B)

Several thousand merchant ships from all nations were lost during the war. Nortraship lost about half of its fleet supporting the Allies. This ship met its fate off the coast of Africa. (13C)

On entering the war, the United States was unprepared to protect merchant shipping. German U-boats deployed off the eastern seaboard scored dozens of hits, and tankers were particularly vulnerable. This tanker was sunk off the New Jersey coast in January 1942. Dozens more met a similar fate. (13D)

Vice Admiral Emory Land (shown with Sir Arthur Salter of Britain on left) led the US Maritime Commission and War Shipping Administration. He was the driving force behind the construction of Liberty Ships. (14A)

America's Liberty Ships were the salvation of merchant shipping later in the war. The ships were smaller and slower than most Norwegian cargo ships, but nonetheless crucial. (14B)

Liberty ships loading at berths in Portland, Maine before heading across the North Atlantic. (14C)

Britain launched the merchant ship *Kong Haakon VII* for Norway on the Clyde in December 1941. She was one of the few ships Norway received to replace the hundreds lost at sea. (15A)

King Haakon returned to Norway on 7 June 1945 to much celebration. He is pictured here in Oslo on that day with Crown Prince Olav, Crown Princess Märtha and their children. (15B)

Minnehallen or Hall of Remembrance near Stavern is Norway's national memorial to its seafarers. Inside are plaques with the names of those who perished on Norwegian ships during the First and Second World War. (16A)

The author was invited to speak and lay a wreath at the Seafarers Memorial in Kristiansund on 17 May 2016. That experience was the genesis of this book. (16B)

they outrun German surface warships. There remained some risk for fast ships as well. The safety provided by convoys far outweighed the loss of efficiency, even though that loss of efficiency increased the need for ships. As an example, by the end of 1939 over 5,700 ships had sailed in British convoys, and German submarines succeeded in sinking only four.[12] Part of the reason for this was that German submarines at the time were hunting independently. That would change.

Failure to join or falling out of a convoy, however, dramatically increased the likelihood of enemy attack, and it was common for faster ships, like those in the Norwegian fleet, to cut their power in order to gain the additional protection of escorts. But slower speeds meant longer voyages. Sailing across the Atlantic and back took about two and a half months, including ship discharge; trips across the Pacific took twice that.[13] Longer voyages demanded greater inventories, until replenishment could occur. It became a planner's nightmare as losses in shipping lanes continued. Convoys and other defensive measures simply were insufficient to meet all the different threats at sea by the summer of 1940. German submarines sank fifty-eight ships off the coast of Britain in June, thirty-eight in July and fifty-six in August. German aircraft sank fifteen Allied ships in August alone.[14] As attacks in the Channel peaked in 1940, one in every three ships was either sunk or damaged.

By the end of 1939 Germany had also begun to lay magnetic mines around the British Isles. This was by no means a new weapon in the history of naval warfare, but these German mines quickly proved devastatingly effective. Sown into minefields by submarines, fast surface ships and planes, they detonated when detecting the magnetic signature of a passing ship. They forced convoys to stop until minesweepers could clear the fields, or to slow down to follow precise navigation routes. It was not unusual for convoys encountering such minefields to have to sail in single or double file in lines miles long, and as they did so they became even easier targets for German attacks.

Because of threats in the English Channel, attempts were made to reduce ship traffic there. It was not possible to eliminate all traffic because the population of southern England relied on the delivery by ship of heavy goods like coal. Before the war started, the British were concerned about threats to shipping off the south coast of England; they had considered shifting as much as 75 per cent of ships from London and other east coast ports to west coast ports and then moving cargo cross-country, but officials determined that the railway and road network could not bear the strain of hauling millions of tons of goods across the country.[15] Therefore, to help safeguard cargo travelling to the east coast, shipping was routed north, around Scotland and then south down the east coast, to avoid the Channel completely. This added more sailing days to each voyage, thereby increasing the frequency of sailings to maintain re-supply of important products. At the time, nearly half of all tanker deliveries headed to ports on the east coast of Britain. Also affected by such routing changes were ships sailing across the Atlantic. They no longer sailed south of Ireland but around the north to avoid German attacks. Such revised routes, although necessary to safeguard ships, reduced the sailing tonnage available.[16]

To counter the new threat of magnetic mines, the British began to cycle their merchant ships out of service so that protective degaussing equipment could be installed to cancel the ship's magnetic field. Degaussing is a process in which systems of electrical cables are installed around the circumference of a ship's hull, running from bow to stern on both sides. A measured electrical current is then passed through these cables to cancel out the ship's magnetic field. Although degaussing helped protect ships, it meant they could not achieve maximum speed near minefields, and installation of degaussing equipment took ships out of service for a period. Extra care still was needed as more minefields were discovered. From September to December 1939, magnetic mines alone accounted for the loss of seventy-nine merchant ships off the coast of Britain.[17] The threat of these magnetic mines significantly slowed the speed of cargo ships around the British Isles. A round trip from the Clyde to the Thames, for example, often took a whopping twenty-four days, about a third of the time it would take an ocean-going ship to sail from Britain to the West Indies.[18] Although degaussing had made magnetic mines less threatening by the summer of 1940, the Germans then introduced a newer acoustic mine, which was detonated by the sound of waves put up by passing ships. They fitted other mines with delay mechanisms so that they exploded days after they were laid, which presented special dangers in constricted waters during peak movements. Mines simply made shipping more complicated; even when ships could avoid them they had to slow down.

Another modification of merchant ships to add defensive capability had begun before the war, and this affected the availability of ships from neutral countries that Britain added to its merchant fleet. The Admiralty's Trade Division established the Defensive Equipment Merchant Ship organization, known as DEMS, which collected old naval armaments and fighting equipment and stored it at ports. The plan was to arm the 5,500 vessels of various sizes in the British merchant fleet with low-angled weaponry to counter attacks by planes and ships. The intent was for installation to take place while ships were berthed for loading or unloading, to minimize the delay to departure times. There are no figures available on how often installation prolonged stays in ports, but it is hard to imagine there were not frequent delays, especially during times when ports themselves came under direct attack. By the end of 1940, about 3,400 British merchantmen had been armed and staffed with trained Royal Navy and Royal Marine reservists.[19] Eventually, merchant mariners were trained to man the weaponry, and the programme was expanded to include ships that Britain had chartered. Installation, manning and training were slow processes. Two years after the start of the war, there was only a single 20mm cannon in the entire Norwegian fleet. A year later, more than 750 cannons had been installed on Norwegian ships, and by the end of the war there were an additional 1,700. The Norwegian Navy's Shooting Department was formed at Dumbarton and trained crew members to fire them.[20]

The challenge of maintaining the flow of imports was not limited to the length of voyages, the threats at sea, the size of fleets or ship losses. The effectiveness of shipping also very much depends on what happens when ships arrive in port. A lot had been written in Britain after the First World War about the problems of shipping in wartime, but hardly anything of value had been produced in the form of lessons learned or actual improvements to ports before the start of the Second World War. In fact, in the early 1930s the Committee of Imperial Defence had examined British ports and concluded that they were sufficient to meet wartime needs. Before the start of the war, however, the Ministry of Transport, which was charged with assessing the readiness of British ports, came to quite the opposite conclusion, indicating it was 'complete nonsense' to think that west coast ports were prepared to handle wartime supply requirements.[21] By the fall of 1940 the British indeed were struggling with severe congestion in their ports.

The congestion had started with the implementation of convoys early in the war. Although armed escorts were effective in reducing losses, convoying meant that ships all arrived in port at the same time, and this resulted in many having to lie at anchor until berths opened. Months later, as the Germans pushed through the Low Countries into France, ships from ports in these countries ran across the Channel for safety, compounding the congestion. Even in the best of conditions, it took many days to offload a ship. There were no such things as 40ft containers or efficient container cranes on piers in those days. All dry-cargo vessels during the war, less those carrying bulk cargo like grain or coal, were known as break-bulk ships. Cargo moved in boxes, crates or barrels, or was just packed loose into the hulls of ships. Sometimes trucks or tanks lined the upper decks and had to be removed before stevedores could open hatches to access cargo down below. Therefore, rates of discharge were slow compared to today. Labour disputes in the years leading up to the war had created tension among dock workers, agreements and regulations still limited working hours in the first year of the war, and it took time for a sense of urgency to develop. Even then, cargo discharge took time, initially averaging only 560 tons per working day per ship, before rising later to about 760 tons.[22] Even with that increase, most ships, other than smaller tramp steamers, would be sitting at piers for up to a couple of weeks before they were ready to depart on another voyage. Meanwhile, other ships were anchored nearby, vulnerable to air attack as they waited for berths to open. By the end of 1940, Churchill was becoming so exasperated at the slow discharge of ships at British ports that he asked the Minister of Transport to take action. The discharge time of a dry-cargo ship at Glasgow was remaining steady at twelve days. At Bristol it had risen to over fourteen days and at Liverpool, to nearly twenty.[23]

Another challenge was finding berths, repair materials and labour to keep ships fit for sea. By June 1940, ships immobilized for repairs accounted for roughly 7 per cent of the entire British-controlled fleet. This figure would rise to 13 per cent by January 1941 before starting to fall.[24] The majority of these repairs were not caused by damage sustained in enemy attacks but the result of mechanical failures. It was not unusual for ships purchased or leased from other countries to require repair when they arrived. And every ship chartered to operate in British waters needed installation of degaussing apparatus to counter detection by the German magnetic mines.

It did not take long for Churchill, still First Lord of the Admiralty and not yet Prime Minister, to see a crisis in the making. He pointed out as early as November 1939 that, even though losses of British-flagged ships had been decreasing slightly, losses of ships from neutral countries supporting Britain had been increasing. He understood that hopes of obtaining more ships from neutral countries had faded after Germany invaded Norway, Denmark and Western Europe, and he realized that Britain's shipyards had become incapable of replacing ships lost. Tankers, as experts had predicted earlier, were no longer available in the market for charter. Nearly one in ten of the tankers under British control had been lost. And although the size of Britain's controlled fleet was about the same as a year earlier, those ships were working far less efficiently.[25] Only two countries remained that could help with more ships. One was the United States, but its Neutrality Act restricted the help it could provide. The other was Norway, no longer neutral and now an ally. It was the only country that could continue bolstering Britain's merchant fleet, and the relationship with Nortraship, both in London and New York, became crucial in gaining additional tonnage.

The crisis in shipping had become so concerning by the spring of 1940 that Britain had concluded it could not continue protecting its merchant ships without help from the United States. Escort requirements for convoys were straining the Royal Navy's capacity, and in May 1940 Churchill asked the Americans for fifty destroyers. President Roosevelt offered them in exchange for being granted bases in Newfoundland and the West Indies, and in September the two countries signed an agreement.[26]

In the interim, though, Britain's relationship with Nortraship remained paramount. The second agreement that Lorentzen approved in May 1940 proved to be a positive step forward in helping Britain gain more ships over the next few months. It was the last agreement the British would reach with Nortraship as a London-based organization under a single leader. Future discussions would become more contentious as offices in New York and London came under two very different characters, who often disagreed. British views were hardening about how much support they should be receiving. King Haakon and his ministers had arrived in London and were establishing a government-in-exile, and Britain now considered Norway as an allied country at war, with its government on British soil and needing protection. Although the two governments were both committed to the war, their priorities would differ. Pressure would mount on Norway to provide additional ships to help, and this would pit the two offices of Nortraship against each other, London focusing more on the war, and New York on revenues for Norway when the war ended. Before the two governments signed their second agreement in October, however, Britain would be fighting for its own survival, relying on Norwegian ships already on charter, as Germany prepared for another invasion

Chapter 6

Nortraship Expands to New York as the Crisis Deepens

As Lorentzen was about to leave for New York to work on improving relations with shipowners, King Haakon, Crown Prince Olav and the Norwegian Government arrived in London. They would take up residence there and establish a government-in-exile in the hope of fostering resistance to the German occupation of their country. But with few warships and planes and only a tiny military force, building up the ability to make a difference would take time. Moreover, the Allies were no longer focused on Norway; Germany and now Italy held their full attention. Shortly after his arrival, the King started weekly radio broadcasts to the people of Norway, trying to bolster morale by encouraging them to persevere and assuring them that their government would return in time. Haakon and his ministers knew that the Royal Decrees released in April and May offered the best hope of helping the Allies win the war and assuring the financial wherewithal to rebuild the country when it finally ended. Nortraship controlled the largest fleet in the world, and he had entrusted the leadership of the new organization to Øivind Lorentzen in the expectation that the ships would support the war effort and build revenue for the future. It is doubtful that any of them knew at the time how difficult that would be or how tumultuous the relationships would become within Nortraship and with the shipowners on which they relied for help.

Lorentzen had gone to New York to meet with the Norwegian Shipowners Committee that he had formed to assess the best way forward to manage Norwegian shipping in America. His priority was to meet the executive committee, which informed the rest of the group. They had rented a small office so that they could meet away from their companies. There can be little doubt that Lorentzen was considering the possibility of finding a much larger office in New York, contrary to what the British desired, even though a team was already in Montreal assessing the viability of an office in Canada. It remains unclear how much thought he had given to the challenges of forming a new organization, with its potential to duplicate the operation in London. When he had arrived in London at the end of April, work already was starting in an atmosphere of cooperation. All were positive, and a sense of urgency prevailed to gain control of a fleet that the Germans were aggressively seeking to seize. The whereabouts of the King and Government were still unknown, and the future of Norway was far from clear. Many shipowners were trapped there now, and their ships were without management. The team pulled together with a sense of purpose and genuine commitment to Nortraship.

The atmosphere in the United States would be different. At the time, dozens of Norwegian shipping companies operated out of the Americas, and many owners lived there. Some, like Thomas Olsen with Fred Olsen Shipping, felt a separate management arrangement was unnecessary. He had set a precedent for non-compliance, and the Norwegian Government had not intervened to stop him. Ships in the States mostly were sailing without threat in profitable trade routes under contracts secured well before Germany invaded Norway. It did not seem necessary for them to take the profits from those contracts and pay them into a Nortraship bank account. Lorentzen needed to explain the provisions behind the Royal Decree and to urge cooperation. The small executive team of Norwegian Shipowners Committee had not developed consensus among shipowners, and it was not in a position to exercise management over a large fleet. The same conclusion had been reached when Erik Colban and Hysing Olsen formed a committee in London immediately after the invasion. The office in London was a direct result of recommendations by members of that committee. They were the ones who convinced Colban and Olsen it was needed. Lorentzen needed no convincing.

The recalcitrance experienced in the States was not just because some shipowners refused to comply. There was genuine confusion on the part of the Shipowners Committee as to what they were supposed to do or even could do, especially when it came to freight payments from ships. The guidance members had received was not clear to all. There was considerable discontent among owners of liners that were operating on long-term, established contracts. The impact on them would be different to that on a shipowner who was looking to charter an individual ship or to

Nortraship Expands to New York as the Crisis Deepens   89

sail a tramp to collect cargo. Therefore, Lorentzen was prepared to discuss in detail his responsibilities as Director of Nortraship and the repercussions if shipowners did not comply; the committee had received a registered letter with this information before his arrival. He arrived in New York on 7 July and started meeting with the Shipowners Committee. Ten days later, he met with committee members and shipowners and explained in detail how Nortraship was formed, his responsibilities as Director, what was expected of them and the potential repercussions of non-compliance. He discussed how the initial priorities of the organization had been to establish the condition and charters of ships and to assure captains that procedures were in place to take care of expenses. He reassured everyone that revenues from shipments prior to the Royal Decree would be kept separate from revenues earned thereafter, but stressed that all operating profits must now be forwarded to Nortraship. He emphasized that the Norwegian Government retained its legal standing and that courts in Britain and the United States would recognize the Government's authority over ships flying the Norwegian flag, regardless of Germany occupying the homeland. He stated that the Government could no longer allow agents of those ships to continue operating if they refused to cooperate fully. And he cautioned that, in accordance with the revised Royal Decree issued on 18 May, Norwegian shipowners who violated its provisions would be subject to imprisonment for up to one year and a fine of up to 100,000 kroner, or both. Moreover, ships involved in violations would be subject to confiscation. Lorentzen provided them with instructions for depositing operating profits in the Nortraship account and told them they needed to comply.[1] Shipowners grumbled after listening to him but, with rare exceptions, compliance followed. The Fred Olsen Company continued to manage its own ships although it relinquished profits to Nortraship, and by the end of the war few could doubt the company's commitment, since half its fleet was sunk while supporting the war effort.

After this meeting, Lorentzen thanked members of the Norwegian Shipowners Committee for their efforts, terminated the committee and announced that he was establishing a second office for Nortraship with himself in charge of both offices, in London and New York, having leased space at 80 Broad Street in Manhattan. This announcement was not popular in London, surprising Hysing Olsen and others, including Lorentzen's boss Trygve Lie and officials in Britain's Ministry of Shipping, who were concerned that split supervision could impact their current and future agreements for Norwegian ships. Arguments about leadership and responsibilities persisted for two months, and over that time Lorentzen's reputation in London suffered, especially after he attempted to reduce Olsen's authority there. When he departed for New York he had left Olsen in charge of the London office with power of attorney to take care of everything that might be needed. In late August, Lorentzen tried to revoke that power, but the Government overruled him.

Three more months elapsed before the Norwegian Government decided what to do about the development in New York. In August, a branch office opened in Montreal under the management of Benjamin Vogt. In future, more than fifty other offices would be established around the world on six continents. Hysing Olsen wanted to remain in charge of the office in London, but Lorentzen was adamant that he should retain authority over both offices. Eventually, Trygve Lie recommended to the King and Norwegian Government that the two operations should become parallel enterprises working independently and reporting to him. The King agreed and issued another Royal Decree on 25 October 1940 to implement Lie's recommendation, thereby dividing Nortraship between offices in the United States and Britain.[2] The whole episode leading to the involvement of King Haakon only worsened relationships between Nortraship's leaders on opposite sides of the Atlantic. The new structure also led to other dramatic changes that fed into British anxieties about securing more Norwegian ships.

Having two offices under different management meant that roles and responsibilities required delineation. The result was two quite different Norwegian fleets. The office in London remained responsible for ships detailed in the Scheme Agreement and others operating as far away as the Far East. Comparatively few of those ships by this time were operating in commercial markets. The office in New York gained responsibility for the rest of the fleet, the vast majority of which were operating commercially on United States trade routes in the Atlantic, Pacific, across the Caribbean and into South America. They became known as the 'free' ships. As the name implied, these were ships that the British viewed as readily available to assist their war effort. In terms of the total number of ships being managed, the new operation in New York under Lorentzen would be much smaller with only 282 ships, including 64 tankers, while the London office under Olsen managed 557 ships, including all the tankers in the Scheme Agreement and the new agreement initialled in May.[3] The London office remained responsible for insurance of the entire Nortraship fleet and for finances.

The New York office retained control of most of the newer and more desirable ships in the Norwegian fleet operating in commercial liner trades, which were producing the highest revenue for the future benefit of Norway. And although it was understood by both offices that these ships should be focused on the best market opportunities regardless of geographical area, there was no interest at Nortraship New York in putting these ships at risk in contested waters. Pressure came now from both Nortraship London and the British Government for Nortraship New York to do more to help the war effort, as Lorentzen and his staff tried to keep revenues growing. It led to perceptions that one office was focused on profit while the other was focused on supporting the war. Tension resulting from this would persist until the war ended. The first few months of Nortraship's existence were filled with confusion and internal conflict as the organization expanded across the Atlantic and worked to hire staff, gain control over the fleet at sea, establish and enforce policies and keep crews on ships. The organization was anything but a perfect marriage of personalities.

Lorentzen had not waited for anyone to agree with his decision to establish the office in New York or to object to his authority. He immediately began hiring staff to fill positions in an organizational structure paralleling that of the London office. Once again, the logical choices became shipowners and staffs from Norwegian shipping companies in the States, because they knew the business well and spoke a common language. These new appointments included, not surprisingly, some shipowners with strong attachments to their businesses.

One such man was a Bergen shipowner by the name of Hilmar Reksten. He had started his company with a single vessel in 1929, and by the outbreak of war had increased his fleet to six ships and gained a reputation as an astute investor. He volunteered for military service when the Germans invaded and led a resistance movement, for which he acquired some notoriety. Four of his six ships had been included in the Scheme Agreement and another became trapped behind German lines, leaving him with a single ship. Before Norway surrendered, he fled to

New York City with the intention of managing his last ship and making some money. Lorentzen selected him to be the head of the Chartering Department in New York. Reksten was a smart businessman and knew that Nortraship was tolerating Thomas Olsen managing his own ships. He therefore formed a Panamanian company for the only ship he had left, thinking he could keep it operating in commercial markets outside of Nortraship. He then chartered his ship along with some others in a new trade lane to Suez, where shippers were seeking options after the closure of the Mediterranean had quadrupled shipping time from Britain to the east. In part, this was a good idea. It would create other Nortraship liner service contracts there as the months went by, with even larger and faster ships, producing nice profits for Nortraship. Unfortunately for Reksten, as the Director of the Chartering Department, he was prohibited from chartering a ship to himself. He also chartered his ship at rates higher than others. When officials learned of this contract, it created an uproar on both sides of the Atlantic, not only in Nortraship offices but with British shipowners whose ships were totally committed to the war effort. They complained to their government that Nortraship New York was profiting at their expense and would shut them out of Middle East markets.

An inquiry found that Reksten had acted inappropriately, and discussions continued for months about what his future role should be, if any, within Nortraship. Trygve Lie and Hysing Olsen in London were incensed by his behaviour and urged that he be sacked. Instead of firing him, Lorentzen removed him from the Chartering Department and put him in charge of the Disbursement Department, perhaps appreciating that Reksten's shipping expertise would be difficult to replace. Many in the Government and in Britain's Ministry of Shipping were adamantly opposed to his remaining in the organization. British shipowners were also angry that Reksten had established a Nortraship-endorsed route in competition with their own ships. The fact that he had chartered his own ship as part of the new service just made it more distasteful.

Reksten's future with Nortraship was not decided in 1940, though. In the interim, Lorentzen proposed to Lie that his son, Per Lorentzen, fill the vacancy as head of the Chartering Department. Per, at the time, was operating the Lorentzen family shipping company Northern Pan-American Line, nicknamed 'Nopal', which provided a scheduled service between Brazil and the United States. Not surprisingly, this recommendation also raised concerns in London, coming as it did on the heels of the uproar caused by Reksten's actions. Minister of Supply Lie nonetheless approved the hiring, as long as Lorentzen's son made no decisions regarding the family business and Nortraship.

Not long thereafter, Hysing Olsen in London raised concerns with Lie about the Lorentzen family business, now exacerbated by Per Lorentzen taking over the Chartering Department. The friction between Olsen and Lorentzen had not lessened since Lorentzen's terse treatment after arriving in London in April. Olsen had harboured suspicions about Lorentzen well before the King appointed him to take charge of Nortraship. When he was Director of Shipping for the Norwegian Government, Lorentzen was responsible for ensuring that Norwegian shipowners complied with an obligation to periodically carry imports to Norway, rather than keep their ships operating exclusively in foreign markets. Olsen believed that, in his role as a policy enforcer, Lorentzen had permitted his family's shipping company to skirt round those rules before Germany's invasion. Nortraship's Financial Department was centralized at the London office, and Olsen kept his eyes on revenues. By the end of the summer he had come to suspect that revenues due to Nortraship from some shipowners and agents were less than expected, and he shared concerns with Trygve Lie about potential abuse by Lorentzen's own Nopal company. Olsen believed that Per Lorentzen, now the new head of the Chartering Department in New York, had not been following Nortraship rules. Rather than confronting Lorentzen prematurely, given the other pressing questions in the new organization, Lie issued guidelines to ensure that no additional agreements be made without all revenues being transferred to Nortraship. Specifically, this meant that if a ship was preparing to leave port not fully loaded as per a contract, and an agent found additional cargo for the ship, revenue from that added cargo became payable to Nortraship. Instead of taking immediate action, though, which would single out Lorentzen and Nopal, Lie instructed that all Nortraship shipping lines should submit their accounts for audit in the spring of the following year.[4]

Lorentzen's decision to establish the office in New York, the uproar that resulted from Reksten's action and the questions now being raised about Nopal were not the only sources of turmoil for Nortraship in the summer and fall of 1940. By then, crew members had started receiving far less pay because of the director's agreement with the British to reduce war-risk supplements. Many had families back in Norway, but they had lost all communication with relatives and did not know whether they were safe or even alive. Pay cuts just increased their anxiety. The Norwegian Government exiled in London had no information to share with them either. Seafarers with families had been advised that on 28 June a sizeable deduction would be made from their pay each month for dependants and deposited in the Norwegian Seamen's Savings Office in London. Some might not have been happy with that, since it remained unclear if families could even access the money. The only way of sending money to dependants in Norway was for the authorities to transfer it to Stockholm and then on somehow to Norway. The plan fell apart. The next month, Norwegian authorities in occupied Norway required shipping companies there to make allotments to families.[5] Deductions continued to be made from the pay of seamen outside Norway, who still did not know whether that money was reaching their loved ones. Meanwhile, they were being asked to sign on to sail in waters where German attacks were becoming more and more prevalent. The coasts of the United States had not yet become dangerous, but the other side of the Atlantic was becoming ever more treacherous.

To aggravate matters even further, hundreds of other Norwegian ships were operating in safe waters between the Americas and elsewhere due to the continuing neutrality of the United States. Crews on those ships were completely unaffected by Norwegian and British wage negotiations. They sailed under commercial contracts, largely without risk and sometimes at higher wages even without supplements. As seafarers sailing under Scheme arrived in America and became aware of such differences and pay cuts, many simply refused to re-board their ships. German consulates were eager to exploit this discontent. By midsummer Nortraship was having trouble keeping ships crewed, especially once they reached the United States. On 8 August, nineteen Norwegian ships remained in ports in the United States and Canada, mostly in New York, Philadelphia and Norfolk, with crews refusing to sail.[6] Strikes broke out as the discontent continued, and news of the situation was soon hitting the newspapers, depicting Norway in a bad light.

Lorentzen was not able to solve the problem on his own. Apparently, Churchill himself, by now Prime Minister, intervened and pressured the Norwegian Government to put a stop to the strikes.[7] Minister of Supply

Trygve Lie eventually travelled to the States in August to negotiate with protesting seamen. He could not go back on the agreement that Lorentzen had made with the British about reducing war-risk supplements, but he met with crews and unions and eventually received approval from the Norwegian Government to reinstate some supplements for specific routes. For example, seamen would receive additional compensation of 300 kroner for a round trip between the United States and Britain and 150 kroner for round trips to the Middle East.[8] The money would be paid from Nortraship revenues, not by the British. This became the only option for Lie to calm protests and get crews back on ships. The Norwegian Government's hands were tied. It had no legal authority to force crews in the United States or anywhere else back onto ships or to enforce compulsory service requirements, as it had for the military before Germany invaded. It was nearly two years later, after the passage of the Allied War Powers Acts, that the Government gained the legal clout to force its seamen to stay on board ship. Listening to crews' concerns and working with their unions remained crucial, and Norwegian ships retained the reputation of having high standards of safety and care for crews. One Danish historian mentioned that Norwegian crewmen 'travelled first class'.[9] It is doubtful whether they viewed it that way, however. Keeping ships fully crewed remained a problem during the war as losses at sea increased. Nortraship would turn increasingly to foreign countries to keep their ships fully manned, and eventually foreigners would comprise over 25 per cent of its seamen, more than double the percentage in 1940.[10]

Nortraship soon discovered that it had a host of other issues to take care of to provide for the wellbeing of its crews. Before the war, all seafarers had been included in the National Health Insurance Programme, which covered treatment of illness or injury in foreign countries as well as a free journey home. Administration of this programme collapsed after the invasion because seamen were cut off from shipowners and insurance offices. Nortraship rushed to set up medical offices in key ports. This was important not only to care for the injured but also to examine crews' health and ensure the working environment on ships remained safe. Other services for seamen were needed in port as well. Norwegian Seamen's Churches and Seamen's Homes had been helpful for many years. The churches had been established in 1864 to help keep seafarers connected to Norway. By 1939, there were twenty-five in Europe, Africa,

America and Asia, but they were no longer sufficient to cater for the many crews circulating through some ports. Nortraship worked with local authorities to provide new homes and reading rooms. Some of these areas, particularly in the United States, became centres from which Norwegian communities would grow after the war.[11]

As these growing pains were being felt inside Nortraship and with crews, Britain was experiencing a threat to its very existence. Although the Royal Navy far outnumbered the Kriegsmarine, Hitler's strategy of interrupting supplies to Britain had proved devastatingly effective. It had become impossible to counter all the threats to Allied shipping. Prior to the start of the war, dozens of German submarines had taken up battle stations to cover the North Sea, the English Channel and shipping routes into and out of Britain. Those submarines had sunk a total of 287 ships from September 1939 to the end of June 1940, but they were only part of the German plan to attack at sea. Mines of various types sank 182 and aircraft another 107.[12] Two pocket battleships had slipped out into the Atlantic before the war started and headed south. A third would join them in the wide reaches of the South Atlantic, where they would spread out and prey on unescorted British merchantmen supporting the Empire or returning with goods to Britain. The *Altmark* had been supporting one of these battleships for months before it headed back north and was intercepted by the Royal Navy off Norway. Germany also replicated a tactic it had used effectively in the First World War by converting ten merchant ships into raiders with cannons for surface and air attack, as well as machine guns and torpedoes. Six of them put to sea in the spring of 1940. These merchant-ship raiders, sometimes separated by vast distances in the Atlantic, disguised their appearance to fool other ships, frequently changing their identities with dummy funnels, adjustable masts, fake superstructures and different colours. The tactic proved remarkably effective in sinking and capturing merchantmen, thereby disrupting the long supply lines connecting British interests and the homeland. They had sunk six ships by the end of June.[13] Fast attack vessels known as E-boats proved effective off the shores of the European continent as well. Essentially heavily armed motorboats with torpedoes and flak guns, they could travel at speeds of 40 to 50 knots, surprise slow-moving merchantmen in the English Channel and escape before warships or planes could respond. These E-boats chalked up another five kills.[14] Shipping around Britain had become ever more precarious as Germany secured ports and bases along the English Channel. The situation demanded the full attention of Winston Churchill, recently appointed Prime Minister.

In June, as German submarines and planes were taking advantage of these new bases in Western Europe, Hitler's focus shifted to Britain with the intention of compelling the British to sue for peace. What became known as the Battle of Britain commenced in early July and continued to the end of October with a continuous bombing campaign. It started with German planes targeting coastal shipping around England, sinking thirty-three ships and damaging many more. Hitler contemplated launching an invasion of Britain across the English Channel in August. Although most of his generals were apprehensive about such a bold venture, given the challenges of moving large ground forces and overcoming the Royal Navy and British defences, Air Marshal Hermann Göring expressed confidence that his Luftwaffe could defeat the Royal Air Force and hold the Navy sufficiently at bay to mount a cross-Channel assault. Hitler approved Göring's proposal to conduct a preliminary air offensive and delayed invasion plans until September. Göring had amassed a large number of aircraft in bases across the Low Countries and into France, about 3,000 planes of various types, which was five times more than the British had available. This weight of numbers appeared to favour his plan to incapacitate the Royal Air Force, and air attacks started on 1 August, targeting airfields and infrastructure. British and Allied pilots, however, unexpectedly succeeded in breaking up German formations with the help of effective early warning systems, and with the added boost of the high-octane BAM 100 fuel their fighters outmanoeuvred German planes. The British lost over 200 aircraft in two weeks; the Germans lost three times as many. Churchill immortalized the heroism of the pilots in thwarting Hitler's plan when he declared to Parliament on 20 August that 'Never in the field of human conflict was so much owed by so many to so few.'

There can be little doubt today that the availability of fuel for those fighters, and the reserve stocks backing it up, would have been much smaller without the help of the 150 Norwegian tankers in the Scheme Agreement and the twenty others arriving after the revision to that agreement in May. They represented a combined volume of more than 1.5 million tons of oil. Ships in the British-controlled tanker fleet were averaging five deliveries per year by the spring of 1940.[15] This average turnaround rate meant that the Norwegian ships were probably contributing well over 7 million tons toward the Oil Board's revised annual requirement in 1939 for 20 million tons of oil. Given the speed of Norway's tankers, they could have been contributing even more. As a result, Britain was able to meet the Oil Board's projected requirements. Consumption had dropped, fortunately, because the Admiralty had overestimated its needs and rationing had proved effective. Imports to the United Kingdom during 1940 amounted to 11.271 million tons; they would increase by two million more tons in 1941. Refineries in the homeland added an additional 8.33 million tons in 1940 and slightly more in 1941.[16] Oil deliveries elsewhere in the British Empire and the replacement of bunker fuel along trade routes significantly increased delivery requirements. Consequently, estimates of the percentage of oil provided by Norwegian tankers to Britain during 1940/41 vary from 30 to well over 50 per cent, with the lower percentages generally found in British accounts and the higher in Norwegian. In either case, Norwegian tanker deliveries proved very significant to Britain in the early years of the war for the military, the civilian population and the Empire. After the summer of 1940, the availability of foreign tankers to Britain would decline, but by 1942 165 Norwegian tankers would still be augmenting the British fleet of 372.[17]

The importance of Norwegian fuel deliveries prompted British politician Philip Noel-Baker to state after the war that 'The first great defeat for Hitler was the Battle of Britain. It was a turning point in history. If we had not had the Norwegian fleet of tankers on our side, we should not have had the aviation spirit to put our Hawker Hurricanes and our Spitfires into the sky. Without the Norwegian merchant fleet, Britain and the allies would have lost the war.' Noel-Baker's statement is debatable. Britain might not have lost the war, but the Battle of Britain and Britain's ability to sustain operations after that fight could have been quite different. Norway's tankers would become even more important as losses at sea increased in the months ahead.

Hitler's attacks on Britain did not stop when the Luftwaffe failed to pave the way for a cross-Channel invasion. The Battle of Britain entered another phase of concentrated bombing by night on London and other cities, this time aimed at terrorizing the British population and destroying more shipping capability. Known as the Blitz, it started on 7 September with raids on London's docks which in one evening sank 21,000 tons of shipping and damaged an additional 48,000 tons.[18] The Royal Air Force did their best to counter these attacks, but they were unable to stop them. As air raids and blackouts began, the offloading of ships slowed and eventually stopped. With ships packing anchorages and awaiting berths, it seems remarkable now that even more vessels were not lost in those air raids. Attacks on ports continued for many months. It was not until the next year, however, that German bombing shifted from east coast to west coast ports, which were the busiest. In May 1941, over eight successive nights, German bombers struck the port area of Liverpool, at one point closing 118 of the port's 130 berths.[19] All such attacks severely damaged a port's ability to offload ships. Additional damage to storage areas, railway lines and roads made it more difficult to clear cargo from ports quickly and create room for more ships to discharge. Congestion in ports eventually became so serious that the War Cabinet took 40,000 troops away from their units and assigned them to ports to help clear cargo.[20]

As the threat of a German invasion subsided, an entirely new battle front opened with even greater shipping requirements, when Italy invaded Egypt in September 1940. As reinforcement of Britain's troops in Egypt and a build-up in East Africa became necessary, demand for more commercial ships emerged. Britain needed faster merchant ships to cut re-supply times for food and other essential stores destined for the Middle East. Of particular interest were the modern, refrigerated Norwegian ships operating in liner trades between the Americas, which were diesel-powered for speed to help keep produce fresh.

Therefore, the British called on the new Nortraship office in New York for help. When the fleet was split between the two offices, London had been allocated 570 ships, but it had few resources to offer. Included in its portion of the Norwegian fleet were 23 ships detained in French ports, 43 trapped in Sweden or Finland, and 151 tankers and 241 dry-cargo ships already on charter to Britain under the Scheme Agreement. That left only about a hundred ships, mostly tramps, operating commercially and available for other use.[21] All the tankers in the London fleet were already on charter to Britain. The London office received a little assistance when five Norwegian ships that had been trapped in Sweden made a daring escape from the Baltic and crossed the North Sea safely to Britain. Another attempt shortly thereafter met with disaster when more Norwegian merchantmen were intercepted by German ships and sunk.

Hysing Olsen and his team could offer no hope of increasing the size of the fleet it was managing.

The situation in the New York office was quite different. Of the 282 ships it controlled, only ten were sailing under the Scheme Agreement. All of those were tankers, which had been added following the agreement in May/June. Three of the ships controlled by the New York office were still detained in French ports. It had 88 liner ships, 126 tramp steamers and 54 tankers in commercial service or on neutral charter.[22] All of these 'free' ships controlled by Nortraship New York were hauling cargo for payment in dollars, not sterling, at freight rates far higher than the London office was banking from the British under the Scheme Agreement. Some of the liner ships were refrigerated vessels operating in highly profitable fruit trades between the Americas. Others were sailing on commercial contracts across the Pacific to Australia. Tankers were making high revenues from oil companies. The New York office remained adamant that it wanted to maintain control of the operation of these ships, insisting that they were essential to the future of Norway. Executives of Nortraship New York knew that it had taken years for Norwegian shipping companies to build up networks in these overseas markets. Ship losses and lack of revenue to re-establish the Norwegian fleet could bring all this hard work to nought. They feared that nations with greater financial resources could step in after the war and take over liner trade contracts if Norwegian ships withdrew from the market to support the war effort.

Part of the challenge facing Britain in its relationship with Norway and Nortraship since Germany's invasion was that it now had considerably less leverage over its ally. Britain had been a vital trading partner of Norway, and Norway relied on Britain and its Empire for many products, most notably coal. In the past, the British could threaten to cut off or reduce coal deliveries as they had in the First World War, but twenty-five years later, they no longer had such leverage. Norway had become an occupied country, and its government-in-exile needed revenue, not coal, to rebuild in the future. The high-paying liner trades to and from the United States helped to offset the lower rates in the Scheme Agreement. That is why Lorentzen tightened his grip soon after establishing operations in New York. It was not just he who was focused on retaining that part of the fleet. Powerful shipping interests also wanted those ships to remain in the American trade as well. They had no interest in abandoning profitable routes and their most desirable liner ships. Thus, the American section of Nortraship, distanced from the turmoil on the eastern side of the Atlantic, began rebuffing demands for more ships to help the war effort. The Norwegian Government had started to become concerned about revenues as well. As revenues began accruing in Nortraship accounts, Minister of Supply Lie complained to Lorentzen that they were less than expected.[23]

Disagreements about the commitment of ships were deepening by November, when an important change of ministers took place in the Norwegian Government. Trygve Lie, who had been the Minister of Supply responsible for both Nortraship offices, became Norway's Foreign Minister. Arne Sunde, who had arranged banking for Nortraship and developed a currency strategy, took his place. Sunde had remained in London and participated in most high-level discussions in the organization there. He was now the boss of both Lorenzen and Olsen, and he was a friend of Hilmar Reksten, who had been moved to the Disbursement Department after being removed from the Chartering Department in the New York office. Sunde took over his new position as Britain was starting to clamour for more ships. He had not been in his position long before he sent a telegram reminding Lorentzen that Britain was at war.[24] It still did not sway Lorentzen's focus on the need to increase revenues as Nortraship supported the war. Trygve Lie had just reminded him of it before changing ministries.

Britain would continue pressing the Norwegians for additional ships, but it needed many more ships than the Norwegians could provide. Ship losses were averaging a hundred per month. By July 1940, even before the worst losses occurred, the British Minister of Shipping had concluded that this rate of loss was unsustainable. He dispatched a team, known as the British Merchant Shipbuilding Mission, to the United States in October to discuss an accelerated shipbuilding programme, and its members met with Rear Admiral Emory Land, Chairman of the United States Maritime Commission. After discussing their needs with Land, they headed out on a whirlwind tour of shipyards and succeeded in striking an agreement with Todd Shipyard Corporation near Seattle, Washington for 120 ships to be constructed in yards on both coasts. The first sixty were promised in twelve months, with the remainder within the following year.[25] This agreement was a welcome relief, but delivery of the ships was still a long way off.

As the end of 1940 approached, both Britain and Norway had been seriously affected by German maritime attacks. Since June, when Norway surrendered to Germany, the British-controlled merchant fleet had lost 719 merchant ships, including nearly one in ten tankers.[26] Of those, 173 were Norwegian ships, constituting roughly 25 per cent of all British-controlled fleet losses.[27]

Churchill continued to concern himself with this deepening crisis. The size of the British-controlled fleet at the end of 1940 was about the same as when the war started, due to the influx of ships from other countries; however, the fleet was working much less efficiently. The increased transit times around Africa to the Middle East for oil, after the Mediterranean was closed, affected tankers twice: first in getting full loads of fuel to Britain, and secondly having to return to the Middle East empty over the same long distance. Unlike dry-cargo ships, which could reload supplies and continue deliveries, tankers unloaded their oil and then returned in ballast over the same route to load with more oil. The nature of their cargo made them inherently less efficient than dry-cargo ships, and increasing distances just made them more so. These distances also affected convoy escorts, which protected tankers whether sailing empty or full, because all ships now consumed three or more times the fuel they had used when transiting the Mediterranean. Since escorts were in short supply as well, it became essential to marshal tankers both in Britain and in the Middle East so that each escort could protect more ships. This meant that ships remained unproductive as they loitered in marshalling areas for other ships to arrive. In essence, the closure of the Mediterranean had the effect of cutting in half the size of the British-controlled fleet.

Another challenge confronting planners was that there were no other countries besides Norway and the United States that could offer help. Britain's shipbuilding industry had slowed almost to a standstill since the war began. It had no hope of making up for the continuing losses without help from the United States, both in building ships and in exerting pressure on the Nortraship office in New York. Churchill sent a letter to President Roosevelt on 8 December 1940 stating that the survival of Britain depended, among other things, on increasing the number of merchant ships supporting the Empire. He advised that Britain's shipbuilding capability had declined to a little over a million tons per year; he urged the United States to commence an immediate programme of building merchant ships, yielding a capacity of more than three million tons per year by 1942; and he requested that 'the United States make available to us every ton of merchant shipping, surplus to its own requirements, which it possesses or controls, and to find some means of putting into our service a large proportion of merchant shipping now under construction for the National Maritime Board.'[28] He did not mention Norwegian ships specifically, but there can be little doubt that Churchill knew that American shippers and Nortraship in New York were controlling many of the liner ships and tankers that his country needed in its controlled fleet. Roosevelt had recently been re-elected President and had developed real sympathy for the plight of the British. His administration would take steps to help them, but before that happened, a new German strategy resulted in even greater losses at sea.

Chapter 7

Britain Looks for More Help as Nortraship Priorities Differ

When Churchill expressed his concerns about merchant shipping at the end of 1940, Germany's strategy for its submarines had just begun to change. For the first year of the war the U-boats had stalked ships independently, mostly in waters close to the British Isles. Convoys had proved quite effective in reducing the threat, but the vast expanse of the Atlantic meant they could not be protected all the way across. Escorts were concentrated on the few hundred miles at each side of the Atlantic, the Canadian navy helping as ships neared North America. In October 1940 refuelling bases were established in Ireland which extended protection about 400 miles to the west. It was not until April 1941 that construction of further refuelling bases in Iceland permitted greater protection in the central North Atlantic.[1] The requirement to protect tankers on the long supply routes to the Middle East continued to deplete the number of escorts available, however, and this offered the perfect opportunity for the new German strategy of employing submarines in groups known as 'wolfpacks'.

After Germany's conquest of France, the Naval High Command in Berlin deployed U-boats to the French coast and established a headquarters nearby to communicate with the fleet at sea and relay commands. The number of ocean-going U-boats had by this time mushroomed from a couple of dozen at the start of the war to about a hundred. By the end of 1940, the fleet would double to two hundred, and although many had still not been deployed because crews were in training, many more were organized into wolfpacks. Most would deploy to the North Atlantic, although some would form off Gibraltar to intercept convoys heading south or trying to enter the Mediterranean.[2] The new strategy employed U-boats in groups of half a dozen to a couple of dozen to patrol a wide stretch of sea in search of convoys. As soon as one spotted

Britain Looks for More Help as Nortraship Priorities Differ   105

a target, it reported the location to the headquarters in France, which then issued orders to other U-boats in the pack to close in. The U-boat which spotted the target would continue shadowing the ships until others arrived, and then captains would initiate individual attacks against the ships they encountered. Attacks generally took place in the evening, when the U-boats could use darkness to their advantage, often surfacing to do so. It did not take long for the Germans to see results. In October 1940, one of the first wolfpacks consisting of seven U-boats attacked a convoy of thirty-four ships with six escorts en route from Sydney, Nova Scotia to Liverpool. It sank twenty of the merchant ships. When it had completed its attack on that convoy it detected another with four dozen ships heading from Halifax to Liverpool. It sank fourteen of those, raising the total losses to thirty-four in a matter of a couple of days.

As 1941 opened, the wolfpacks continued to be deployed. It was not long before losses of ships crossing the Atlantic exceeded those around the British Isles. In January, sinkings in the North Atlantic amounted to forty-two, compared to fifteen around Britain; in February they rose to sixty-nine, compared to twenty-six.[3] As these losses were accruing, the Luftwaffe continued its terrorizing bombing of British towns and ports, causing havoc to offloading operations. There was one small piece of good news at the start of the year for the Allies and Norwegians, however. Five Norwegians ships had broken away from Gothenburg, Sweden, where they had been trapped since Germany invaded Norway. They reached Britain safely.

At the beginning of the second year of the war, even more shipping was needed to supply essentials to other parts of the Empire. Italy had attacked British-controlled territory in Africa and presented a potential threat to oilfields in the Middle East, and Australian and Indian forces had been deployed there to help. The continued closure of the Mediterranean and the opening of this new theatre had created difficult conditions in Egypt, which was vital for supplying British military operations in the area and for protecting oil interests in Persia. Egypt was heavily reliant on imports of British coal as well as agricultural fertilizer, and its total imports including those raw materials dropped from three million tons at the start of the war to one million by the end of 1940.[4] Support of Egypt and the Empire would become known as the Cross Trades, and as the war progressed an ever greater effort was needed to keep cargoes flowing to these places and to keep supplies of fuel in place for bunkering ships.

Concern about shipping led to fresh discussion in Britain about the need for more Norwegian ships, while contrary attitudes were starting to harden even more in New York. On his appointment as Minister of Supply, Arne Sunde visited New York in 1941, shortly after the allegations had surfaced against Lorentzen's son in the Chartering Department. Lorentzen bent his ear over frustrations with the negotiation process in Britain; he was becoming more and more concerned that Olsen was getting too close to the British, and he criticized the negotiating process to his new boss. Lorentzen wanted ships in the Nortraship fleet to receive full market rates payable in dollars. There was no easy solution to giving up ships without causing adverse results. Simply providing more ships at much higher rates, regardless of where they came from, would annoy British shipowners since they already were receiving lower rates than the Norwegians, and would lead to more complaints about Norway profiteering in time of war. Most ships controlled by the New York office were receiving favourable market rates from commercial customers. He pointed out to Sunde that if his office allowed any more of its ships to work at lower rates, like those in previous agreements, then Norway would be losing significant revenue. At a minimum, rates had to be comparable. If payments were made in sterling instead of dollars, then the financial impact would be worse, since the fleet in the States was presently receiving payments in dollars. He alleged that the British had been using some of the ships under the original Scheme Agreement in places where they were benefiting from free market rates, at times even competing with Nortraship. Lorentzen argued that Norway's situation was very different to the challenges faced by other countries. Belgium and the Netherlands, with ships in the British-controlled fleet, enjoyed revenues from their colonies around the world, while Britain had its extensive Empire. But Norway's industries, other than its merchant fleet, had been lost, and it had no colonies. Nortraship was the country's only source of revenue in the foreseeable future.[5] Sunde was answerable to the Norwegian Government for the revenues Nortraship produced, so Lorentzen's arguments would certainly have piqued his interest. Sunde also had the political responsibility of ensuring an acceptable relationship between the Government and its two key allies. He agreed with Lorentzen that future agreements needed to consider the financial needs of Norway now and in the future.

While Sunde was visiting the New York office, Olsen was in the process of negotiating on his own with the British Ministry of Shipping, much to Lorentzen's irritation. He was adamant about being involved in any agreement involving ships in the fleet, insisting that he should be the one to determine which if any ships to provide the British with. In London, Olsen had been haggling with the British over a variety of issues from off-hire rates to insurance subsidies. He tried to get them to commit to including Nortraship in their programme of building new ships, even though construction was slow. There were 2.2 million deadweight tons of ships in the New York fleet and 3.3 million in the British. The Ministry wanted about half a million deadweight tons, including 50,000 deadweight tons of tankers, as well as some of the modern liner ships in the New York fleet. Olsen and the British reached a tentative agreement on 19 March 1941, and the London office started providing ships from its fleet.[6] The agreement included some favourable rate adjustments to previous agreements, but Olsen had not succeeded in gaining any commitment for Norway to be included in new ship construction. Nor had he coordinated the agreement with the New York office.

At the time, there were six Norwegian liners operating out of New York to Britain. They had become very important in increasing turnaround times, because these ships, with speeds of 16 to 18 knots, were fast enough not to need convoying. Britain agreed to subsidize the ships even more to keep them in service, but the British expression of a desire for fourteen more fell on deaf ears when the terms of the agreement were shared. Lorentzen and Sunde agreed that liners needed to stay in the American markets, although Lorentzen offered two of the less desirable liners and provided Olsen with a list of fifty-five other ships totalling 214,000 deadweight tons that could be transferred to the British.[7] They represented the smallest and least desirable vessels in the fleet. Olsen suspected the offer would upset the British. He was correct. Lorentzen and Sunde headed to London to discuss the matter further.

Upon arrival, Lorentzen demanded that he be involved in all future negotiations. Nor did he stop at that. He also insisted that Olsen provide him with daily reports on the status of charters and other topics of importance. This was more than Olsen could stand, and he informed his boss Sunde that he could no longer remain in Nortraship if he had to answer to Lorentzen as well. Sunde calmed him down and assured him that he still supported him fully as the head of the London operation. The British remained very upset, though. In a meeting on 5 May, Chancellor of the Exchequer Sir Kingsley Wood demanded that Britain be given the rest of the Norwegian ships to support the war effort. He insisted that the faster liner ships were essential to services across both the Pacific and the Atlantic because of their speed and ability to outrun German U-boats. Sunde countered that the ships in America were assisting the war effort already because they were helping the United States, and he pointed to the problem of inefficiency in British ports which had been affecting turnaround times.[8]

Both the Norwegian Government and Nortraship understood what the result would be if revenue from liner operations was forfeited without due compensation. Aside from the potential impact on future markets if these ships were pulled from service, liners brought in much more revenue than tankers or tramps. The value of a ton of cargo on a liner ship was just over £322 compared to £242–£258 on a tanker, depending on location.[9] Tramp revenue per ton was considerably less. Twenty-two of twenty-five shipping companies operated out of the New York office. Together the office controlled eighty-three liner ships and fifty-five tramps. The British named eleven of the liners that they wanted and requested negotiation for the remaining seventy-two. They also wanted thirty of the fifty-five tramps. They decided not to pursue the remainder because they were operating in the bauxite trade between the United States and Canada.[10]

The meetings generated much acrimony. By this time, the British Ministries of Shipping and Transport had merged to become the Ministry of War Transport. Lord Frederick Leathers, who had just taken over after the unexpected death of Ronald Cross, set everyone back when he claimed that Roosevelt himself had agreed to intervene on Britain's behalf if ships were not being utilized fully.[11] It is not clear whether this was a bluff. There is no question that Roosevelt was fully aware of the position of merchant shipping and of Britain's concerns, since he met regularly with Rear Admiral Land of the United States Maritime Commission. The threat of Roosevelt's involvement was sufficient to make the Norwegians realize that they needed to soften their approach. They and the British decided to examine ship availability and utilization together and to stop pointing fingers as they continued to negotiate. They formed committees to focus on dry-cargo ships and tankers. At one point, Minister of Supply Sunde suggested to Lorentzen and Olsen that perhaps it would be best to offer the British two dozen tankers. Lorentzen was quick to point out that a representative from the United States needed to be included in discussions before any decision was taken affecting tankers chartered to American companies.[12] The Norwegians therefore suggested that the committees be expanded to include the Americans, since they deserved a say in decisions involving ships that were serving them. Reluctantly, the British agreed. Americans joined the committees, starting in June, and as negotiators worked to come to an agreement, implementation of agreed measures began while discussions continued.

Although the war was far from over, Nortraship officials believed that Britain might discriminate against Norway after the war because of these ongoing disagreements about ship allocation and deployment. British negotiators had already dismissed Norwegian efforts to be included in shipbuilding programmes. Britain always had been the most important trading partner of Norway. Were it to cut off trade sometime in the future, it would have dramatic effects on Norway's merchant fleet and economy. The Norwegians expressed their concerns about not being included in shipbuilding plans, but Lord Frederick remained noncommittal.

Turmoil within the Nortraship organization continued in the first half of 1941 and was not limited to Lorentzen's frustration at being left out of negotiations. The uproar surrounding Hilmar Reksten and his tenure remained very much active at the start of the year. The issue had garnered attention at Government meetings, and various people spoke up for and against him. Two of the chief supporters of his staying in post were Director Lorentzen and the new Minister of Supply Sunde. It is highly doubtful that Lorentzen would have done so if he had been able to see into the future, because Reksten would become the source of unending allegations about his management and decision-making. Debate over Reksten's future with Nortraship became so heated that the Norwegian Government took a vote over whether he should remain in post. The ministers were evenly split, but Prime Minister Nygaardsvold decided in favour of Reksten remaining, probably due to the support he had received from Lorentzen and Sunde.[13] Later that spring, when shipowners submitted their accounts for audit as Trygve Lie had required before leaving to become Minister of Foreign Affairs, Sunde appointed Reksten to work with the audit team to assess results, much to the consternation of ministers and some in Nortraship. The audit of Nopal proved that there were irregularities in the Lorentzen family shipping company's accounts, and further examination confirmed that Nopal had received some commissions that should have stayed with Nortraship. Lorentzen disagreed with the findings of wrongdoing but admitted that some payments had been erroneously made to Nopal. He agreed to reimburse Nortraship for the improper payments and to cease any further involvement with his family's shipping company.

However, the discovery of the commissions paid to Nopal darkened the cloud over Lorentzen even further. Anyone who harboured concerns about his leadership style now had another reason to distrust the director. Sunde had already fostered some doubts about Lorentzen; however, he chose not to remove him, in all probability because Lorentzen had developed good relations with many in the States. Removing him would bring unfavourable attention to bear on Nortraship and, with everything that was under way, it could be challenging to replace him quickly. Sunde gained even more respect for his protégé Reksten because of his findings and asked him to continue providing feedback on operations in New York. Reksten became highly critical of Lorentzen's management, believing he was ill-suited to running such a big operation. When Reksten returned to his position in the New York office he continued examining practices there with the full blessing of Sunde and with unrestricted access to documents he deemed important. This back-channel of communication between one of his subordinates and his boss proved to be a lasting irritant to Lorentzen.

It is not known to what extent President Roosevelt was kept informed about Nortraship or the status of Norwegian ships operating in the United States at this time. It is clear, however, that the letter Churchill sent to him in December had found a very sympathetic ear, and he was looking to help the British. Roosevelt shared Churchill's maritime interests. He had served as Assistant Secretary of the Navy under President Woodrow Wilson during the First World War, specializing in merchant shipping and convoys, and was very much aware of the shipping crisis developing for Britain. In November 1940 Roosevelt was re-elected for a third term, and three months later, he directed Admiral Land at the Maritime Commission to provide him with regular updates on the progress of shipbuilding and the status of merchant ships in the war. He knew that during the first full year of the war Britain had lost over a thousand ships and that its shipyards were incapable of making up even a third of the losses.[14] The first half of 1941 would prove to be one of the most consequential periods of the entire war because of action taken by Roosevelt. It would produce dramatic effects for Britain, and although it helped the Norwegians as well, it also set in motion events that would eventually lead to the full commitment of Norway's ships.

The President had wanted to help the British for some time and he pressured others to increase the availability of merchant ships to support the war effort. He had directed previously that the nation should construct seven new shipyards and over 400 Liberty ships by the end of 1942, with a further forty shipyards and 1,200 more ships by the end of 1943.[15] But Roosevelt had been hamstrung since taking office by Neutrality Acts dating back to the mid-1930s which severely restricted the assistance that his country could provide to warring nations. The Acts did not distinguish between aggressor nations and victims. When the first one was passed in 1935 it imposed an embargo on war materials to all nations at war. The following year, a revision forbade loads or credits to belligerents. In 1937, a new Neutrality Act prohibited American ships from transporting supplies or passengers, but included a 'cash and carry' clause permitting the sale of supplies to belligerent countries providing they arranged for the transportation of the supplies and paid in cash. This clause was renewed by the start of the Second World War, but it became a major problem for the British as the war progressed, because Britain was running short of cash and the value of the pound had plummeted.

Without question, the biggest boost for Britain came in March 1941, when the United States Congress, at the urging of President Roosevelt, passed the Lend-Lease Act. He and his Secretary of War, Henry Stimson, argued to Congress that lending much needed supplies and capabilities to allies was a key step in buying security for the United States while the nation prepared for what seemed likely to be its own entry into the war. The Act also eliminated the requirement for countries to pay cash. Its initial aim was to help Britain, but Lend-Lease would eventually be used to assist Russia and China as well. By the end of the war, the new Lend-Lease Act would enable the United States to provide $50 billion to more than thirty nations around the globe. This was the reason, as the benefits of the new programme became more and more apparent, that America came to be dubbed 'the Arsenal of Democracy'.

In effect, after the passage of Lend-Lease, the United States could lend material to a warring nation like Britain with an open-ended line of credit, payable in ways other than cash and with unlimited payback periods. It became a legal way of giving other nations what they needed, and in return it produced opportunities for the United States. For example, Lend-Lease led to the opening of bases for the American military later in the year, from Iceland and Greenland south to Bermuda, which eventually became important for extending the air protection of convoys. It also enabled the transfer of ships to the Royal Navy to help it strengthen escort services, and allowed the repair of British ships in American shipyards. The Act did not help to alleviate Britain's urgent need for merchant ships, however, since shipbuilding programmes in the States were only just beginning, and Nortraship New York remained adamant that it wanted its fleet to continue earning dollars.

Therefore, the British again proposed an innovative solution, this time to the United States Maritime Commission, to appease the Norwegians and to take advantage of the terms of the Lend-Lease Act. What resulted was an agreement between Norway, Britain and the United States for seventeen dry-cargo ships. The Commission chartered the ships from Nortraship and paid for them in dollars provided by the Lend-Lease Administration. Then it made the newly chartered ships available for use by the British. This was a win for all three countries and the first step toward a partial thaw in the frigid relationships that had developed between Nortraship offices in New York and London and between the Nortraship organization as a whole and the British Government. It did not, however, reduce the British desire to gain access to all remaining Norwegian ships.

Tankers remained an immediate need for Britain since, due to continuing threats in the Mediterranean, delivery times from oilfields in the Middle East had quadrupled. Britain needed over a half a million tons of oil to meet its requirements, and efforts to coerce Norway into freeing up more tankers operating out of the States were still getting nowhere. All tankers in the fleet controlled by the Nortraship office in London were already sailing in support of Britain. Early in 1941, the British therefore asked the United States to build thirty tankers for them over the next few years. The Americans agreed, and construction commenced in April. This was a positive step, but the British need for tankers was much more urgent. To try to compensate for the lack of tankers, they focused on shortening the oil supply line by shifting deliveries from the Middle East to oilfields in the Gulf of Mexico and the Caribbean. That saved a couple of thousand miles and made re-supply more efficient; the time for a tanker to make a round trip to Britain fell by 30 to 50 per cent, depending on the weather.[16] Although this helped, Britain needed still faster turnaround times for the tankers in its fleet to reverse the decline in petroleum reserves.

Fortunately, the British were able, with the help of the Americans, to reduce oil delivery times from the Gulf and Caribbean even further through an innovative shuttle programme. Britain rented oil storage tanks in New York, Baltimore and Halifax, and the United States deployed fifty tankers, including Nortraship tankers serving American oil companies, to deliver oil from wells in the Gulf of Mexico and Caribbean to these facilities. The British then used tankers in their fleet to transport oil from the storage tanks across the Atlantic. The British Petroleum Board set up a Shuttle Department specifically to manage these shuttles and transfers. The new service started in May and reduced the cycle times of the British tanker fleet by ten days. From May to July 1941 alone, 2.5 million tons of oil were shuttled into these tanks.[17]

Another benefit of this arrangement was that tanker travel became safer. Given the continuing neutrality of the United States in 1941, ships operating for the Americans were not under threat of German attack. Since Hitler did not want to provoke America into entering the war, U-boats had not been deployed across the Atlantic. As a result, the shuttle service from the Gulf and Caribbean to the British-rented tanks on the east coast operated with relative impunity, thereby reducing the overall threat to British oil deliveries significantly, since their ships only became targets in areas away from the western Atlantic.

On 27 May, to free up more merchant ships, Roosevelt declared an unlimited state of emergency for transportation in the United States. This was precisely the type of decision which the British had hoped for. After this declaration, Admiral Land withdrew many cargo ships from domestic coastal trades, and transportation of cargo previously carried on merchant ships shifted to roads, rails and pipelines. Cross-country movement replaced long, circuitous ship routings to deliver oil to east and west coast ports. All this helped to release more vessels to satisfy British needs. Then, on 6 June, Congress passed the Ships Requisitioning Act, and Roosevelt delegated requisitioning authority to the Maritime Commission. Land immediately requisitioned foreign tankers from European countries overrun by the Germans which were sitting idle in American ports. The requisition was not applied to Norwegian ships, but it must have registered with Nortraship officials that the United States had put in place procedures which would enable them to do that whenever they deemed it necessary for the war.

Another pivotal event with great potential to affect Nortraship was the passage of Public Law 173, known as the Ship Warrants Act, by the United States Congress in the summer of 1941. The Act was designed to bring all ships engaged in the foreign trade of the United States under a coordinated national defence programme administered by the Maritime Commission. The Commission was authorized to give priority in the issue of ship warrants to those companies that agreed to comply. Warrants governed the use of dry-docking and repair facilities, cargo handling and refuelling. To secure a warrant and continue doing business with the States, shipping companies had to agree to coordinate their trades, voyage and cargo with the Commission. They also had to agree to fair and reasonable hire and off-hire rates for vessels. In essence, the Warrants Act enabled the Maritime Commission to set up and enforce the priorities demanded by the strategic and critical needs of the United States.[18] It meant that Nortraship and other foreign companies had to comply or risk the likelihood that the Commission would simply requisition their ships. It was becoming clear that the Americans intended to control all shipping from here on in their ports.

The Warrants Act was perhaps the first hard notice to the Norwegians that they could lose all leverage in the commercial marketplace. If they were refused warrants, their business in the States would collapse and their ships would face requisition. And if they strong-armed the British too much, then Churchill might very well give King Haakon or Norwegian Prime Minister Johan Nygaardsvold in Britain an ultimatum about the future use of Norwegian ships. Accepting warrants meant that shipowners had also to accept the rates determined by the Maritime Commission.

By this time Nortraship had established a good relationship with Admiral Land from the Maritime Commission, although the Norwegians realized that these good relations would not prevent him from doing what was best for the United States. He was aware of how important Norwegian ships were to the commercial trade in the Americas and of the contributions Nortraship had already been making to the war effort. He, more than anyone else, knew that the United States remained dependent on foreign shipping for its strategic as well as day-to-day needs. Shortly after the passage of the Warrants Act, he welcomed a group of Norwegian seamen at the Department of Commerce building in Washington DC. He went around the room shaking each man's hand and thanking him for what he was doing for the Allies. He talked about the challenges of shipping, the difficulty of meeting demands for oil and the difference Norwegian tankers were making. Then he heaped praise on each of them and their country, saying, 'I think it was a British publication which said that the Norwegian merchant marine was worth as much to the Allied cause as a million soldiers. Well, I want to say that this is no exaggeration. You are worth more than a million men.'[19] Land was referring to an article in the June issue of the British magazine *Shipping World* which had attributed the remarks to Churchill.

In the summer of 1941 the American people were still staunchly opposed to entering the war, but the British had succeeded in establishing a strong relationship with the US government. The British Merchant Shipbuilding Mission, which had visited the States at the end of 1940 to contract for ship construction, had shifted its focus to shipping in general and taken on the name the British Shipping Mission under the supervision of Sir Arthur Salter, the Parliamentary Secretary to the Ministry of War Transport. In the spring of 1941 the Mission rented offices in Washington DC adjacent to the Maritime Commission. Dozens of staff worked with Salter to establish relations with the Commission, Congress and the State Department. Although Lorentzen and others in Nortraship had many contacts in the capital, they had not succeeded in penetrating the White House to the same extent. Salter not only maintained frequent contact with Land; he also enjoyed regular communication with other close advisers to President Roosevelt, something which Lorentzen and others in Nortraship lacked. It was Salter's suggestions that led to the innovative tanker shuttle programme. He pressed the Maritime Commission repeatedly for additional ships, stressing that Britain still needed dozens more tankers to build up its oil reserves for the winter. On 11 April, after having dinner with Salter and listening to more requests for ships, Land relayed to Roosevelt his alarm at Salter's demands: 'If we do not watch our step, we shall find the White House en route to England with the Washington Monument as a steering oar.' The President responded to him three days later with a terse reminder of how important support for Britain remained: 'Which would you rather do, give away the White House and the Washington Monument and save civilization, including American independence and the democratic system, or have the White House and the Washington Monument taken over by people under a different regime'?[20] Roosevelt remained attentive to British needs, and it was not unusual for him to call Land and direct the disposition of specific ships to help Britain.

Salter had conveyed to some that Norway had agreed to transfer all its tankers. That was far from the truth. Nortraship had agreed to look at all options, but the tanker committee formed at the May meeting in London was still assessing possibilities. The committee had asked American oil companies to participate in discussions. There were sixty-three tankers managed out of the New York office at this time, and the British wanted half of them now and the rest later, as well as six whale-oil processors, which had nearly twice the capacity of the tankers.

Nothing happened quickly. Committees continued to assess options and ship utilization. Although during the summer some American oil companies agreed to transfer tankers to aid the British, others did not. One Texas company threatened to sue Norway for breach of contract. Attempts to secure tankers operating in foreign markets presented added difficulties. Companies in Chile and Uruguay had chartered Norwegian tankers and protested at their removal, but the committee still came close to meeting British demands, agreeing to provide twenty-five additional tankers from the New York fleet. The committee believed Norwegian whale-oil processors were unsuitable for transatlantic convoys, so it agreed to use them in coastal routes in the United States to help free up other tankers. The other committee focusing on dry-cargo ships also proposed changes to help the British. The Americans decided to sacrifice twenty-seven of the Norwegian liners the British wanted so badly, as well as twenty-three of the thirty tramps they had requested. The Norwegians mostly succeeded in receiving market rates for their ships, payable in dollars provided by the Lend-Lease Administration. Since it could not provide money directly to the British, the Maritime Commission chartered the ships and turned them over to Britain.[21]

The collective agreement resulting from negotiations by the two committees and involving the Americans was signed on 10 October 1941 by Lord Leathers and Arne Sunde in London. Like previous agreements, this one had a duration of six months. Ships covered by the agreement were called 'Plan' ships to distinguish them from the 'Scheme' ships included in the agreement at the start of the war. With this latest deal, the first between Norway and Britain that also involved the United States, Nortraship committed to 'give absolute priority to the transport of vital war supplies'.[22] The Norwegians had wanted American participation in the negotiations, contrary to the desires of the British, but the result might have proved different to what they expected. The Americans would remain involved in all subsequent discussions about the commitment of the Nortraship fleet, and Britain's contacts in the States had helped create a partner to leverage more ships from the Norwegians.

As these events were occurring and the newly formed committees were assessing the employment of fleets, the war had taken a dramatic turn. In June, the attention of the world shifted to the east, with Germany's surprisingly swift invasion of the Soviet Union. Despite initial victories, Hitler would discover the fighting there to be much tougher than his forces had experienced in the Low Countries and France the year before. As fighting with the Russians became bogged down, he shifted naval and air forces from the Western to the Eastern Front, including hundreds of planes to support the advance and dozens of submarines to intercept supply lines. This created a temporary reduction in shipping losses both in the Channel and in the North Atlantic. The Russians were in dire need of immediate help against the German invasion and they tried to charter Norwegian ships, but Britain held out against it.[23] Although Churchill, Roosevelt and others harboured great distrust of Stalin, they knew that the Soviet Union was important to the alliance, and Churchill pressed for immediate help to the Soviets from Lend-Lease, using ships mostly from the British-controlled fleet. Re-supply by sea via the Baltic or Black Sea proved impossible, and shipments into Vladivostok in the Far East or from the Persian Gulf required lengthy transport by rail to reach the front. The solution took the form of convoys, commonly originating from Iceland and travelling through the Norwegian Sea and Arctic Ocean to Murmansk and Archangel. These started in August 1941 and continued until May 1945. The first convoys arrived safely, although some ships had to turn back because of bad weather. The routes became deadly, however, from 1942, when Germany shifted U-boats, warships and aircraft to intercept the convoys, succeeding in sinking 102 vessels. Numerous Norwegian ships participated in the convoys; none was lost.

Meanwhile, on the other side of the world, tension was peaking between Imperial Japan and the United States and Britain. This had its origins well before the beginning of the Second World War. British colonization and influence on the Pacific Rim had been an irritant for many years to the Japanese, and as the influence of the United States expanded into the Pacific at the turn of the century, with the Philippines eventually becoming an American protectorate, concern at Western encroachment deepened, and the Japanese, like the Germans in Europe, looked to strengthen their position. Their aggressive expansion started in 1931 when they provoked a war with China in Manchuria. Five years later, they invaded the rest of China and joined the Germans in condemning communism in the Comintern Pact of 1936. Then, in 1937, Japan mounted a full-scale invasion of China. When Germany swept across Western Europe with ease three years later, Japan saw their opportunity to capitalize on German successes and increase their own standing in the Pacific. In September 1940 they attacked French Indochina. The same month, they signed a Tripartite Pact with Germany, Italy and others, pledging mutual support for new world orders in Europe and East Asia. By then, Roosevelt had made the decision to move the US Navy's Pacific Fleet to Pearl Harbor to try to deter further Japanese aggression.

Japan is a country with few natural resources of its own and was totally dependent on the United States, the British Empire, the Netherlands and others for a wide range of materials from coal and iron ore to rubber and metals, without which it had no hope of establishing its new world order in the Far East. The United States, for example, provided Japan with more than half the copper, scrap metal and tooling required for making steel, as well as 80 per cent of the fuel oil the country needed and 90 per cent of high-grade petroleum products like aviation fuel.[24] The Allies now began reducing exports in response to Japan's belligerence, and in 1941

Roosevelt closed the Panama Canal to Japanese shipping, froze Japanese assets in the States and embargoed further shipments of oil and gas to Japan. The British and Dutch followed by imposing embargoes on oil shipments from fields in Borneo and the East Indies. Without oil, Japan could not execute its plans to expand, unless it took over the actual sources of supply in the region.

All of this led the Japanese to attack Pearl Harbor on 7 December 1941. Japan rightly suspected that any attack on the strategically positioned Philippines would provoke an American reaction, and their own military would require weeks to prepare for counter-attacks. It therefore aimed to pre-empt the ability of the United States to react quickly by taking out the Pacific Fleet in Hawaii, and simultaneously seizing islands that were stepping stones between there and the Philippines, as well as the Philippines itself. The Japanese also attacked further south to gain control of territories in South-East Asia with valuable natural resources, and the success of these invasions eventually forced the withdrawal of American, British and Australian forces. On the same day as the attack on Pearl Harbor, the United States declared war on Japan. Four days later, Germany declared war on the United States. The war had turned global almost overnight as Japan continued to advance into Dutch Indonesia, Burma, New Guinea and Sumatra.

After the attack on Pearl Harbor, the situation of shipping throughout the world changed rapidly as all the oceans became potentially unsafe. The next day, Roosevelt created the Strategic Shipping Board under his own supervision, with the Chairman of the Maritime Commission, the Army Chief of Staff and the Chief of Naval Operations as co-chairs. Its purpose was to plan future shipping policy and to allocate merchant ships to meet military and civilian requirements.[25] Within the next two months, however, he would come to realize that this board, chaired by three strong personalities with different viewpoints and reporting directly to himself, had become unworkable. An organization under a single leader with greater authority would take its place, and the immediate formation of the Strategic Shipping Board demonstrated the focus of the President on the importance of merchant shipping. He and Churchill were conversing regularly by this point in the war, and Roosevelt was aware of how many ships were being lost and the effect of these losses on Britain's ability to feed its citizens and continue fighting. He directed Admiral Land of the

Maritime Commission to build 8 million deadweight tons of merchant ships by the end of 1942 and an additional 10 million by the end of 1943.[26]

Commercial traffic declined rapidly after the Japanese attack. Lend-Lease shipments that had started from the west coast of the United States into Vladivostok now shifted across the globe into Murmansk. In the months leading up to Pearl Harbor, Norwegian liner ships on charter contracts had been crossing the Pacific to Australia with a wide range of goods, some smaller vessels had been sailing the coastal waters of China and Japan and many others had been on contract to the British in Indonesian waters and in the Indian Ocean. When the Japanese attacks continued in the Pacific in December, Nortraship held its liners on the west coast of the United States, like other commercial shippers, to keep them out of danger. Once again, Norwegian ship captains began receiving messages enticing them to sail to new ports, this time sent by the Japanese. Hysing Olsen from the Nortraship London office wired all Norwegian ships in the Far East after the attack on Pearl Harbor, telling them to disregard such messages, although he hardly needed to do so, because the Japanese Navy had already sunk several Norwegian ships and captured others. All the Norwegian captains knew that their country was now at war with Japan as well. As before, none was taken in by the enemy's messages.

During the month of December, both offices of Nortraship distributed binders to ship captains standardizing many procedures to be followed. Nortraship staff had been providing guidance as best it could to captains once their ships were located and captains committed to follow directives. These binders, referred to as 'Captain Books', became the source of standard operating procedures for the entire fleet. They included an introduction by Lorentzen and Olsen with details about the formation of Nortraship and its organizational structure, as well as location and contact information for the two main offices in London and New York, and for branch offices. Most importantly, the binders contained a variety of information on ship security and safety: procedures to be adopted during enemy attack, evacuation, reporting and convoy procedures, care of seamen, safeguarding of confidential documents, insurance, and much more.[27] They were an important step forward in establishing expectations and improving communications.

As 1941 came to an end, President Roosevelt and Prime Minister Churchill agreed that the priority in the new global war was to defeat

Hitler in Europe. Losses to the British-controlled fleet had proved staggering: a total of 1,299 ships during the year, including 432 to U-boat attacks and 371 to aircraft.[28] Of the total ship losses, 496 occurred in the North Atlantic, an increase of about 50 per cent over 1940, and 350 off the coast of the United Kingdom, a decrease of about 50 per cent over the same period. The U-boat wolfpacks had proved very effective as German focus shifted to the Atlantic. Nortraship lost 106 ships throughout the year, but managed to acquire two tankers and ten dry-cargo ships of various sizes. By the end of December, its fleet had declined to 718 ships of all types and sizes, a 30 per cent reduction since the outbreak of war.[29] Over 70 per cent of its fleet was now directly serving Britain. Japanese and German attacks that same month had, however, proved exceptionally devastating to all shipping. From January to November 1941, fifteen British, Allied and neutral merchant ships had been lost in the Indian Ocean and only five in the Pacific. In the month of December alone, losses increased dramatically to 246, all but five in the Pacific.[30] That was merely a precursor. The worst losses at sea, for both the British and the Norwegians, were yet to come. Concerns about shipping would peak, and Allied pressure on Nortraship to provide more ships would continue to increase.

Chapter 8

Global War Leads to Cooperation and More Ships

The cloud that had formed over Øivind Lorentzen as a result of allegations in 1940/41 darkened further in the first half of 1942. Hilmar Reksten had continued his personal inquiries into various aspects of business in the New York office of Nortraship, with full approval from Arne Sunde. He insisted that Lorentzen lacked the knowledge and leadership necessary to manage such a large global operation. He also started sharing with Sunde his dissatisfaction at Olsen's management of the London office. In early spring, Lorentzen and his son Per travelled to London to defend themselves once more against Reksten's allegations about the family's shipping company. Nothing was proved this time, but continuing concern about Lorentzen led the Norwegian Government to solicit the help of Johan Ludwig Mowinckel, someone with a background in shipping who had also served three times as prime minister and who now went to New York to lead the committee advising Lorentzen. He and Lorentzen developed a collegial working relationship, and Mowinckel could see that Reksten was causing problems to the organization and was a thorn in the side of the director. He advised Lorentzen to find a way to marginalize him and to stand up to Sunde, who had been fostering the continuing investigations and back-channel communications.[1]

Distracting as these internal squabbles must have been at the top of Nortraship and for the Government, they did not affect the support being provided to Britain and the Allies. Negotiators from the Ministry of War Transport and Nortraship had disagreed on many things, but Britain had no complaints about the hundreds of ships put at its disposal. Norwegian ships of all types, especially tankers, were contributing immensely to meeting British needs. In April, Philip Noel-Baker, Parliamentary Secretary to the Ministry of War Transport, stated, 'Norwegian tankers are to the Battle of the Atlantic what the Spitfires were in the Battle of Britain.'² Also in that month, British Foreign Secretary Anthony Eden broadcast over the radio to citizens in Norway his pride in what Nortraship had been doing: 'The Norwegian merchant fleets have been famous down the ages. At no time in their long, proud history have they played a more glorious part than in this present struggle ... The ships of the Norwegian merchant fleet totalling over three and a half million tons of shipping, ply day and night in fair weather and in foul, in their country's cause, which is the cause of free men everywhere.'³ By then, however, the war at sea had shifted dramatically to the other side of the Atlantic, and many more ships would be lost. Meanwhile, President Roosevelt would issue more directives to control the merchant ships then in service and to construct thousands more. Pressure would mount on Nortraship to provide additional ships to support the war effort directly.

Up to this time, the British and Americans had viewed the Norwegian fleet from different perspectives. While the British Government tried its best to charter as many Norwegian ships as possible, the US Government had not intervened in any discussions about the allocation of ships within the Nortraship organization. American officials and shipping interests remained focused on the commercial benefits of the Norwegian ships operating on their behalf over multiple trade routes throughout the world. By December 1941 an even greater difference had developed between the fleets managed by the two Nortraship offices. Ship losses had been suffered far more heavily by the fleet managed by the London office. These included thirty-nine of the forty-five liners lost, thirty of the thirty-five tankers, and eighty-five of the eighty-nine tramps.⁴ Nearly 90 per cent of the ships managed by the London office had been committed to the British by this time, whereas most of the 237 ships managed by the New York office continued sailing on commercial contracts, mostly in safe waters. These ships, and other merchantmen, now came under intense attack as the war at sea broke out in waters off the coast of the United States.

By the time Germany declared war on the United States it had achieved much success in attacking convoys crossing the Atlantic. The Germans knew that these convoys were at their most vulnerable once they neared the Canadian coast, and they suspected that merchant ships travelling further south down the Atlantic seaboard to the Caribbean and Gulf of Mexico would make even easier targets. They also thought that the

United States was ill-prepared to protect ships in or near those waters, and this belief could not have been more accurate. Germany started the year with 91 U-boats operational out of a fleet of 249. It ended 1942 with 212 operational in a fleet of 393.[5] Only a fraction of that fleet moved to the western Atlantic, seldom more than a dozen at any one time, but those U-boats proved remarkably effective, because the United States Navy failed to protect merchant ships for the first six months of 1942.

Admiral Ernest King, the head of the Navy at the time, believed there were insufficient ships available after the losses at Pearl Harbor and with the new requirement to escort ships in convoy in the Pacific. He contended that any attempt to do so would only dissipate the resources of the Navy even further. The few escorts available had already been sent to the Pacific in preparation to take on the Japanese. King might have been correct in some of his conclusions, but his reluctance even to try to protect merchant ships off the east coast led to substantial losses, much to the frustration of the British, now America's allies in war. Britain had learned the importance of convoys in the First World War and was quick to establish them at the start of the Second. The United States, unfortunately, did not share that experience.

German submarines enjoyed immediate success in waters off the east coast, not just, however, because merchant ships were sailing without protection. The United States had not taken basic precautions to limit the exposure and vulnerability of ships near its coasts. It had not enforced black-out conditions in cities, as Britain had; in many locations, the lights of towns and cities along the coast silhouetted passing ships and made them easily detectable targets; waterways remained clearly illuminated with channel markers; there was no restriction on the use of communications, thus enabling U-boat captains to monitor transmissions and determine the location of ships, even if they could not see them. In the first two weeks of January the Germans sank thirteen merchant ships off the east coast. In February they sank twenty-eight more, and another fifteen further south in the Gulf of Mexico and the Caribbean. By the middle of April, the losses off the east coast alone had exceeded 1.2 million tons, over half of which was represented by tankers.[6] The U-boats moved around at this time, shifting to the Caribbean or to the Gulf of Mexico to target tankers sailing to or berthed at refineries, then returning north to prowl for targets off the east coast again. It was a profitable hunt for them, and their tactics kept the shipping authorities and the US Navy off-balance. By midsummer a small number of German U-boats had succeeded in sinking 495 Allied ships off the eastern seaboard, in the Gulf of Mexico and in the Caribbean, including sixty-eight Norwegians.[7] This was a staggering setback for the Allies, but especially for Britain, which had been struggling to build up oil reserves and to increase imports in the hope that it could ease the severity of rationing. Losses also seriously affected its shuttling of oil from tanks on the east coast and from refineries in the Caribbean and Gulf of Mexico. As these attacks were underway, the Germans had renewed their air assault on shipping in the Mediterranean and the Japanese had started sinking merchant ships in the Indian Ocean.

As the first German submarine successes were starting to hit the news, President Roosevelt and Prime Minister Churchill agreed to enhance the cooperation between their countries, in order to meet the new requirements of a global war. On 19 January 1942 the two nations established a coordinating body named the Combined Shipping and Adjustment Board; it consisted of two divisions, one in Washington and the other in London, each co-chaired by senior officials from both countries. Its purpose was to ensure full cooperation between the two countries in the use of shipping to support the global war effort and to prevent competition for scarce shipping resources. In principle, the ships serving the needs of the United States and of Britain became pooled for the benefit of both, although they were managed separately. As the war progressed, the two allies would divide up the world in the attempt to reduce the number of ships needed and to improve efficiency in moving supplies and equipment where required in multiple theatres. The British generally handled what was needed in the Atlantic and eastern theatres of Europe, and the Americans took the Pacific and western European theatres. But there was some overlap, with the United States carrying supplies to Africa, and Britain to Australia and New Zealand.[8] Overall, this split focus was especially helpful to Britain, given its extensive supply lines. The American theatres of responsibility were only about half as far from the States as they would have been from Britain.

In January, the first American forces started arriving in Britain. There was both good and bad news underlying that move. The British certainly welcomed the added military strength, and a steady stream of men would continue to arrive for many months in preparation for Operation Torch, the invasion of North Africa, which would take place towards the end of the year. The bad news was that the United States was ill-prepared to provide transport to carry its own forces overseas. The timing was unfortunate. The Allies were still reeling from the first U-boat attacks off the east coast of the United States, but the Ministry of War Transport needed to help get the Americans across the Atlantic. This added to its burgeoning list of other requirements stretching across the world, and shipments elsewhere would have to be reduced until more ships became available.

In early February, Roosevelt ordered another major change affecting the authority behind merchant shipping and ship construction in the United States. The Strategic Shipping Board, established after Pearl Harbor to coordinate shipping needs for the military services and industry, had proved ineffective in its short existence. Headed by the Chairman of the Maritime Commission, the Army Chief of Staff and the Chief of Naval Operations, its direction suffered from differing viewpoints and a lack of decisive authority short of the President. It was quite unlike Britain's Ministry of War Transport, which exercised absolute authority over the British-controlled merchant fleet. Therefore, on 7 February Roosevelt issued an executive order establishing another new organization to be called the War Shipping Administration, to manage both shipping and ship construction. Three days later, he appointed Rear Admiral Land, Chairman of the Maritime Commission, to be its sole administrator. Land kept his position as head of the Maritime Commission, which focused on the aggressive ship construction plans dictated by Roosevelt. Combined with his authority over the Ship Warrants Programme started the previous summer, Land's responsibilities now covered the operation and chartering of all merchant vessels operating from the United States, the requisition of vessels when needed, shipyard and ship construction, vessel repairs and modifications, administration of marine and war-risk insurance, and training of crews, as well as the loading and discharge of ships at terminals. Simply put, nothing happened in merchant shipping and construction without Land's oversight. The official policy of the United States at this time was that shipping should not be exploited for commercial purposes during time of war. This policy and the extensive authority of the War Shipping Administration meant that Nortraship New York could no longer direct the destiny of its ships without Admiral Land's approval.

Roosevelt instructed the new administrator to organize the construction of new shipyards and to build 24 million tons of new ships in 1942 to help meet British and American needs, twenty times more tonnage than the United States had produced in all of 1941. The rate of building would double again in 1943, leading to the construction of 1,500 new merchant ships.[9] Under Land's direction, the number of shipyards mushroomed in the next eighteen months from a dozen at the start of the war to over eighty. The time taken to build a Liberty Ship fell dramatically from 244 days to 53 in 1943, and eventually to 40 before the end of the war.[10] Although the United States was quite ill-prepared for war in many ways, its industries were able to crank up without the threat of air attacks, as suffered in Britain, and in the years following generated an astounding output: 2,700 merchant ships, 82,028 landing craft, 10 battleships, 18 fleet-carriers, 9 escort-carriers, 2 large and 10 heavy cruisers, 110 escort-cruisers, 33 light cruisers, 358 destroyers, 504 destroyer-escorts, 211 submarines and 80,000 naval aircraft.[11]

The War Shipping Administration took responsibility for many of these remarkable achievements. Ship construction would take many more months before it could start making an impact on what was required. In the interim, obtaining more ships from somewhere became imperative, and in the months that followed, the Administration exercised its authority to take firm control of merchant ships flying the United States flag. Although it did not requisition ships per se and place them under separate management, the Administration began determining what cargoes merchant ships carried and where ships went. In essence, shipping companies in the United States became operating agents for the War Shipping Administration and carried cargoes wherever they were told, mostly for the military services. By 30 June 1942 the Administration had acquired more than 300 large US-flagged merchant ships with a total capacity of more than 3 million deadweight tons, as well as smaller vessels. Many of the larger ships had been operating in profitable trade routes.[12]

American shipping companies, which had forfeited lucrative commercial contracts to concentrate instead on defence needs, started complaining about foreign merchant ships continuing to operate without constraint. Soon fingers were pointed at the Nortraship office in New York, and also at Dutch shipping companies that were operating commercially. As the

American companies saw it, it was not fair for Nortraship to continue operating for profit in trades around the world, when they could not.

The Norwegians could see that storm clouds were gathering on the horizon because of these and other concerns. They had been surprised to learn of the formation of the Combined Shipping Adjustment Board in late January, believing this new body would be a duplication of committees established previously to assess ship needs; they did not realize that it was created by the United States and Britain because of shared concerns about merchant ship shortages and the need for closer cooperation. The American representatives on the Board were Admiral Land in Washington, with whom the Norwegians had maintained good relations, and Averell Harriman in London. Harriman was Roosevelt's special envoy to coordinate Lend-Lease requirements for Britain and other countries, a programme that had already helped Nortraship to garner more revenues in dollars. The British co-chairs on the Board must have created some concern, however. They were, in Washington, Sir Arthur Salter, who had been establishing close ties with Land and others in the nation's capital as he pushed for more merchant shipping help from the Norwegians, and in London, Lord Frederick Leathers, the head of the Ministry of War Transport, who had pressed Lorentzen, Olsen and others the previous May for more ships. The British position regarding the Nortraship fleet had remained consistent over the past year: they wanted all remaining Norwegian ships committed directly to the war effort.

Soon after the formation of the Combined Shipping and Adjustment Board, pressure increased on Nortraship New York to contribute more ships to the war effort in line with Britain's wishes. At the time, its liners were operating out of the west coast of the United States to Australia and the Far East, from the east coast into South America and Caribbean, and across the Atlantic to India, the Middle East and Britain. The British claimed there were surplus liners on the west coast of the United States and wanted some shifted to the east coast to carry cargo across the Atlantic to Britain and India. As they had in the past, Lorentzen and Olsen opposed the removal of the liner ships from existing trades. They argued that even though they were not serving the military directly, the liners were moving important cargoes for the Allies and should therefore remain in their current service. The Norwegians had always been concerned that removing liner ships from commercial trades, after shipowners had dedicated years to establishing contracts and networks of agents, would prove detrimental in the future. They feared that once liners were removed from routes and agent networks were lost, the liner trades would be lost permanently, because British and American shipping companies would rush to fill the gap in the market after the war. They anticipated that both Britain and the United States would have more ships available to do so at that time, especially if Norway failed to secure commitments for replacement vessels. One of the few dissenters to this view was Hilmar Reksten. He believed that Nortraship overstated the importance of the liners and proposed they be removed from commercial trades and, because of their increased speed, be devoted to supporting the war effort directly. He considered that chartering the liners at good rates for long periods was the best solution. Sunde, whose title had changed from Minister of Supply to Minister of Shipping, listened to all the concerns, eventually siding partially with Reksten and approving the transfer of some liners from the west coast of the United States to the east coast to serve the British directly.[13]

Also of interest were Norway's new refrigerated vessels carrying fruit and other produce from the Caribbean and South America. These ships, less than a decade old and capable of 17–18 knots, had temperature-controlled compartments to keep fruit and vegetables fresh, and the British wanted them for the transatlantic route between the United States and Britain. Again, both Olsen in London and Lorentzen in New York objected to the use of these specialized ships over that route, because the ships would either need to cut their speed in half to sail with convoys or sail at higher speeds on their own but at greatly increased risk. Sunde overruled their objections once more and approved the transfer of ships. To the surprise of the two directors, no one from the War Shipping Administration objected on Nortraship's behalf when the authorities in Argentina and Brazil complained to the State Department about the pending transfer. Britain gained control of eight of the refrigerated ships and put them immediately into service on the Atlantic run. The New York office started monitoring the use of the ships, and it was not long before they noticed that some of those sailing to Britain were not full and, quite surprisingly, not even carrying refrigerated cargo. As a result, Nortraship in New York hardened its position on the transfer of any more ships to the Ministry of War until utilization of the Norwegian ships improved.[14]

By June, Nortraship leaders were becoming more and more concerned that the British members of the Combined Shipping and Adjustment Board were having an increasingly adverse influence on the future of their fleet. The Maritime Commission had been focused on ship construction for quite some time. Neither it nor the War Shipping Administration had developed experience in managing the employment of thousands of merchant ships. This task was new to Admiral Land as well. Managing the construction of ships and calculating requirements based on input from the military services remained quite a different job to ensuring the efficient use of ships and adjusting their employment as losses occurred. It was quite understandable, therefore, that Lord Leathers and Arthur Salter should be guiding many of the discussions within the divisions of the Board in Washington DC and London. Leathers had been in charge of the Ministry of War Transport for over a year by this time, and Salter and his team at the British Shipping Mission had been focused on ship requirements and on establishing relationships in Washington DC for even longer. They and staffs had been trying to balance requirements with ship availability for over two years.

While the Americans came to understand better the complexity of sustaining multiple theatres of war, given their own shipping shortages, British participants on the Combined Shipping Adjustment Board became valuable sources of information as the two countries tried to sort through issues together. The vastly different requirements of the military forces of the two countries dominated many discussions. At a very basic level were the supply planning factors used by the Americans and the British. The British, for example, based their supply needs on 0.6 measurement tons per man per month; Americans calculated theirs on 1.3 measurement tons.[15] That alone dramatically affected shipping requirements. The Board could not resolve such differences, but it eventually found ways to improve the utilization of ships which led to some improvements.

Given their inability to gain a seat on the Combined Shipping Adjustment Board, some in Nortraship started believing that a new committee, one that excluded the British, was needed to jump-start negotiations with the Americans. Even a representative from the Maritime Commission had suggested that the United States should charter the remainder of the Nortraship fleet and allocate whatever tonnage it wanted to Britain.¹⁶ Should not Nortraship at least negotiate the future of its liner ships, if not the entirety of its fleet, with the Americans? That question dominated Nortraship's internal discussions during June. By the end of the month, Sunde and most others in Nortraship had agreed that direct negotiation with the Americans was a necessary step to protect the long-term interests of Norway. They felt, however, that such a proposal to the Americans should come from the Norwegian Embassy, not from Nortraship or from the Ministry of Shipping, and that it should be addressed to the Department of State. Sunde, who was in New York with Lorentzen at the time, sent a note to Olsen in London to ask the Norwegian Government to put such a proposal. Thinking that to do so would be an inappropriate blindside to the British, Olsen held on to the note with the intention of discussing it further with Sunde, since he and Lorentzen would be arriving in London together in the next couple of weeks.¹⁷

The two divisions of the Combined Shipping Adjustment Board had been meeting in Washington DC and London periodically for over six months by this time and had considered that negotiations with the Norwegians should commence as well. The Board believed, however, that both the United States and Britain should be involved. Although the Norwegians had not secured a seat on the Board, they had received assurances that they would be invited to participate whenever discussion focused on Norwegian ships. When Minister of Shipping Sunde and Director Lorentzen arrived in London towards the end of July, they received a surprise from the Combined Shipping Adjustment Board there, in the form of an invitation to join the Board for a meeting in London on 6 August. Olsen had still not informed the Norwegian Government that Sunde, Lorentzen and others wanted to seek negotiations separately with the Americans.¹⁸ It was now too late.

The Norwegians might have thought the meeting they would be attending concerned new contracts, and if so, they were partially correct. The agreements they had signed in October 1941 were scheduled to expire during the summer of 1942 but had been extended until October. Replacement contracts were needed, and Nortraship had been hoping that the agreement from the previous October could be extended again, perhaps until the fighting ended. The Japanese bombing of Pearl Harbor had started a series of events that altered worldwide requirements for shipping and increased the need for the Allies to cooperate more actively.

The short meeting that day turned out quite differently than either Sunde or Lorentzen expected. The British had convinced the Americans that it would be best to have a single entity negotiating for additional ships, be they from Norway, the Netherlands or any other country. The Allies agreed not to compete against each other as they had been doing. Rather, they decided to approach ship chartering together, with a single voice, and to require rates that did not vary between countries. That day, Lord Leathers explained that the War Shipping Administration no longer desired to act as a charterer of Norwegian vessels. Instead, the Board had agreed that all future chartering would be accomplished through the British Ministry of War Transport. He explained that a new committee could be formed in Washington DC to discuss ships and concerns, but that in the end all negotiations now would take place only with Ministry of War Transport representatives.[19] The two Norwegians were stunned by this new development. Leaders in Nortraship and officials in the Norwegian Government found the announcement at the meeting unacceptable and conveyed that to the Board the following day. For the next three months Norway tried to get the State Department involved. Since the ships in question were all operating out of American ports, they did not believe that the British needed to be involved, so they started focusing their efforts on diplomatic channels directly to the State Department. Meanwhile, no negotiations took place.

Nortraship's relationship with the Americans had been much better than with the British. Since the start of the war there had been many disagreements between the Norwegians and the British about ships. There had been none with the Americans, simply because the United States had not become involved in the war directly and thus had less need for additional ships. Nor had the US sustained any losses at sea until the start of 1942. Crown Princess Märtha had been in the States for quite some time and had formed a friendly relationship with President Roosevelt. That had led to more attention by the President to the predicament of Norway, occupied as it was by the Germans, and to the issues it would face when the war ended. Nortraship had been pursuing commitments from both the United States and Britain to help replace its hundreds of ships lost since the start of the war and had failed to receive assurances that they would do so. Finally, on 6 September 1942, in a handover ceremony at the Washington Navy Yard, President Roosevelt personally presented an escort ship named *King Haakon VII* to Norway's Crown Princess Märtha. It was during this ceremony that he offered his legendary tribute, praising Norwegians for their resistance to German aggression: 'If there is anyone who still wonders why this war is being fought, let him look to Norway. If there is anyone who has any delusions that this war could have been averted, let him look to Norway; and if there is anyone who doubts the democratic will to win, again I say, let him look to Norway.'

The gift that day, even though it was a warship not a merchantman, was taken by Nortraship as a sign of American attitudes, and Roosevelt's words proved inspirational to all Norwegians. They helped sway Allied public opinion, which had been influenced by some news articles criticizing Norway's rapid surrender to the Germans and its possible profiteering from shipping in America. Norwegian diplomats subsequently received assurances from the State Department to the effect that Roosevelt had also agreed that Norway needed assistance to replace its merchant ships. This was especially important to the Norwegians, and they felt that continued negotiations with the Americans regarding the future of the fleet would be beneficial.

By the end of October, after more discussions with members of the Combined Shipping Adjustment Board, Sunde concluded that, given the need for new contracts, negotiations with both the British and the Americans must commence, and that if the Norwegian position became too entrenched, the War Shipping Administration would simply exercise its authority to requisition Nortraship's entire fleet in the States. Everyone else in Nortraship, this time including Sunde's protégé Reksten, disagreed with this decision. Efforts to get State Department participation had continued through diplomatic channels. The Norwegian Ambassador had met several times with the Secretary of State and his staff and eventually received word that State Department representatives would be willing to discuss a list of concerns with the Norwegians. Those at the top of Nortraship interpreted this gesture as a willingness to be involved in bilateral discussions about ships.

Given Sunde's change of mind, the question for the Norwegians became who would be most suited to negotiate the best solution for Norway's future. Sunde, Lorentzen, Olsen and others had participated in negotiations in the past, but there had been strong disagreement on several occasions. Some hard feelings had also developed in the Combined

Shipping Adjustment Board because of Norway's intransigence since the August meeting. The Norwegians felt that the cards would be stacked against them when they entered negotiations, since the British and Americans seemed to share the same view of shipping requirements. They felt that a new person would be helpful to represent their interests, someone with an in-depth understanding of shipping and the potential issues involved, and preferably capable of a little diplomacy.

Attention therefore focused on Erling Dekke Næss, another shipowner and businessman. Although a proud Norwegian, Næss had been one of the early users of 'flags of convenience' for his ships, registering them in Panama to avoid the high taxes in his own country. He had made his mark early in the whaling industry with one of the world's first whale factory ships. These ships were sometimes twice as large as tankers, including their processing equipment for extracting whale oil. At the start of the war he had half a dozen tankers and a whale factory ship in his company and had acquired a reputation as a smart businessman. He happened to be in Oslo on the day of the invasion but escaped to England, where the British had tried to coerce him into relinquishing his ships. He refused to do so unless they permitted him to continue managing them, much as Thomas Olsen had demanded from Nortraship two years earlier. When officials refused to let him leave Britain, he agreed to pay them over a million dollars for a travel permit to the States, where he quickly established a good relationship with Admiral Land at the Maritime Commission. He proceeded to charter his ships to the Commission and to Britain. One of his tankers was torpedoed by a U-boat in January 1942 off New York, becoming the first ship to be sunk on the western side of the Atlantic. That sinking had resulted in Næss receiving much favourable press coverage.

Lorentzen had tried to entice Næss to accept a position at the New York office after he arrived in the States, but Næss declined and continued to operate his shipping business. Months later, former Prime Minister Mowinckel, who had joined the committee in New York advising Lorentzen, also talked to him about joining the Nortraship management team. After much discussion, Næss finally agreed to do so and accepted the position of Deputy Director. Mowinckel and others believed he would be a good complement to Lorentzen. Næss was experienced, level-headed and generally well-liked. He became the man chosen to negotiate the final disposition of the Norwegian ships.

Meanwhile, the Combined Shipping Adjustment Board had also named their negotiators. They were William Weston from Britain, a skilled negotiator with vast shipping and financial experience, and David Scoll from the Maritime Commission within the War Shipping Administration, a lawyer with comparatively little experience of shipping. The Board had been working on an initial proposal for the Norwegians to consider as a starting point, and they passed this to Nortraship in late November. There were several provisions in the proposal that could be beneficial to the Norwegians. For example, the Board recommended that insurance of Norwegian ships would be based on ship valuations by the War Risk Insurance Office in London, because these were nearly 60 per cent higher than the same valuations in the United States. Except for a group of ships that would be needed immediately, most vessels would be able to continue in their commercial service until required. Payments would be in dollars, and rates would mirror those from the Plan Agreement in October 1941. The Ministry of War Transport would remain the central point of contact for the Allies. It would charter the ships and then re-charter them to the War Shipping Administration. This arrangement would be particularly favourable to the British, because payment could be made using Lend-Lease dollars, which would ease Britain's monetary problems. And the proposal included a provision for the formation of a shipping committee in the States, whereby the Americans could exploit Norwegian knowledge of the capabilities and best employment of those ships contracted.

Much in the proposal seemed favourable to the Norwegians.[20] However, their initial reaction to it was hostile, and they informed the Board that the proposal was unacceptable. They continued to be concerned at the Ministry of War Transport being the charterer, but their specific worry was the suggestion that some ships would be needed for immediate charter. Although only twenty-six were listed in that group, twelve were liners currently operating in high-revenue routes. They were convinced that this was a deliberate effort to drive Norway out of liner trades so that either the British or the Americans could position themselves to take advantage of these opportunities once the war was over. This continuing worry hardly seemed warranted. The liner ships were the fastest in the Nortraship inventory, and the Allies wanted them because speed was important for the long distances to multiple theatres, particularly across the Pacific. The Norwegians were also still expecting State Department participation in bilateral discussions. Therefore, they rejected this proposal and others. On 4 December Weston expressed to Næss his concern about the lack of progress and suggested to him that if the Norwegians were not willing to negotiate, then perhaps the Norwegian Government needed encouragement from someone at a much higher level.[21]

Admiral Land had learned of Norwegian efforts to get the State Department involved in discussions regarding ships and other related issues. He succeeded in convincing the Department that negotiating with the Norwegians over ships was the responsibility of the War Shipping Administration and Combined Shipping Adjustment Board, not of the State Department, even though the Department had conveyed to the Norwegians a willingness to discuss matters with them. To appease the Norwegians, Admiral Land arranged a meeting between the State Department and Nortraship executives, including the Norwegian ambassador, Lorentzen and Sunde, in his office in Washington DC on the afternoon of 10 December. The discussion covered Norwegian concern to protect trade routes, the continuing need for sufficient rates, and Lend-Lease provisions, but not the chartering arrangements for ships. The Norwegians received assurances from the State Department representative that talks could continue in the future. The meeting then broke up, and negotiations on the proposal commenced in earnest the following day, with Weston, Scoll, Næss and some other department heads from Nortraship involved.[22] Land had succeeded in breaking the stalemate by satisfying the Norwegian desire for some State Department involvement.

Lorentzen and other executives in the New York office had spent considerable time with Næss explaining the background of previous agreements and the issues to anticipate when meeting with Weston and Scoll. When the meetings started, Næss was well prepared. Negotiations took place throughout December up to New Year's Eve, at which time Næss, Weston, and Scoll initialled a final agreement. It became known as the Hogmanay Agreement, after the Scottish tradition of presenting a gift to the first person crossing the threshold at the start of the new year, supposedly to ensure good fortune for the rest of the year.

The Norwegians, British and Americans certainly had much to celebrate on the evening of 31 December 1942. The last five months had been contentious for all involved, but they now had an agreement covering all remaining ships in the Nortraship fleet. The agreement did not mean that the Norwegians lost control of managing their ships or that all carried military supplies. Nortraship retained control of ship management, ironically much as Thomas Olsen had insisted on for Fred Olsen Company ships after the formation of Nortraship in 1940. Nortraship vessels would carry cargo specified by the War Shipping Administration and Ministry of War Transport. An important promise from the Americans as the agreement was being finalized was that the Norwegians would receive two new ships from the United States. The Norwegians hoped many more would follow. The agreement provided for the chartering of all ships to the Ministry of War Transport for re-chartering to the War Shipping Administration, the fees payable in dollars to the British. Insurance was paid entirely by the War Shipping Administration based on higher ship valuations from the War Risk Insurance Office in London. Three categories of ship remained, but the ships involved changed significantly. Group A consisted of fifty-three ships to be time-chartered immediately, more than double the number in the original Board proposal. These included thirty-six tankers along with seventeen dry-cargo ships. The dry-cargo ships only included three liners, instead of twelve. All ships received rates comparable to those in the October 1941 Plan Agreement, with daily supplemental additions nearly twice the amount in the first Board proposal. The addition of the tankers was particularly beneficial to the British because of their need for oil. In Group B were sixty-three ships, five tankers and fifty-eight dry-cargo ships, including the rest of the liners. They would continue in service until needed. If Nortraship wanted to add any of them to Group A, it could do so. In Group C were twelve small boats, mostly whalers, that were provided on bare-boat charters (without crews) to the War Shipping Administration for use in American waters, at a flat rate of 10 per cent of insured values. What was hidden between the lines for ships in Group B was the provision that they could be chartered only on a per-voyage basis, not for months at a time.[23] This would prove contentious later.

The Hogmanay Agreement offered a final shaft of optimism in what had been a dismal year for merchant shipping and British imports. As the end of 1942 approached, only 300,000 tons of commercial bunker fuel remained for the fleet under Britain's control, with consumption averaging about 130,000 tons per month.[24] The Admiralty had another million tons for the Royal Navy, but all of it was needed for warships. By this time the British had curtailed shipments to other parts of the Empire and started directing forty-ship tanker convoys from Aruba in the Caribbean to the UK. Total imports had dropped to nearly 30 million tons for the first time since the start of the war, meaning that even tougher rationing would be needed. In all theatres in 1942, the Allies had lost 1,664 ships amounting to 7.79 million tons of cargo space, and although they were able to secure about 7 million tons of new shipping, that still meant a net loss of nearly a million tons.[25] It was the worst year for shipping losses by far. Nortraship's losses had been equally staggering. It lost 182 ships throughout the year, including 49 more tankers. Although it was able to add 30 more ships to its fleet, including 11 tankers, it ended the year with a combined fleet of 566 ships managed by the offices in London and New York. Since the establishment of Nortraship in April 1940, the size of the Norwegian fleet had been cut nearly in half.[26]

Fortunately, there had been some positive developments in the war, despite the horrendous losses of shipping. In fact, the momentum had started shifting in the Allies' favour. British forces had finally succeeded in pushing Rommel back in the North African desert, and the advance of Hitler's armies on the Russian front had stalled as a bitterly cold winter began to set in. Germany had suffered the loss of many ships, too, greatly affecting its own imports. It had not given up trying to coerce shipowners in Norway to stop their ships from serving the Allies, but no shipowner in Norway obeyed the Germans, leading to the arrest of some and imprisonment of others in the summer of 1942.[27] And in the Pacific, the United States Navy had defeated the Japanese at the Battle of Midway. The war was very far from over, but the losses to Allied merchant shipping would drop considerably as newly constructed American warships were launched to provide protection and to target the Germans and Japanese.

Chapter 9

The War Ends but Nortraship's Work Continues

The Norwegians had much reason to be pleased with the outcome of the Hogmanay Agreement, particularly with the new terms skilfully negotiated by Næss to protect the country's liner trades. The Agreement gave the Allies ample reason to be satisfied, too, since they now had access to all remaining Norwegian ships. However, losses at sea during 1942 and the requirement to support new and distant theatres overshadowed any optimism generated by the year-end negotiations. Shipping shortages continued to plague Britain. Since the start of the war, British imports had been decreasing steadily as ship losses rose and military requirements increased. Annual imports had declined from 50 million tons at the start of the war, to 42 million at the end of 1940, 31 million in 1941, and then 23 million in 1942. They would drop below 20 million unless something was done. Churchill had expressed his concern to Roosevelt before the start of 1943 and received the President's promise to assist with 7 million tons of imports; but help had still not arrived.[1] In January, the Prime Minister therefore took the drastic step of diverting dozens of cargo vessels from routes serving colonies around the Indian Ocean in order to bolster imports and ease the privations being suffered by the British people. Monthly sailings to that area dropped from ninety-two to fifty-two.[2] The British were still awaiting word of America's plan to help alleviate their concern about imports when an important meeting between the two leaders and their staffs took place that month. The British anticipated some answers, but confusion developed when the President's senior planners failed to realize the extent of the commitment their boss had given.

The Casablanca Conference became pivotal in charting a grand strategy for the Alliance. Stalin had received an invitation to join Roosevelt and Churchill, but the Red Army was fully engaged in fighting the Germans at the time. The President and Prime Minister agreed to concentrate immediate efforts in Europe in order to shift Germany's focus from the Eastern Front, to plan an invasion of Sicily in order to knock Italy out of the war, to increase bombing of Germany to destroy as much of its war industry as possible, and to begin moving a million men with weapons and equipment to Britain in preparation for a full-scale cross-Channel landing in France. They also agreed that Russia needed more shipping help to hold off the Germans and that a new campaign against the Japanese in Papua New Guinea was needed to open supply lines to Burma. These decisions all increased the need for shipping and raised additional British concern about when they would receive help to arrest the decline in imports. The subject of Roosevelt's commitment to help did not, apparently, come up in discussions between the two leaders, but it did become the focal point of a side session at the conference. The President's staff had clearly arrived in Casablanca with a different understanding to the British of what Roosevelt's commitment signified. When the conference ended, the British had still received no assurance that additional shipping would be made available.

The next couple of months only heightened Britain's concern about shipping requirements and imports. Rommel routed the Americans at Kasserine Pass in Tunisia, resulting in the loss of many lives and much equipment. British and American commanders in the South Pacific disagreed about whether to re-supply the Chinese by air across Burma or by sea. And, especially disturbingly, German U-boats experienced great success again in the North Atlantic, sinking eighty-two ships in March alone, the highest losses in four months.[3]

Disagreements about the ability to help Britain without jeopardizing America's own military requirements led to a session between the President and his senior advisers in late March aimed at clarifying Roosevelt's commitment to Churchill. The President told them emphatically that the United States would provide even more than the 7 million tons he had promised to the Prime Minister at the end of 1942. Furthermore, he directed the War Shipping Administration a little over a month later to provide Britain with fifteen to twenty cargo vessels per month for the next ten months, a whopping total of 150 to 200 additional merchant ships in less than a year.[4] The Administration fulfilled the President's promise, and the additional ships became key in reversing the decline of imports to Britain.

The construction of new ships in the United States was starting to accelerate by this time. The stunning output of merchant ships and warships not only helped British imports. It also enabled the Allies finally to establish control of the oceans and protect their convoys, which ultimately meant that shipping became far less dangerous from later in the year until the end of the war, although issues persisted about the efficient and proper use of ships. The success of the American new-build programme made reliance on the Nortraship fleet far less important from 1943 onwards, despite how critical it had been for Britain ever since the outbreak of war.

The Hogmanay Agreement, much to the frustration of the Americans, had proved very difficult to implement as the year progressed. The fifty-three ships included in Group A of the agreement, referred to as the 'Hogmanay ships', had been put into service for periods of time, commonly referred to as 'time charters', to support military needs. The sixty-three other ships listed in Group B had become the source of concern because the terms of the agreement prevented them from being contracted in the same manner. According to Hogmanay, the War Shipping Administration would gain ready access to the ships in Group B whenever they wanted, but use of the ships required a separate contract for each vessel and every voyage. Staff in the War Shipping Administration had become so frustrated at the onerous administrative process needed to bring one of the vessels from Group B into service to support war needs that, by the end of 1943, some wanted to restart negotiations. That did not happen. The agreement remained in effect as originally negotiated until the end of the war. What this meant, however, was that comparatively few extra Norwegian ships were added to directly serve military needs. Instead, the Hogmanay ships in Group B maintained trade routes carrying cargo needed by the military but not delivering it directly to military theatres. Whether that was the intent behind the negotiating strategy of Næss remains unclear. Losses to the Nortraship fleet after 1943 decreased noticeably, however, since fewer ships sailed into high-risk areas as the Allies took control of the seas. From the beginning of 1944 until the end of the war, Norway lost only nineteen ships.[5] In previous years, they had sometimes lost that many in a single week.

The Agreement produced frustrations for the Norwegians as well. When ships were damaged or lost, the British, Americans and Norwegians disagreed on who should pay the insurance and in what currency. For example, vessels were insured against war risks by the British, who insisted that payments for loss or damage be made in sterling not dollars, because of their country's poor financial situation. They expected the War Shipping Administration to accept sterling and then pay the Norwegians in dollars, which the Norwegians wanted. It was finally agreed in September 1943 that marine insurance for the Hogmanay ships would become the responsibility of the Ministry of War Transport payable in sterling, and that war risk insurance would become the responsibility of War Shipping Administration payable in dollars. For the other two groups of ships, responsibility rested with the British, with payment in their currency.[6]

Other issues of concern for the Norwegians included the commitment of certain types of ship. They remained sensitive about the inefficient use of their ships and especially about the removal of any of their liners from trade routes in which other liners from the United States continued operating. The final agreement had improved their ability to protect the liner ships. In the summer of 1943, the War Shipping Administration wanted two specific ships to be transferred from Group B to Group A to help transport troops across the Pacific. Both were capable of speeds of 17 knots or more, making them particularly suitable for crossing the Pacific quickly, but they also had refrigeration capability and were currently operating in the highly profitable banana trade routes. Nortraship took issue with the request, contending that these specialized ships were unsuitable for troop transport. When the War Shipping Administration persisted in its demand, the Norwegians asked to be provided with some new-build ships in return. After being informed that President Roosevelt had threatened to withdraw his previous commitment to them for new ships in the future, the Norwegians reluctantly backed off and relinquished the ships for troop transport.[7]

Dissension within the Nortraship organization continued in 1943 and by the end of the year again necessitated the involvement of King Haakon and Prime Minister Nygaardsvold. In previous years, Director Lorentzen had been the target of most criticism, often instigated by Hilmar Reksten with support from Minister of Shipping Sunde. Although some disagreements had surrounded the appointment of Næss as Lorentzen's deputy, his success in negotiating more favourable terms with the British in the Hogmanay Agreement had increased his stature among some Nortraship executives. This proved short-lived, however. By this time, Sunde had become more and more involved in decision-making in both the New York and London offices, directing that he be provided with the minutes of all staff meetings, much to the consternation of Lorentzen and Olsen. The minister had not warmed to Næss and felt that he was overstepping his authority and encroaching on the responsibilities of others. In March 1943, while Lorentzen was away on vacation, the relationship between the two men became openly confrontational during a staff meeting. Prior to the meeting, Næss had asked Reksten for an update on his efforts regarding new ship construction, but Reksten had refused to provide him with one. During the meeting, the topic of ship construction arose, and Sunde asked that Reksten join the meeting to provide an update. Næss objected and refused to discuss the topic with Reksten present since he had not provided him with an update earlier as asked. This obstinacy prompted Sunde to suspend Næss as deputy and to appoint a department head as his replacement.[8]

Discussion about the Minister of Shipping's role in and authority over both offices was taken to the level of Prime Minister Nygaardsvold and continued for months. Although hard feelings had developed between Lorentzen and Olsen since the formation of Nortraship, this new confrontation with Minister Sunde brought the two heads of Nortraship closer than they had been before, and they would remain close for the rest of their time in Nortraship. Both complained about the difficulty of working in an environment in which their boss was repeatedly undermining their efforts and collaborating with subordinates. They refused to permit Reksten to continue working in Nortraship. Olsen went so far as to state openly at a conference that he did not trust Sunde, after which King Haakon himself instructed Olsen to apologize. Discussion about the dismissal of Næss continued for months. The Prime Minister eventually concluded that there was insufficient reason to dismiss him, even though Sunde had the authority to do so. Næss was reinstated with the title of Secretary General of Nortraship, rather than Deputy to the Director. At the end of 1943, over forty months since the provisional degree establishing Nortraship and appointing Lorentzen as director, a Royal Resolution finally clarified the responsibilities of the Minister of Shipping and the heads of Nortraship offices in New York and London.[9]

It was long overdue. Reksten left Nortraship at the end of the year, but not before issuing more allegations about Director Lorentzen and his son Per, none of which were substantiated. Despite all the allegations and investigations, Per Lorentzen remained as the head of the Chartering Department in the New York office from the fall of 1940 until he left Nortraship in 1945.

There can be no doubt that these quarrels were a distraction for Nortraship and the Norwegian Government at an important time. With all its ships committed to the war effort and revenue accruing, it was time to focus on the future of the organization and of Norway itself. The Nortraship fleet had been reduced by nearly half. Hundreds of millions of dollars and pounds had been deposited in banks from contracts and insurance payouts for the loss and damage of ships. What was now of paramount importance was rebuilding the country's merchant fleet, once the fourth largest in the world. How fast that could happen, and how quickly shipowners could re-establish commercial contracts, would have a direct bearing on the future economy of Norway. No other revenue streams existed after the Germans took control of the country.

Throughout the war, the Norwegians had been pressing the British and Americans to include them in new ship construction programmes undertaken in both countries. They had received some promises but had little to show for them. The British had made their first offer of ships to Norway in the spring of 1941 as losses in the Norwegian fleet steady increased. It included six old ships received from the United States in the First World War, and six tankers and seven dry-cargo ships of standard construction from British shipyards. Nortraship saw little value for future commerce in the old American ships and only limited value in the British-built vessels. Nonetheless, they accepted the offer as interim replacements until purchase of better ships became possible. The purchase price was to be the cost of construction of the ships. On 19 December 1941, the British provided the first and only merchant ship built specifically for Norway when *Kong Haakon VII* was launched, in the presence of the King himself. In 1942 the British offered eighteen more ships, five older tramps built in the United States and thirteen new standard-built British ships. The cost of these was much higher and only payable in dollars.[10] Norway refused this second offer, preferring not to invest in ships which would be less competitive in commercial markets after the war was over, and not wishing to surrender dollars to pay for them.

Discussions with the United States proved no more promising for Norway's future. With the signing of the Hogmanay Agreement, the War Shipping Administration had confirmed that Norway would receive two new ships. The United States had become the new leader in merchant shipping with its accelerated construction of Liberty Ships, and Admiral Land of the War Shipping Administration intended to maintain his country's edge in shipping for the future. Although Roosevelt had given the Norwegians assurances that they would receive some new ships, it remained unclear whether that meant more than the couple previously promised. Land kept a tight rein on the new ships coming out of shipyards.

Norway had signed a Lend-Lease agreement with the United States in the summer of 1942 covering the repair of ship damage and installation of defensive equipment, but the agreement provided no commitment for new ships. In the exchange of notes, the American Government again agreed to help the Norwegians replace ships lost in war. In October of that year, the War Shipping Administration offered the Norwegians five of its older ships, but they rejected the offer. When the Norwegians asked for more help, Admiral Land told them that under the Lend-Lease programme they could only rent ships, not purchase them. A Norwegian appeal to President Roosevelt to be able to purchase ships proved to be of no avail. The Norwegians could hardly complain about the leasing arrangements since Liberty ships were rented for just a dollar, although the ships could not be used as Nortraship desired. They had to be chartered back to the War Shipping Administration, with reimbursement only for operating expenses. The arrangement could keep crews employed, but the ships would not provide any revenue. Nonetheless, the Norwegians eventually rented twenty-six ships from the War Shipping Administration from 1943 to 1945 in the hope of opening the door to more rentals and purchases. Norway received no other offers of new merchant ships during the war.[11]

The focus remained on creating conditions for Norwegian shipowners to be capable of competing again in world trade once the war ended. This purpose had been the backdrop to all negotiations with the British and Americans. Because Nortraship had been unable to replace many of the ships lost, shipowners would have to assume responsibility for rebuilding their own fleets as soon as possible after the war. The Norwegian

Government had tried to help, but there was little it or Nortraship could do to make up for the large number of losses.

Sweden had been the primary source of shipbuilding prior to Germany's invasion. Before April 1940, Norwegian shipowners had signed contracts with Swedish shipyards for twenty-six new ships, but most shipowners holding those contracts were trapped behind enemy lines in Norway. The Norwegian Government realized the importance of keeping these contracts in place, in order to protect the investments of its shipowners and to prevent the ships from being sold elsewhere. After arranging banking agreements in London for Nortraship, Arne Sunde had travelled to Stockholm in August 1940 to secure guarantees from the Swedish shipyards that they would continue the building of these ships for Norwegian shipowners. There was a minor problem, however. Shipyards in Sweden required payment in Swedish kronor, and the Norwegian Government in exile in London had no access to its own banks. It had to rely on banks in Britain for currency conversion, and British banks would accept only dollars. It took until February of 1941 before arrangements could be made to satisfy both Sweden and Britain.[12] Fortunately for the shipowners, their investments in new ships became protected, but how much Sweden would or could help when the war ended remained an open question. Other countries would also be looking to have ships built at that time.

It soon became apparent that not all of Norway's merchant ships would be entering commercial trades immediately after the war, even after the termination of contracts with the War Shipping Administration and Ministry of War Transport. As fighting continued around the world, the Allies committed themselves to avoiding had what happened after the First World War. Some countries were left in ruins at the end of that war, with populations displaced elsewhere and transport networks destroyed. Not surprisingly, ships were needed in many places to move supplies, but no plans were in place to give help immediately after the fighting stopped. The Allies anticipated such needs well before the end of the Second World War. President Roosevelt proposed the formation of an organization to provide such assistance in June 1943 and obtained endorsements from the leaders of forty other governments. What resulted became known as the United Nations Relief and Rehabilitation Administration (UNRRA). Countries with the wherewithal to assist, especially those with financial and shipping capability, agreed to help for a period of six months after the war ended. This meant that Nortraship and shipowners had to factor in these potential shipping requirements as well.

The fighting against Germany and Japan was far from over, though. After epic battles and a huge loss of life, the Soviets had defeated the Germans at Stalingrad, raised the siege of Leningrad, recaptured Kharkov and were now advancing westward through Poland. Britain and the United States had finally halted Rommel in North Africa, successfully landed in Sicily and forced Italy to surrender. Although the Germans were resisting the Allied advance in Italy, the country had officially had joined the Allies. Over a million American troops had deployed to Britain, with a mass of assault ships and planes, and were preparing to surprise Germany with an amphibious landing on the beaches of northern France. In the Pacific, despite earlier retreats from Burma and the Philippines, the Allies had defeated the Japanese at Guadalcanal and in the Solomon Islands, and had weakened their strong naval forces. Fortunately from an important strategic perspective, the vast output of warships from American shipyards had enabled the Allies to establish firm control of the oceans. Concerted efforts to reduce threats at sea with more convoy escorts and extended coverage by aircraft were succeeding in making shipping lanes safer. A credible threat to merchant ships crossing the Pacific had never materialized, and the danger from U-boats in the Atlantic had largely vanished. Even the Indian Ocean was becoming safer. Also important for Britain, the Mediterranean was again open to shipping, greatly shrinking the delivery times of oil from the Middle East. By the end of 1943, with these positive developments and the help of additional shipping tonnage, British imports had taken a noticeable turn upwards for the first time since the start of the war.

By the beginning of 1944 the tide had certainly begun turning in favour of the Allies, but the challenge became maintaining that momentum. Shipping remained a continual concern, not so much because of the lack of ships, as in previous years, or threats at sea, but more because ships were often not being used effectively. Norwegians, noticing ships not sailing full and then having to wait to discharge their cargoes, sometimes complained that neither the British nor the Americans knew how to manage merchant shipping effectively. New problems were now appearing that were self-inflicted. Military commanders, mostly

American generals, had started holding on to ships after they arrived to use them for storage, instead of offloading them quickly and sending them back for re-use. Roosevelt himself became so frustrated with his commanders that he sent a scathing directive telling them, 'The use of ocean-going shipping for storage purposes, whether loaded in the US or in the theatre, is prohibited.'[13]

As the year ended, it was clear that the 'Europe First' strategy agreed by Roosevelt and Churchill and formalized at the Casablanca Conference had proved effective. The war had required Norwegian and other seafarers to perform unusual missions at times. Some crews on tankers found themselves in large fleets following warships and refuelling them at sea, something they had not done before. In advance of D-Day, the amphibious landing of Allied forces across the Channel in June 1944, Nortraship and the Norwegian Seamen's Organization reached a particularly unusual agreement: sixty Norwegian ships would take part in the Normandy operation, and crews agreed to give up all rights related to regular work and to perform whatever duties became necessary. They received an extra 20 kroner per week in addition to their wages and were not permitted to resign. During the first days of the invasion there were no temporary quay facilities; ships would simply run ashore on the beach at high tide. When the tide receded, the ships stood aground, and the crews unloaded cargo directly into waiting trucks.[14]

The landings in Normandy and the subsequent advance into France pushed the Germans back toward their own western border, as the Soviets did the same from the east. Norwegian forces from Britain had joined the Soviets in northern Norway to expel the Germans. But hard fighting continued for close to a year before the end finally came. Germany surrendered unconditionally to the Allies in the early hours of 7 May 1945 at Reims in north-eastern France. That evening, at 2240 hrs, the Norwegian cargo ship *Sneland* was the lead vessel in a convoy just off the east coast of England when a U-boat hit her with two torpedoes before heading back to Germany. She became the last Norwegian ship lost in the war, and Captain Johannes Lægland and six of his crew were the last Norwegians to perish in the war at sea. After the Americans bombed Hiroshima and Nagasaki, Japan surrendered unconditionally on 2 September 1945. When the Second World War finally ended, over 4,000 seafarers had perished and nearly half the Nortraship fleet had been lost.

The end of the war meant that Nortraship – with its offices in New York and London, its fifty branch offices on six continents and close to a thousand employees – now faced all the tasks associated with closing down its operation. By the end of the war about half the staff of the New York and London offices were occupied with accounting and insurance, and much work remained for them to settle accounts and claims. Phasing out management of Norway's ships and transferring responsibility for them back to shipowners, with hundreds of ships still under contract and spread throughout the world, posed many problems. Some of those ships would continue to support the United Nations Relief and Rehabilitation Administration requirements until March 1946, six months after the surrender of Japan. Ships leased from the War Shipping Administration needed to be returned. All required inspection for damage. Defensive and degaussing equipment needed to be removed. Similarly, shipowners would require inspections and the removal of military equipment from their ships before taking them back. There were concerns about the condition of ships, because most had been pressed into continual service for years without the benefit of inspection or the routine repairs common in peacetime. Tankers were an especial worry, because they were prone to rust after prolonged use. Accounts needed to be settled with the War Shipping Administration and the Ministry of War Transport. Complicating the settlement process further were changes scheduled to take place in the United States. Admiral Land, who had been key to many discussions and agreements in the past, would retire from the military at the end of 1945. Six months later, the War Shipping Administration would cease to operate, making the United States Maritime Commission the focal point of residual actions and settlements. Such changes meant that Nortraship would be dealing with new people as it started downsizing its own staff.

Settlement took time, not surprisingly, because of the many requirements. It was less complicated with Britain's Ministry of War Transport, because Lend-Lease was not involved. Except for insurance issues, settlement was finalized in March 1947 and proved to be simple, since British and Norwegian claims balanced each other out. Insurance settlements took another half-dozen years. Settlement with the United States took much longer. The two governments did not reach a final agreement until August 1958, with $5.2 million granted to the Norwegians. They had wanted more.[15]

Norwegian shipowners wanted to regain control of their remaining ships and receive reimbursement as soon as possible after the war. Arriving at settlements presented a host of different considerations aside from inspection and repair of ships. Shipowners were due reasonable compensation for the use of their ships and insurance payments covering loss and damage. Most ships had been requisitioned while sailing with cargo destined for customers. Shipowners also had rights to the revenue from deliveries under contracts that had existed before the establishment of Nortraship in April 1940. Figuring out these details was difficult. Of course, shipowners had received no insurance payouts thus far and wanted this money in order to invest in new ships. But shipbuilding opportunities were limited, and the condition of Norwegian shipyards after the long German occupation remained unclear. Thus, shipowners would have to look elsewhere and face competition with other countries wanting to rebuild their fleets.

Well before the end of the war, Nortraship had anticipated issues over settlements with shipowners. Hysing Olsen had travelled to Stockholm in the fall of 1943 to discuss the question with shipowners in Norway who could get across the border safely; they had been subject to intense pressure from the occupying forces. Although some shipowners still feared that the Norwegian Government intended to retain control of the consolidated fleets, Olsen emphasized to them during the meeting, as he solicited their opinions about the future, that this should not be a concern. Lorentzen and others at Nortraship were adamant on one point as they started considering these many issues, understanding that owners in occupied Norway could be disadvantaged. They agreed that no Norwegian shipowner should be allowed to benefit at the expense of others.[16] This ultimately meant that shipowners would not be allowed to use insurance payments from the war or revenues from Nortraship to invest in ships until all were able to do so.

Olsen's meeting with the shipowners helped lay the groundwork for solutions to complex problems of compensation beyond insurance payments. Nortraship, with shipowners on its staff, wanted the Norwegian Shipowners Association involved in the solution. Those in Norway established a secret committee after the meeting with Olsen and issued further recommendations. The Norwegian Government then formed another committee in London to consider proposals and make recommendations for settlement. There was not unanimous agreement, since the views of Government officials differed from those of the shipowners. Some officials argued that revenues from the use of ships during the war should remain with the Government, because it had absorbed all expenses over that time. Shipowners, of course, saw it quite differently. They felt that their ships had produced the revenues and that therefore all should come to them. Lorentzen and other shipowners on the staff of Nortraship supported the view that revenues belonged to shipowners. They pointed to Section 105 of Norway's Constitution, which stated that any time the State took over property for public use it should provide full compensation, and to the provisional decree of April 1940 that stated shipowners would be compensated. Profits made by shipowners prior to the war had been subject to high taxation, which formed the basis of much government revenue. A further point of discussion about compensation concerned whether shipowners should be taxed on any of the compensation they received. Since the Government did not tax its own income and the Ministry of Finance received and managed all revenues from Nortraship, the feeling was that shipowners should not inherit a tax liability. The Government eventually agreed, after much discussion, that shipowners would be allowed tax-free compensation for the use of ships, including allowances for the value of ship location at the time of takeover, for the value of bunkers and provisions or equipment on board at the time of takeover, for amortization, for lost income and for damage to ships that had not been repaired when returned to owners.[17]

The Norwegian Government passed a Compensation Act on 19 July 1946 laying out the principles for settlement. Calculation of settlements to shipowners required detailed assessment of every one of the thousand ships in the inventory of Nortraship at its formation six years earlier. To ensure owners were treated equitably, the compensation for loss of income became based on 5 to 6 per cent of the ship's value for its time in service according to the ship's size. Compensation for depreciation and wear and tear was 6 or 7 per cent, depending on whether ships were diesel, steam, tramps or tankers.[18] Not unexpectedly, some shipowners were unhappy with their settlement offers. Determining what was due to owners of whale ship fleets presented additional complications, because their fleets were a combination of whale processors and whalers. Most processors were full of oil when requisitioned, and Nortraship had sold that oil to the United States and Britain. The Government did not forget that ships trapped in Norway had been lost and damaged as well. Although not part of the Nortraship fleet, those ships had helped import supplies into Norway which proved vital to sustaining the population. The Government factored in an anticipated settlement of 205 million kroner to those owners.[19]

Nortraship had accumulated a sizeable sum of money during the war. By the time Germany and Japan surrendered, this totalled 4.5 billion kroner, which included 2.8 billion in operating profits from contracts and 1.34 billion in loss and damage compensation for ships. Settlements to all shipowners were not completed until nearly two decades after the war. Cargo and tanker shipowners shared 1.9 billion Norwegian kroner of Nortraship's operating profits in addition to loss and damage compensation. Owners of whaling fleets shared 24 million kroner. After those settlements, the Government was left with a surplus of over 800 million kroner to pay its own debts and to help with the rebuilding of Norway.[20] There can be no doubt that Nortraship had met its mission of generating money for the country's future as it helped the Allied war effort.

As shipowners looked to rebuild their fleets after the war, they initially found there were few opportunities to do so. Most of the ships they received back from Nortraship required considerable maintenance given their recent constant use. Commercial opportunities remained minimal because most of the world's shipowners also were focused on rebuilding. Much of the transport network, as well as many ports and shipyards in Europe and Asia, were badly damaged and needed repair as well. Nations wanting more ships waited for America to decide what to do with the thousands it had built during the war. Commitments to the United Nations Relief and Rehabilitation Administration finally started tailing off at about the time that the United States Congress passed the Ship Sales Act in 1946, which permitted the sale of Liberty and other ships.

Out of necessity, shipowners thus focused on acquiring used ships and the standard-built ships from the United States and Britain. Nortraship sold the ships that it had purchased from the two countries during the war to shipowners and helped with their purchase of other vessels it had chartered. It also received forty-two German ships taken over by the Allies and offered them to shipowners as well. Germany had confiscated many ships itself during the war, and these were returned to their owners in various countries. After the Ship Sales Act passed, Norwegian shipowners purchased sixty-five Liberty ships on favourable terms from the Maritime Commission and a variety of other vessels from Britain. This combination of war-built and other second-hand vessels amounted to 565 ships, but with a combined capacity of only a million gross registered tons. Some were purchased for rebuilding, and most were suitable for use only in domestic trades. The first new-built ships to be added to Norway's fleet were the twenty-six diesel vessels that shipowners had contracted for with Swedish shipyards before they war. Sweden delivered these in 1945. Norwegian shipowners also had the opportunity to purchase ships that Norwegian shipyards had been building for the Germans during the occupation. In search of more ships and with some settlement funds in hand, the shipping companies looked for opportunities in foreign shipyards untouched by the war. Of particular concern were tankers because the loss of those ships during the war had been especially high. By the end of 1946, shipowners had invested 2.3 billion kroner in contracts for the construction of another two million gross registered tons of shipping. Even with those additions, Norway's merchant fleet remained a million tons below its pre-war size.[21]

Norway's competitive edge in shipping therefore declined considerably as the composition of the world's ocean fleets changed after the war. The United States and Britain did not face the same urgency to rebuild. The fleet of the United States had increased by a whopping 369 per cent since pre-war years, and that of Britain had increased by 72 per cent.[22] Even with the small additions to the Norwegian fleet during the war, the country's total ocean-going fleet, including ships in Nortraship and those captured by the Germans, had declined by 40 per cent since 1939. As construction picked up in the United States, Britain, Canada and Sweden in the late 1940s, the Norwegian fleet finally reached the size of a decade earlier. Its composition had changed considerably, however. Roughly 40 per cent of the fleet consisted of standard ships built in the United States during the war which were far less desirable for commercial use. A decade after the war, the size of Norway's tanker fleet remained well below the pre-war level even though it had become equally modern.[23]

Unfortunately for Norway's shipowners, the Norwegian Government became concerned about the sharp rise in foreign loans to build more ships outside the country and re-established import licence requirements for ships built elsewhere. That put a damper on new ship contracts.

Consequently, Norwegian shipowners were ill-prepared to take advantage of new shipping opportunities starting in 1950 with the outbreak of the Korean War. By the time the Government had relaxed licensing regulations, those opportunities had passed, and the cost of ship construction had risen well beyond prices at the end of the 1940s, even though opportunities for shipbuilding in Norway had increased. As investment continued over the next decade, Norway finally found itself, in the early 1960s, with the third largest fleet in the world, behind the Americans and the British.[24] It had taken nearly twenty years for the country to regain its competitive place in world trade.

Even before settlement proceedings and efforts to re-establish the fleet, Nortraship had started to adjust its organization, and after the war it downsized rapidly. Employees in New York and London were anxious to return to their homes in Norway, uncertain of what they would find there. With Germany's surrender, Nortraship established a small office in Oslo to provide continuity as the New York and London offices began to curtail operations. Some staff moved there the same month. Director Lorentzen had informed Minister of Shipping Sunde in August 1944 that he intended to resign directly after the war in Europe ended. He left New York on 25 May 1945, leaving Erling Dekke Næss in charge, and arrived in Oslo on 31 May with other members of the Norwegian Government. King Haakon and his family returned from exile in London on 7 June. A new Prime Minister took office on 22 June, and that same day, Sunde resigned his position as Minister of Shipping. Lorentzen submitted his resignation on 4 July and left Nortraship on 15 August. Two days later, the Government revoked the powers of the director, since a curator of ships was no longer needed and shipowners were beginning to assume control of their fleets.[25] In the space of three months, much of the top management of Nortraship departed, leaving small contingents of staff to continue working out settlement arrangements as the transition to peacetime operation took place.

Hysing Olsen in London became the new leader of the staff remaining in New York and in the new office in Oslo. Næss remained as his subordinate in charge of the New York office until November 1946, while ships came off charters and work continued on settlements with the United States and Britain. By then, most employees had departed. Staff remained in London to work with the War Risk Insurance Office for several more years to settle claims. The bulk of the London office moved to Oslo to head departments handling shipowner settlements. When the London office closed in April 1948, Olsen finally left the organization he had helped to set up with Erik Colban as the King and Norwegian Government were fleeing from Germans across Norway eight years before. He had been the first and last leader of Nortraship. The Oslo office remained open until 30 July 1958, at which time the Nortraship organization officially closed down, and responsibilities for remaining actions and final settlements transferred to the Ministry of Trade.

There had been a rapid and relatively orderly transition in the Nortraship office as the war came to an end. Staff dealt with a variety of complex issues as they worked out final settlements with shipowners and settled accounts elsewhere. One thing which was lost in all the activity during those final months was the account established in the early summer of 1940 when Director Lorentzen was preparing to leave for New York. The 'Secret Fund' with British deposits to compensate for reduced war-risk supplements to Norwegian seafarers had been growing steadily ever since that time. Word of the fund had spread to the crews on Norwegian ships by then. As Nortraship was downsizing and making settlements so that shipowners could rebuild their fleets, those seamen were focusing on what would happen to that money. It had grown to more than 43 million kroner, about enough to purchase twenty brand-new ships if those crewmen had been shipowners. This large fund would become the cause of a controversy lasting far beyond the life of the Nortraship organization, eventually pitting seamen against their own government and legal system.

Chapter 10

The Struggle of Seafarers Tarnishes the Legacy of Nortraship

After five years of German occupation, much in Norway needed repair. In the far north, the Germans had torched the regions of Finnmark and Troms while retreating from the Soviets, destroying the town of Kirkenes. No telecommunications remained in the area. Some residents had fled south looking for shelter, while many others took to the woods to seek refuge in caves. Coastal villages in central Norway, heavily bombed when the King was fleeing from the Germans, still lay in ruins. Food shortages and rationing had pushed much of the population to the brink of starvation. Most had been burning whatever they could find to keep themselves warm. The country's economy was in a shambles as well, since the proceeds of remaining businesses had been devoted more to the occupying forces than to the inhabitants. Any Norwegians who had voiced opposition over the years had been killed or imprisoned, and there was understandable bitterness toward the occupiers who had been treating them so harshly. On 7 May 1945, when Germany surrendered to the Allies, its occupation force in Norway still numbered close to 400,000. Some Norwegians had befriended or even collaborated with Germans over the years, to the dismay of others. For a variety of reasons, the situation was ripe for the exaction of revenge.

Fortunately, the Norwegian Government in exile anticipated the possibility that things might rapidly get out of control. In the absence of a domestic police force, it arranged for the Norwegian resistance to assist in maintaining law and order around the country until the police could be re-established. An Allied military mission arrived in Oslo the day after the surrender to give orders to the German leaders which included disarming and segregating the military all over the country. Crown Prince Olav, then the Supreme Commander of Norway's Armed Forces, returned a week later with some government ministers and military forces to implement the plan for a peaceful, disciplined transition to the establishment of a new civil administration. King Haakon returned to much fanfare the following month, and the celebration of the end of the war in Europe and Norway culminated in a large parade on 30 June in Oslo honouring the Norwegian, British and American military. The stage was set for hundreds of thousands of Norwegians to return to their now peaceful country and to begin rebuilding for the future. Much remained to be done, though. Conditions in Norway were quite different to before the war, and anyone anticipating a rapid return to pre-war times would have been sorely disappointed. This was certainly true for the many seafarers still at sea supporting the Allies.

There was immediate action to hold Nazi leaders and Norwegian collaborators to account, and trials began that same summer. Prosecutors called for the death penalty in two hundred cases of treason, and thirty people received sentences of execution, twenty-five of which were carried out. The first to be tried and convicted was Reidar Haaland, a member of the *Nasjonal Samling* party who had joined the Gestapo. He was executed on 17 August 1946, a little over three months after Germany's surrender. Vidkun Quisling was convicted the following month and executed by firing squad on 24 October 1945. There was a widespread backlash against women who had slept with German soldiers and given birth to children. Many were humiliated by having their heads shaved. Shipowners and crews of vessels that had sailed for the Germans were subjected to denunciation and occasional prosecution. But no attention was paid to those seamen outside of Norway and anxious to come home.

Unlike most of the Norwegian military, these sailors did not return to Norway immediately after the war in Europe ended. They remained spread throughout the world and only returned home when their ships were ready to do so. Generally, they trickled back with little notice and no fanfare. And when they finally made it home they found themselves in a country focused on other issues, not on what might have happened to them over the past half dozen years. Few in Norway understood what they had endured in their years at sea during the war. Seafarers and their families had been without communication with each other for over five years. There were no crowds or parades to welcome them home. They might not have expected much more, but they certainly anticipated being able to receive all the money deducted from their pay over the years. The rebuilding of Norway was just beginning, and Nortraship was settling its own accounts and phasing itself out of business. A new Nortraship office in Oslo was in the process of setting up, with few employees, the institution responsible for paying crewmen.

This organization was the Norwegian Deposit and Accounting Office. It had established offices in London and New York to handle crew pay after Germany invaded Norway. At any one time during the war, those two offices held accounts for 30,000 to 50,000 seamen. Whenever Nortraship made changes to sailors' pay, officials updated the ledgers accordingly. Seamen were able to draw from their accounts at various locations in the world if they needed money, and these transactions were recorded on balance sheets at Norwegian Deposit and Accounting Office locations. Each sailor maintained a small account book with details of pay and any deductions and withdrawals, as people did with personal bank accounts. Some sailors held multiple accounts due to changes of location and employment. The system worked during the war, but when it ended and accounts in various locations required reconciliation, the process took time. Eighty years ago, accounting offices could not correlate details of pay electronically. Entries were manual, based on information received by telegraph or mail. Complicating matters for those sailors returning home and wanting access to their money, there was nowhere in Norway to provide them with a banking service until a new Deposit and Accounting Office was set up in Oslo two months after the surrender. The handful of employees in that office could not have anticipated the problems awaiting them.

Seafarers' pay had undergone several adjustments since the start of the war, all of which contributed to many changes and complicated the accounting process. Those who were married had required deductions for families taken out of their wages well before the war started. As access to families terminated with the German occupation, these mandatory deductions began to accumulate. If a man's marital status had changed by the end of the war, that affected what could be due to him. The families in Norway of some seamen had been lucky enough to receive some remuneration during the war. That, too, might have affected accounts if seafarers needed to provide reimbursement to shipping companies which operated in the occupied country. The change to war supplements in the summer of 1940 also affected accounting. Bonuses were no longer based

The Struggle of Seafarers Tarnishes the Legacy of Nortraship 159

on monthly allocations according to areas of risk, but on voyages over certain routes. As the war progressed, Nortraship mandated savings plans for all seafarers, and these sums had accrued interest. At the beginning of the war, taxes were deducted from wage packets. Then the Norwegian Government decided not to penalize seamen with taxation, but instead of eliminating deductions, it added money back into accounts, doubling the entries. If a seafarer was unfortunate enough to become a prisoner of war he stopped receiving any actual pay, but his wages kept accumulating. That became potentially confusing as well, because halfway through the war the Government decided that it would no longer be responsible for prisoners' wages, and that Nortraship should assume responsibility for them.

All of this and more complicated the process of accounting and repayment. By the summer of 1945, the Deposit and Accounting Offices was holding considerable sums for those at sea. The London office alone held 300 million kroner for seafarers and another 6.6 million for prisoners of war.[1] There was some good news awaiting those with accounts in London. The exchange rate for their savings deposited in sterling was 17.7 kroner per pound throughout the war. When the war ended, that rate increased by over two points, meaning that they received a bonus on savings of about 12 per cent.[2] That would not prove sufficient, however, to offset bigger frustrations when it came time for seamen to withdraw their money.

The net result of all this was that the first seamen who showed up at the new Norwegian Deposit and Accounting Office in Oslo departed in frustration. Some received small stipends of several dozen kroner, but the office was prevented from providing full settlement to any seafarer until ledger sheets from the other offices had arrived in Oslo and been reconciled. Employees of the woefully understaffed Oslo office were required to verify the net amounts due to each man before making a final settlement. With tens of thousands of sailors eventually showing up to collect their savings, there was little they could do to alleviate the men's distress other than offer small sums as interim payments. This applied equally to the families of men who had died at sea, who also needed money. Long delays followed as the New York and London offices waited for final payments from ship captains before forwarding all the information to Oslo. It was not until the autumn of 1946, over a year after the end of the war in Europe, that the first boxes of financial statements from New York and London arrived in Oslo.[3] Only then could the small staff there start calculating the balance due to each seafarer, as they sifted through entries for tens of thousands of men. It was a horrendous task. As sailors returned to discover how difficult it was to retrieve their money, they found they had no place to turn for recourse or appeal.

These early frustrations at not being able to access their accounts only exacerbated the hard feelings over what came next. As they struggled to get paid, they became aware of other money which they thought was due to them as well. Few knew about the so-called 'Secret Fund' established early in the war; they only understood that they had started receiving less pay because war-risk supplements were greatly reduced, which had led to the refusal by many to re-board their ships and Trygve Lie's subsequent hurried trip to New York to resolve the continuing strikes. Although men had started receiving small increases in supplements following negotiations with him, these fell far short of what they had been getting before. Now word spread around ships that all the money withheld from their pay had gone into a separate account. That was not entirely true, because the British payments were based on tonnage not on withheld supplements. The payments the British had been making over the years had, however, grown considerably. Eventually, the sailors discovered that the accumulated balance in that separate account totalled 43.7 million kroner, and most believed that it belonged to them. The balance had been much larger earlier in the war, but Nortraship had withdrawn 90 million over the years to pay the additional supplements Lie negotiated with crews in August 1940. Finding out about the fund became the start of a prolonged effort by sailors to get what they thought was theirs, while they continued to struggle to retrieve their savings and other pay from the Oslo office.

Whether it was rightfully theirs is debatable, but the use of the account to pay the additional supplements certainly added ammunition to the seafarers' argument. Seamen's unions organized protest marches demanding that the fund be allocated to surviving sailors, and demonstrations disrupted discussion of the fund in the *Storting* on one occasion. Public sentiment nonetheless remained muted during this time, because some communist groups had thrown their support behind the sailors, and many countries, including Norway, had become concerned about Soviet intentions after the war ended. As the sailors garnered more attention, the Norwegian Government was forced to reckon with their concerns. By then, the press had started referring to them as '*krigsseilers*' (war sailors), which must have generated some pride. The Government formed a committee including members of the four major maritime unions and chaired by Arne Sunde, the Minister of Shipping during much of the war with direct responsibility for Nortraship.[4] Discussion focused on the original purpose of the fund and how it should be used. For the sailors, the answer to that was obvious. It was less clear, however, to others. Back in June 1940, when Øivind Lorentzen agreed to adjust war-risk supplements, neither he nor others in Nortraship or the Norwegian Government had specified the exact purpose of deposits by the British. The agreement merely spoke of 'a suitable sum representing part of the difference between the bonus at the old and new rate, which additional sum would be credited to the Norwegian Mission to a fund for the benefit of seamen after the war'.[5] Did that mean the fund belonged to the sailors and should be apportioned to them or surviving families for the time at sea? Or did it mean the fund should be used for the benefit of all seafarers and families in need?

Most sailors would have anticipated a favourable decision from the committee, since their own union representatives had been appointed to serve on it. They were therefore disappointed when Sunde issued a recommendation in November 1947 that the funds should not be distributed to the sailors or next of kin, as they had asked. Rather, the committee proposed that the money be used for the benefit of any seamen and families in need. A decisive majority of the *Storting* supported the committee's recommendation the following month. As part of its findings, however, the *Storting* further directed that 186 million kroner be allocated from the final settlement of Nortraship accounts to subsidize seamen's pensions in the future.[6] Although this was a substantial amount for pensions, it was very different to what the sailors were demanding. It was difficult to qualify for pensions. Many ailments did not meet the criteria, and all applications became subject to rigorous review. The men wanted the money from the Secret Fund to be parcelled out to them and to the families of deceased seamen. Instead, the *Storting* decision made the fund a legal entity to be administered only for the benefit of sailors and families in need. The Ministry of Trade appointed a board to start receiving applications for pension payments from the fund, and by the summer of 1948 it had received 2,400 applications, mostly from the widows of seamen who had perished, and the fund began paying its first pensions.[7] But the dispute was far from over.

This action by the *Storting* infuriated the sailors even more. They began a campaign to mobilize support and to solicit donations to fight the legislature's decision in court. Many contributed to the cause, and expectations soon ran high that they could overturn what they saw as an injustice. Three years after their disappointment at the *Storting*'s decision, by which time there were supposedly thirty-seven different action committees supporting the cause, a legal team representing the sailors filed a suit to overturn the decision. On 19 September 1951, to their dismay, a court in Oslo ruled unanimously in favour of the *Storting*. Although disappointed once more, the seamen were not finished. Over 10,000 of them had joined the cause by this time, insisting the money was rightfully theirs, and their lawyers appealed to the Norwegian Supreme Court. Three years later, on 13 February 1954, that court also ruled against them.[8] This final decision proved to be a demoralizing blow to men who had been fighting to achieve allocations from the fund for eight years or more. Meanwhile, some had discovered their names had been removed from electoral rolls because they had been away from Norway for so long. Others received conscription notices, since military service remained mandatory for Norwegian citizens and they had not actually served in the military. Those without families also discovered that it was difficult even finding a place to live, since they had no previous residence other than their ships to give as a reference.[9]

The sailors had been reasonably well protected if something catastrophic happened to them at sea. If a man perished at sea, his dependants received a one-off payment of 15,000 kroner and a pension. Those who became 'invalids' received the same one-off payment and a pension amounting to 60 per cent of wages.[10] Many others, however, only started developing serious health problems long after returning home, and this increased their bitterness.

Today, physical and mental ailments caused by Post Traumatic Stress Disorder or PTSD are well known. That was not the case in the Second World War or for decades thereafter. Norwegian seafarers not only returned home without the fanfare given to military units, they also carried with them health issues that without treatment became much worse over time. Few others in Norway or elsewhere had experienced the sustained emotional and physical stress which they had during the war. Most seamen had been sailing on ships in hostile waters for many years by the time they arrived back home. Some of them had survived multiple attacks at sea, been on ships that sank, sometimes more than once, and spent weeks in lifeboats desperately hoping to be rescued. Few resources and little help were available for them upon their return. They were not alone, of course. Those who had been fighting in military units or in resistance movements suffered as well. Regardless of where one served, the law at the time required that medical authorities verify that any debilitating condition was, in fact, the result of participation in the war. Whereas that could be relatively straightforward in the case of a physical injury, the same was not true for mental ailments. The behaviour of the person with the illness was insufficient on its own. The condition had to be tied directly to something that happened in the war, and a medical authority had to verify the connection. What exacerbated the plight of Norwegian seamen with illnesses was that existing laws restricted their eligibility for disability pensions. An ordinance dating back to 1941 covering injuries and pensions for seamen provided coverage only of those sailing for Norway, not those sailing in other countries' ships. That seemingly minor stipulation directly affected all seamen in Nortraship, because they were sailing for Britain or the United States during the war, not for Norway. Strangely enough, this ordinance meant that Norwegian seamen on ships in occupied Norway sailing at the behest of the Germans were eligible, while the thousands of Nortraship seafarers were not.[11]

After the war, a newly appointed War Damages Committee proposed to the Ministry of Social Affairs that seamen with war injuries who had sailed for Nortraship should be covered by accident insurance policies. Perhaps not surprisingly, by September 1945 this led to 12,000 claims being submitted to Norway's National Insurance Administration. In the same year, the Ministry of Social Affairs appointed another committee to examine the possibility of a special pension for sailors, but nothing substantive ensued. A new law in 1946 reiterated that injuries to seafarers must be verified to be the result of a war accident, such as a torpedo striking a ship, an air attack or an exploding mine. Two decades later, only 377 Norwegian seamen from the Second World War, out of the tens of thousands who sailed on ships supporting the Allies, were receiving war pensions.[12]

By the late 1960s numerous studies had substantiated the debilitating effects, both mental and physical, that certain experiences in war could have on individuals over time. These findings led to significant pension reform in Norway. No longer did medical authorities have to verify a causal connection between a seafarer's ailment and his wartime experiences for a pension to be approved. Rather, the focus shifted to the illness itself. Although such developments came much too late for some, the shift in perspective had a dramatic effect. Medical authorities assumed that conditions were linked to what happened in the war. Between 1968 and 1972, over 5,000 seafarers applied for disability pensions, and over 80 per cent of the applications were approved.[13]

About the same time that these positive developments were taking place, seamen received some unexpected support for their claim that the money in the Secret Fund belonged to them. A recently retired admiral named Thore Horve started looking into decisions taken by the courts and concluded that Norway's social welfare programmes were designed to take care of those in need and that the money in the fund need not have been specifically allocated for that purpose. He felt that the seafarers' cause was just, and not long afterwards, given his stature and connections, the admiral was able to gather support for reviewing the purpose of the fund. Newspapers took up the story, public interest was aroused, and on 30 January 1970 the Norwegian Government appointed another committee to review what had happened in the past, assess whether there was an overlap between the disposition of the funds and welfare programmes and decide whether the seamen were due any direct reimbursement.[14]

The economic situation of Norway at this date was very different to the time when the seafarers had argued their case in court. Oil had recently been discovered in the North Sea and production was just beginning. The country was still years away from becoming as wealthy from oil as it is today, but there was much optimism about the future, and belief in social welfare had taken a firm hold. Sympathy grew for the seafarers, given how they had been treated when they returned from the war.

The committee's first recommendation, just a few months later, was that pension benefits for the seamen be doubled. Over a year went by before the committee further recommended that the Norwegian

Government allocate money to compensate them for their service. It did not recommend dissolution of the fund itself, which by then was providing support to several thousand people. Rather, it recommended that the Government allocate additional funds. Voting in the *Storting* was unanimous this time in support of the committee's recommendation. On 27 April 1972 it agreed to allocate 135 million kroner spread over budget years 1972, 1973 and 1974 for payments in gratitude to seafarers who had sailed at some time during the period 1 July 1940, the date when war-risk supplements were reduced, to 30 July 1945. Seamen would receive a one-off *ex gratia* payment of 180 kroner per month sailed, so a man who had sailed for the full fifty months during the period would be entitled to a payment of 10,800 kroner. By the end of 1976 the Ministry of Trade had received 26,000 applications for payment and approved over 90 per cent of them.[15]

Not all who went to sea were pleased by the payments that the merchant seamen started receiving. Many sailors who had served on Norwegian Navy ships felt that they should be entitled to such payments as well. Their applications, however, were denied, unless they had sailed on merchant ships, either as crewmen or as gunners manning defensive weapons. Those who did also received proportional payments for their time at sea with the merchant fleet.

Money from the original Secret Fund continued to provide benefits for seamen and families who needed assistance. By the end of the 1990s, since interest had increased the sum over the years, the fund had paid out more than double its original value and was averaging over 800,000 kroner per year in payments to seamen, widows and families. As the money eventually began to run out, the Government topped it up to keep payments continuing for those in need.[16] Applications have dropped off significantly as ageing seafarers and their families pass away. Eventually, social welfare programmes will replace it completely.

Admiral Horve brought Norwegian seafarers back into the public eye, but not much had been written by then about what merchant seamen had experienced during and after the war, other than reports of how they had had to fight for their pay and pensions. It took another forty years before the public started to learn more about what had happened to them in the war at sea. Credit for that must go to Jon Michelet. Born in the small coastal town of Moss in 1944, while the Germans were still occupying his country, Michelet went to sea himself as a young man in the 1960s, before becoming a writer of crime fiction in the 1970s. But the memories of his days on board ship working with foreign seamen had a lasting impact on him, and he later moved from crime writing to historical maritime fiction. His book *Skogsmatrosen*, written in 2012, became a bestseller in Norway. It is the story of a young Norwegian who signed on as a crewman on a merchant ship in December 1939, just months after the start of the Second World War. Five more books followed, describing the perilous existence of seafarers during the war, the last one published just before Michelet passed away in 2018. These six books, known as the 'Hero of the Sea' series, proved a raging success. Surprisingly, none of them has yet been translated into English, but millions of copies have been sold elsewhere. More than anything else, these books finally made the Norwegian public aware of what their seafarers had endured during the war.

Michelet also was the inspiration behind the belated recognition of others who had sailed on Norwegian ships. He was invited to give two speeches in 2013, the first on 8 May at the War Sailor Monument in Oslo and the second on 17 May, Norway's National Day, at the Seamen's Hall of Remembrance in Stavern. This large stone monument overlooking the ocean from a hillside in south-west Norway was built in 1926 to commemorate the 1,748 seafarers who perished in the First World War. Each sailor's name was engraved on copper plates on the walls inside the Hall. In 1952 the authorities started adding the names of men who had lost their lives in the Second World War. What Michelet discovered in researching those speeches was that many others, not just Norwegians, had died when sailing on Norwegian ships during the war. In his remarks in Oslo he proposed that they be recognized as well: 'We must honour our own sailors from the war. But I think the time is ripe to honour the sailors from other nations who sailed on Norwegian ships for the Allies and risked their lives as well . . . My proposal is to create a memorial record or a memorial album in the Seamen's Hall of Remembrance where the names of the fallen foreign sailors are recognized.'[17] Others joined the effort to 'lift their names from oblivion', as Michelet would later say.

Those efforts paid off. Perhaps the most remarkable act of recognition arrived shortly after Michelet gave his speeches. Norway's Minister of Defence, Anne Grethe Strøm-Erichsen, issued a public apology on 3 August 2013 for the way her country had treated its seamen. She said,

The Struggle of Seafarers Tarnishes the Legacy of Nortraship 167

'The story of our war sailors is a shocking story. About a society that was not well enough prepared to take care of some of the greatest war heroes. About rejection and denial. You the war sailors cannot be blamed. You assumed that society would value your efforts. But you were disappointed. As a society, we disappointed you. Today, therefore, on behalf of the Norwegian state, I apologize for the treatment the war sailors were subjected to after the war. What has happened, or not happened, is also our story. It will lie there as an imprint and as a lesson for posterity. We need to learn about history. And we must learn from history.'[18] Her words reverberated throughout Norway.

In 2014, the prominent Norwegian newspaper *Verdens Gang* conducted a poll to determine who people thought were the most important Norwegians since the signing of Norway's constitution a hundred years before. The public cast the most votes for the war sailors. They had come a long way since walking off their ships in the aftermath of the war and experiencing those years of disappointment. Most had passed away by then and did not know of the vote of appreciation.

The following year, Bjorn Tore Rosendahl's book *Foreign Seafarers Remembered* was published, first in Norwegian and then in English. It contained a full accounting of all foreign seafarers who perished on Norwegian ships. Research had identified 953 foreign seamen and women from thirty-six nationalities who died aboard Norwegian merchant ships in the Second World War. British sailors topped the list with 323, followed by Chinese with 253. Two of those foreigners who perished were women, one from Australia and another from the United States, married to and sailing with their seafarer husbands. Both couples perished when their ships sank while supporting the Allies. Norma Nergaard, the young lady from the States, is believed to be the first American woman to have died during the war.[19] In 2018 the names of these 953 foreign seafarers finally joined the other fallen war sailors from the First and Second World Wars in the Seamen's Hall of Remembrance in Stavern.

Today, there are a number of Norwegian towns with memorials honouring war sailors. A restored merchant ship that sailed in the Nortraship fleet, the SS *Hestmanden*, is now anchored at Kristiansand and serves as a floating museum and memorial to seamen. In the United States, communities with memorials on east and west coasts honour fallen Norwegians at annual occasions. Ceremonies in Norway have become more poignant in recent years, with the national recognition of the difficulties seafarers faced upon their return and the growing awareness that so few of them are still alive. In September 2021, survivors received invitations to a ceremony in Oslo to honour them in commemoration of the seventy-fifth anniversary of the end of the war in Europe. It had been delayed for over a year because of the COVID pandemic. War sailor attendance at the event declined from about 150 at similar events in the past to fewer than a dozen. The few who attended enjoyed dining and talking with King Harald V and other dignitaries before the ceremony. They could hardly have imagined such an honour in earlier years.

Although merchant seamen finally received recognition of their service in the Second World War, the organization for which they sailed has almost been lost to history, not just in Norway but throughout the world. Those Norwegians who remember Nortraship today often think of it more in connection with the seamen who suffered and less with reference to its impact on the war. Both memories are important. The legacy of Nortraship is not a simple one. It was riven with controversy from the beginning, and the struggles of seamen after the war just made this worse.

The executives at the top of Nortraship must share some blame for the post-war controversy. It is not that the organization mistreated or underpaid their seamen. In fact, Norwegian crewmen were paid as much as if not more than seafarers of other nations, even without the bonuses they received for sailing in dangerous waters. They sailed on the best of ships with high standards of safety and excellent life-saving equipment. Rather, it is because Nortraship, like the rest of the Norwegian Government near the end of the war, simply did not give as much attention to seamen as it did to shipowners. The seamen's union had tried to gain a seat on committees advising Nortraship executives well before the end of the war so that those serving at sea would have a voice, but both Lorentzen and Olsen refused to let that happen. They thought that the inclusion of people without experience in managing the business of shipping would not be helpful.[20] Whether it would have made a difference or not is unclear. It certainly would not have helped to quell the uproar that developed after the war about the Secret Fund. The money was flowing into that account long before then.

As the end of the war approached, shipowners on the Nortraship staff hurried to re-establish their own fleets. Their earnest desire to do so is understandable. There were not many shipyards ready and capable of building ships, and the condition of yards in Norway remained unclear. Shipowners in other countries were just as eager to start replacing ships. Norwegian shipowners were anxious to receive settlement and insurance payments for ships lost or damaged, in order to make new investments. By the time Germany surrendered, many had already started signing contracts for replacement ships. The Government was focused on helping them, and it secured the immediate release of ships built in Sweden, facilitated the purchase of ships from the United States and Britain and lifted barriers restricting foreign construction. Some would say the shipowners, if not the Government itself, focused on ships at the expense of the crews who had made shipping so successful. Concentration on rebuilding the country's fleets continued as seamen were starting to return home, only to discover they were not even able to withdraw their savings. By the 1950s, when shipowners were on the road to full recovery, seamen were losing their battles in the courts. And in the 1960s, as many of those seafarers were feeling the physical and emotional impact of years at sea in the war, magnates in the Norwegian shipping industry were increasing in number. The two extremes represented by the plight of seamen and the growing wealth of shipowners tarnished, more than anything else, the post-war legacy of Nortraship.

As a result, for some at least, Nortraship has become associated with the suffering of its own seamen. That is understandable, particularly since it took the *Storting* in 1947 to decide that some of the settlement money from the Nortraship account needed to go towards crew pensions. Had Nortraship proposed that itself two years earlier, seamen might have felt more positive, at least until they learned of the money deposited in the Secret Fund. Instead, most shipowners within Nortraship, including Lorentzen, were arguing that all Nortraship profits belonged to the shipowners.

When Øivind Lorentzen agreed to reduce the war-risk supplements for Norwegian seafarers in the summer of 1940, he set the stage for the outcry five years later. His decision was not made in a vacuum. Hysing Olsen and Trygve Lie were involved in the discussions, the seamen's union was aware, and there were certainly many pressing matters at the time that made the decision seem less important. Nortraship was still recruiting staff while locating ships at sea; the Norwegian Government remained in isolation at Tromsø as the battle for Narvik raged; the British were evacuating Dunkirk, France was on the verge of collapsing to Germany, and shipowners in New York were refusing to abide by Nortraship mandates. Nonetheless, it was certainly shortsighted to think that seamen would not be upset by such sharp reductions in pay when sailing in dangerous waters. Trygve Lie was able to appease them a little later in the summer, but no one should have been surprised that the seamen were upset when they discovered tens of millions of kroners had been stashed away as their wages declined. Nor did it create an impression of impartiality when Arne Sunde was appointed to lead the commission to determine what should be done with the fund in the summer of 1945. Ultimately, the problem that resulted was as much the fault of the Norwegian Government as it was of any individual in Nortraship. Many knew about the agreement and the fund. It just took years for the seamen themselves to find out.

What was happening in Nortraship was new to everyone at the time. There was no precedent for setting up a company from scratch to manage close to a thousand ships at sea. No country had ever done such a thing before. Nortraship started out with fewer than a dozen volunteers in a single location, but it would grow to employ nearly a thousand people spread over dozens of offices on six continents. Those present at its birth set up an organizational structure on the pattern of a shipping company with much larger personnel needs and a broader scope of responsibilities. They had to hire people quickly so that Nortraship could establish the whereabouts of ships and keep them out of German hands, figure out previous contractual arrangements and deliver or redirect cargo, arrange for banking and book-keeping, and much more, while dealing with shipowners angry at losing control of their businesses.

No one in that fledgling organization suspected that the war would spread so rapidly in Western Europe, leading within the first four months of Nortraship's existence to the fall of the Low Countries and France, to Italy entering the war and closing the Mediterranean to shipping, or to the destructive attacks on Britain. The only thing clear was that merchant shipping was in grave danger. Norwegian shipowners had already lost dozens of ships, and a couple of hundred were supporting the British. Meanwhile, ships were sinking almost daily, and crews were being lost.

The provisional decree directing Øivind Lorentzen to proceed to London and set up an office provided little direction, other than the requirement to establish control of the Norwegian fleet not presently on contract to the British and French and to make ships available to support the war effort. The fledgling organization performed remarkably well in making this possible. The decree of 18 May, replacing the provisional decree, provided no further direction, although it expanded the requisition to include all Norwegian ships and provided Director Lorentzen with the authority to act as curator. There was no mention in either decree of ships operating from locations outside of Europe, for example in the United States, and whether they too should be dedicated to the war effort. Such lack of detailed instructions therefore gave the new director wide discretion in implementing his brief. Therein were sown the first seeds of dissension, because those in London, led by Hysing Olsen and pressured by the Ministry of War Shipping, sometimes took a different view to those in New York. Lorentzen certainly understood the importance of supporting the war, but he also believed that shipping revenue was vitally important for the future of his country and therefore that Nortraship must be mindful of how the fleet was employed. To some, he became overly protective of the fleet in the States. The Norwegian Government, however, never stepped in to change his approach, although on a couple occasions Minister of Supply Sunde overruled their recommendations. One must assume, therefore, that the Government fully appreciated the revenues from Nortraship pouring into government accounts, regardless of the controversy this caused.

Given the disagreements between the London and New York offices in the early stage of the war, it seems surprising that the Norwegian Government did not intervene more directly, particularly since it had close relationships with British Government ministries. It provided no more guidance about the use of ships and left it up to Lorentzen and Olsen to manage the fleet and to work together to negotiate contracts. It is hardly surprising that the two met resistance to their efforts. Neither they nor anyone else in Nortraship had any experience of managing fleets larger than a few dozen ships or of leading organizations staffed by hundreds of people. Some very smart shipowners joined their teams, arriving with varying experiences of and approaches to business, many with dominating personalities and strong opinions, and they were not afraid to make their feelings known. This was particularly true in New York, where many owners opposed Nortraship taking over their ships.

Lorentzen was not a person to take criticism in his stride, so the situation there became particularly tense by the end of 1940.

By then, Arne Sunde had taken over as the minister responsible for both the London and New York offices. Unlike most other senior leaders in Nortraship, Sunde did not come from the shipping industry. His background was in banking and law. The fact that he found a sounding board on shipping in Hilmar Reksten, a subordinate of Lorentzen, only exacerbated tensions in New York, which eventually spilled over into London and required the direct involvement of the King and Prime Minister multiple times before the end of the war. It took that high-level involvement to confirm the responsibilities of the Minister of Shipping and the directors of Nortraship, but it seems extraordinary that, a little over a year before the war ended, the Norwegian Government was still having to sort out the job descriptions of executives in the organization that it created four years earlier.

What seems remarkable today is that all this turmoil did not sidetrack the operations of Nortraship. Could Nortraship have run more smoothly? Without a doubt. But despite the loss of ships and seamen week after week, the many contract negotiations and pressure to provide more ships, as well as concerns about the future, Nortraship continued to function effectively and to manage the largest fleet the world has ever witnessed under single 'ownership'. Much credit for that surely goes to the hundreds of employees who stayed focused on the job at hand despite the distractions happening at the top. Lorentzen, Olsen and their executives deserve much credit as well, because they too fulfilled their roles effectively, notwithstanding repeated involvement in some of those distractions. This success helped shipowners re-establish their fleets after the war so that they could again support the nation's economy, and it helped the Norwegian Government pay its bills and rebuild the country. It remains unfortunate that, in the rush towards a new future, some tended to ignore the welfare of the seamen responsible for manning the ships successfully at sea.

The saga surrounding Nortraship remains one of the least known yet more important behind-the-scenes stories to come out of the Second World War. It is hard to imagine what would have happened if King Haakon and the Norwegian Government had not escaped the Germans and taken control of their country's merchant fleet. Nortraship took part in all the naval operations of significance during the war, carrying

145 million tons of cargo for the Allies. Over 33,000 seamen sailed on Norwegian ships during the war, with 2,600 of them serving continuously from its beginning to end.[21] Norwegians today should be proud of the contributions of their country's seafarers during that war, and they should be equally proud that their government had the vision and determination to protect the nation's large merchant fleet and use it for the benefit of the Allies and the future of Norway. Without the help of those ships, it is certain that the war would have taken a different turn for the Allies, and Norway would have struggled more after it ended. Britain would have received far less food and fuel. The United States and Britain might have been forced into a totally different war strategy. It is difficult to judge all the ramifications or whether the outcome of the war would have been different; however, it is certain that the path to victory would have become far more complicated. For that, everyone, as well as the Norwegians themselves, should be thankful.

Appendix I

Nortraship Fleet from April 1940 to May 1945

Type of Ship	9 April 1940*	31 Dec 1940	31 Dec 1941	31 Dec 1942	31 Dec 1943	31 Dec 1944	8 May 1945
Tankers	242	210	192 (2)	154 (11)	135	138 (5)	137
Steam Ships	226	186	176 (5)	139 (7)	132 (10)	131 (1)	131
Diesel Ships	430	366	314 (4)	143 (11)	225 (7)	214 (3)	207
Small Ships	11	8	8 (1)	6	5 (1)	7 (2)	7
Whale Factories	12	9	6	4 (1)	3	3	3
Whale Boats	107	33	22	20	20	19	19
Total	1028	812	718	566	520	512	504

Notes
* Prior to Germany's invasion on 9 April 1940, Norway already had lost 57 ships and 377 seafarers. When Nortraship was formed on 22 April, the exact number of ships outside Norway was unknown. The above number comes from Nortraship's 'New Ship Employment Register' completed in September 1943 and showing 1,028 ships as of 9 April. When King Haakon VII and the Norwegian Government arrived in London on 8 June, the fleet had declined to 985 ships due to losses.

Numbers in parentheses indicate replacement ships obtained by Nortraship. They are included in the numbers.

Sources
Hegland, Jon Rustung, *Nortraships Flåte*, 1940-1941, Vol 1 and *Nortraships Flåte, 1942–1945*, Vol 2, Dreyers Forlag, Oslo, 1976.

Appendix II

Translation of the Provisional Royal Decree issued by King Haakon on 22 April 1940

In accordance with the Royal Decree of 20 April 1940, I, Trygve Lie, confirm as the head of the Royal Norwegian Government Ministry of Supply that Director of Shipping Øivind Lorentzen has been appointed by the King to head the Department of Supply's Shipping Directorate in London. This directorate, which begins its operations as soon as Mr Lorentzen arrives in London, has the task of concluding an agreement with the British and French governments in chartering Norwegian tonnage by provisional arrangement of today, whose first, second and third points read as follows:

1. All ships entered in the Norwegian ship register and are over 500 gross register tonnes and not already in the service of the Norwegian, British or French governments are from today made available to the Norwegian, British and French governments to promote war operations and secure supplies.
2. For the purpose of this provision, a joint office shall be established in London. This joint office manages the ships on behalf of the Government.
3. The Norwegian Government shall immediately intervene in the rights of charters and other licensees in the obligations of shipowners or licensees according to employment contracts of all kinds. The British and French governments take effect from the day they take over ships.

This letter serves as a power of attorney to Mr Lorentzen to terminate all contracts and take all other steps to carry out the Directorate's task thus specified.

Source
Jon Rustung Hegland, *Nortraships Flåte, 1940–1941*, Vol 1, Dreyers Forlag, Oslo, 1976, pp. 254, 257–8.

Appendix III

Translation of the Royal Decree issued by King Haakon on 18 May 1940

Paragraph 1. All ships registered in Norway or domiciled there and located outside areas in Norway which are occupied by enemy force and which belong to

   a) persons who are resident in the occupied territory or who carry on their business from an office there,
   b) partner shipping companies, corporations, joint stock companies or other companies that are registered in or have their board in the said area or that conduct their business from an office there

are regarded as requisitioned by the Norwegian Government, which hereby takes over the right of use of the ships.

Paragraph 2. The Norwegian Director of Shipping in London, or the person or persons he authorizes to do so, has the authority to take over or demand the transfer of possession of any ship as mentioned in Paragraph 1, or to require that any such ship be made available to the Government or to the person or persons determined by the Government. The Director of Shipping is further authorized, either by himself or through the representative or representatives he appoints, on behalf of the Government to take over the ownership of any such ship, as well as in the same way to take over ships under construction outside occupied territory, and contracts for shipbuilding when these belong to persons, partner companies, corporations, joint stock companies or other companies as mentioned in Paragraph 1.

Paragraph 3. The owner does not have the right to use or otherwise dispose of, mortgage, encumber or dispose of ships as mentioned in Paragraph 1, or to transfer a part or share in such ship. The same applies to the owner of a ship under construction as mentioned in Paragraph 2.

Holders of a contract for the construction of ships as mentioned in Paragraph 2 are not entitled without the consent of the Director of Shipping to forfeit over, mortgage, encumber or dispose of the contract.

Ships as mentioned in Paragraph 1, part or share in ship, ship under construction or contract for construction of a ship as mentioned in Paragraph 2 cannot be sold by forced auction or otherwise during forced collection.

Paragraph 4.

1) The Director of Shipping is authorized on behalf of the Government to exercise control over ships and contracts which have been taken over in accordance with the provisional arrangement of 22 April 1940 or which are taken over in accordance with this arrangement. He is called in this capacity curator.
2) With the exclusion of the owner's right, the curator exercises control over all property outside the occupied areas belonging to owners as mentioned in Paragraphs 1 and 2, and has in all respects the right to dispose of and conclude and approve contracts for future such property, unless this according to law or other legal provision is controlled or handled in another way by the government or by a person appointed by the government.
3) Insofar as it does not contravene the law or provisions as mentioned above, the trustee has the right to collect claims belonging to owners as mentioned in Paragraphs 1 and 2, to recover through litigation or other ways all claims such as these have in advance or later acquired, enter into settlement or accept settlement and give a valid receipt.
4) The provisions in the second and third paragraphs only apply to property that the owner had used in shipping business and claims that have been acquired through this business.

5) All payments that have taken place or may have taken place to the Special Norwegian Shipping Account in the Bank of England shall be considered as payment to the curator.

Paragraph 5. Compensation for what has been taken over by the government according to the provisional decree of 22 April 1940 or which is taken over according to the current decree is determined in accordance with current Norwegian legal rules. Further provisions on the procedure for determining compensation with be given by separate decree.

Paragraph 6. The Minister of Supply may issue further regulations for the implementation of this decree.

Paragraph 7. Violation of this decree or of regulations issued pursuant to it shall be punishable by imprisonment for up to one year or by fines of up to 100,000 kroner or both of these penalties, if the situation is not affected by stricter penalties. The same applies to complicity in such a violation. Violation is a misdemeanor. Attempts are punishable. If the violation applies to a ship or contract as mentioned in Paragraphs 1 or 2, the ship or the contract may be confiscated for the benefit of the Treasury.

Paragraph 8. This decree shall take effect immediately. At the same time, the provisional ordinance of 22 April 1940 on the requisitioning of Norwegian ships, etc. is repealed. Ships taken over by or on behalf of the Government pursuant to the Ordinance of 22 April shall henceforth be regarded as taken over in accordance with the next provisions. The Government's takeover of employment contracts of all kinds on the basis of the ordinance of 22 April 1940 also remains in force.'

Source
Jon Rustung Hegland, *Nortraships Flåte, 1940–1941*, Vol 1, Dreyers Forlag, Oslo, 1976, pp. 260–2

Appendix IV

Evolution of Departments within Nortraship Offices During the War

London

1941*

Accounting (Leadenhall Street)
Accounting (Sunningdale)
Chartering
Disbursements
Financial
Insurance
Legal
Maritime
Passenger
Ships' Positions
Statistical
Tanker
Technical
War Risk Insurance (Premium Collections)
Whaling

New York

Accounting
Chartering
Charter Hire
Disbursements
Insurance
Legal
Liner
Maritime and Vessel Operations
Public Relations
Ships' Positions and Ships' Mail
Statistical
Tanker
Technical
Whaling

1945**

Branches Control
Accounts (Leadenhall Street)
Accounts (Sunningdale)
Disbursements
Dry Cargo
Financial
Information
Insurance
Legal
Maritime
Office Management and General Staff
Protection and Indemnity
Statistical
Tanker
Technical
War Risk Insurance Premium
Whaling

Accounting
Disbursements
Dry Cargo
Freight and War Insurance
Insurance
Legal
Liner
Maritime
Master and Crew Accounts
Medical
Office Management
Protection and Indemnity
Public Relations
Statistical
Tanker
Technical
War Loss
Whaling

* Jon Rustung Hegland, *Nortraships Flåte, 1940–1941*, Vol 1, Dreyers Forlag, Oslo, 1976, p. 264
** Atle Thowsen, *Nortraship: Profitt og Patriotisme*, Vol 1, *Handlesflåten I Krig* 1939–1945, Grøndahl Dreyer, 1992. p. 494

Image Credits

1A   Hans Petter Nielsen, National Library of Norway, (public domain)
1B   Conrad Alfred Erichsen, postcard c. 1910, (public domain, brown tones changed to black and white)
1C   Photographer unknown, Pa 0982 Esso Norge N/S, Stavanger State Archive, Creative Commons Licence BY
2A   'Norway's Floating Empire', 1942, Royal Norwegian Government's Information Office
2B   'Norway's Floating Empire', 1942, Royal Norwegian Government's Information Office
2C   'Norway's Floating Empire', 1942, Royal Norwegian Government's Information Office
3A   'Norway's Floating Empire', 1942, Royal Norwegian Government's Information Office
3B   Ansgar Theodor Larsen, Vestfold Country Museum Digital Archive, (public domain)
3C   Ansgar Theodor Larsen, Vestfold Country Museum Digital Archive, (public domain)
4A   Photographer unknown, Flickr File 8620293422, National Archives of Norway, Creative Commons 1.0 Universal Public Domain (https://creativecommons.org.publicdomain/zero/1.0/deed.en)
4B   Photographer unknown, Flickr File 8617530282, National Archives of Norway, (no known copyright restrictions)
4C   Photographer unknown, SA Photo, Finland, (public domain)
4D   Norwegian News Agency, File 266847, National Museum of Denmark, Creative Commons Attribution – Share Alike 4.0 International Licence (https://creativecommons.org/licenses/by-sa/4.0/deed.en)
5A   Photographer unknown, http://www.nrk.no/kana/nrk_gull/1.486844, (public domain)
5B   Photographer unknown, NTBs War Archive, National Archives of Norway, Creative Commons Licence BY
5C   Photographer unknown, Flicker File 6829235893, National Archives of Norway, (no known copyright restrictions)
6A   Courtesy of the Royal Court, Norway
6B   Norwegian Official Photo, National Archives of Norway, Creative Commons Attribution – Share Alike 4.0 International Licence (https://creativecommons.org/licenses/by-sa/4.0/deed.en)
6C   David E. Sherman, NTBs War Archive, National Archives of Norway, (no restrictions)
7A   Atelier Rude, Image No. OB.RP18239a, Oslo Museum, Creative Commons Attribution – Share Alike 4.0 International Licence (https://creativecommons.org/licenses/by-sa/4.0/deed.en)

Image Credits   181

7B   Ernest Rude, Image No. OB.RP20232, Oslo Museum, Creative Commons Attribution –Share Alike 4.0 International Licence (https://creativecommons.org/licenses/by-sa/4.0/deed.en)
7C   Photographer unknown, NTBs War Archive, National Archives of Norway, (no restrictions)
7D   Photographer unknown, Oslo Museum, Creative Commons Attribution – Share Alike 3.0 Unported Licence (https://creativecommons.org/licenses/by-sa/3.0/deed.en)
8A   Courtesy of Jan Lorentzen
8B   Courtesy of Jan Lorentzen
8C   Photographer unknown, NTBs War Archive, National Archives of Norway, Creative Commons Licence BY
9A   Courtesy of Jan Lorentzen
9B   Photographer unknown, Wikimedia File: Reksten1949.jpg, (public domain)
9C   Courtesy of Jan Lorentzen
10A   Stephen Richards, geograph.org.uk photo 2557537, Creative Commons Attribution – Share Alike Licence 2.0 (https://creativecommons.org/licenses/by-sa/2.0/deed.en), (image changed to black and white)
10B   Berenice Abbott, htttps://www.flickr.com/photos/nypl/3110607948/, New York Public Library, (no known copyright restrictions)
10C   Photographer unknown, NTBs War Archive, National Archives of Norway, Creative Commons Licence BY
10D   Photographer unknown, National Archives of Norway, Creative Commons CC0 1.0 (public domain)
11A   Ole Friele Backer, National Archives of Norway, (public domain)
11B   Photographer unknown, NTBs War Archive, National Archives of Norway, Creative Commons Licence BY
11C   Ole Friele Backer, National Archives of Norway, (public domain)
11D   Ole Friele Backer, National Archives of Norway, (no restrictions)
12A   Photographer unknown, NTBs War Archive, National Archives of Norway, Creative Commons Licence BY
12B   Ole Friele Backer, NTBs War Archive, National Archives of Norway, (no restrictions)
12C   Ole Friele Backer, NTBs War Archive, National Archives of Norway, (no restrictions)
12D   Photographer unknown, NTBs War Archive, National Archives of Norway, Creative Commons Licence BY
13A   Photographer unknown, Convoy in Bedford Basin, Department of National Defence, Library and Archives, Canada, Creative Commons Attribution – Share Alike 2.0 Generic Licence (https://creativecommons.org/licenses/by-sa/2.0/deed.en)
13B   Ole Friele Backer, National Archives of Norway, (public domain)
13C   John Atherton, (https://www.flickr.com/photos/gbaku/3418426627/), Creative Commons Attribution – Share Alike 2.0 Generic Licence (https://creativecommons.org/licenses/by-sa/2.0/deed.en)
13D   Courtesy of Joseph Bilby
14A   Photographer unknown, National Archives, Washington DC, (public domain)
14B   Photographer unknown, US Office of War Information, Overseas Division, US Library of Congress, (public domain)

14C   Albert Freeman, US Library of Congress, (public domain)
15A   'Norway's Floating Empire', 1942, Royal Norwegian Government's Information Office
15B   Photographer unknown, Oslo Museum, Creative Commons Attribution – Share Alike 4.0 International Licence (https://creativecommons.org/licenses/by-sa/4.0/deed.en)
16A   Torstein Frogner, Creative Commons Attribution – Share Alike 2.0 Generic Licence (https://creativecommons.org/licenses/by-sa/2.0/deed.en)
16B   Author's photograph

Notes

Chapter 1: Norway Emerges as a Giant in Shipping
1. Lise Lindbaek, *Norway's New Saga of the Sea*, Transl. by Nora Solum, Exposition Press, New York, 1969, p. 138
2. Kaare Petersen, *The Saga of Norwegian Shipping*, Dreyers Forlag, Oslo, 1955, pp. 47–8
3. Stig Tenold, *Norwegian Shipping in the 20th Century*, Palgrave Macmillan, 2018, Open Access Publication, p. 27
4. Ibid., pp. 26–7
5. Petersen, p. 48
6. Ibid., p. 48; Bård Kollveit, *Trade Winds – A History of Norwegian Shipping*, Dreyers Forlag, Oslo, 1990, p. 188
7. Tenold, p. 33
8. Ibid.
9. Steve R. Dunn, *Southern Thunder: The Royal Navy and the Scandinavian Trade in World War One*, Seaforth, Barnsley, 2019, Kindle, pp. 21–2
10. Tenold, p. 34
11. Dunn, p. 22
12. Claus Ahlund, (ed.), *Scandinavia in the First World War: Studies in the War Experience of the Northern Neutrals*, Nordic Academic Press, Lund, 2012, p. 9
13. Dunn, p. 7
14. Petersen, p. 59
15. Dunn, p. 38
16. Petersen, pp. 65–6
17. Dunn, p. 78
18. Ibid., p. 130
19. Petersen, pp. 67–8
20. Kollveit, p. 243
21. Petersen, pp. 67–9; Kollveit, p. 269
22. Kollveit, p. 269
23. Tenold, pp. 121–3, 136
24. Kollveit, pp. 269–70
25. Tenold, p. 136
26. 'Norway's Floating Empire,' Royal Norwegian Government's Information Center, Montreal, 1942, p. 16; Petersen, p. 92
27. Tenold, p. 126
28. Ibid., p. 36
29. Petersen, p. 86
30. Kollveit, p. 288
31. Lindbaek, p.18; Tenold, p. 132

184 The Norwegian Merchant Fleet in the Second World War

Chapter 2: Norway Becomes a Battleground
1. Atle Thowsen, *Nortraship: Profitt og Patriotisme*, Vol 1, *Handlesflåten I Krig 1939–1945*, Grøndahl Dreyer, 1992, pp. 46–50; Tenold, *Norwegian Shipping in the 20th Century*, p. 169
2. Kaare Petersen, *The Saga of Norwegian Shipping*, p. 116
3. 'Norway's Floating Empire,' p. 27
4. D J Payton-Smith, *Oil: A Study of War-Time Policy and Administration*, HMSO, 1971, Celsius eBook, p. 79
5. Ibid., pp. 7, 162, 185, 192
6. Ibid., p. 162
7. Jordan Siemianowski, 'Behind the Scenes in Norway's Role in the Second World War: The Norwegian-British Tonnage Agreement from 11 November 1939', *Folia Scandinavica*, Vol 11, 2010, pp. 53–4
8. Thowsen, pp. 63–4
9. Ibid., p. 86
10. Ibid., p. 60
11. Ibid., p. 89
12. Ibid., p. 62
13. C. J. Hambro, *I Saw it Happen in Norway*, Appleton-Century, London, 1940, p. 116
14. Ibid., p. 145
15. Ibid., pp. 67–9
16. Greene and Massignani, *Hitler Strikes North*, Frontline, 2013, Kindle, p. 107
17. Ibid., p. 316
18. Thowsen, pp. 48–50; Hambro, p. 124
19. Greene and Massignani, pp. 272, 276

Chapter 3: A National Fleet Develops as Norway Falls
1. Atle Thowsen, 'Business Goes to War: The Norwegian Merchant Navy in Allied War Transport', in *Britain and Norway in the Second World War*, HMSO, London, 1995, p. 54
2. Geirr H. Haarr, *The German Invasion of Norway*, Naval Institute Press, Annapolis, 2009, pp.112–13; Halvdan Koht, *Norway Neutral and Invaded*, Macmillan, New York, 1941, p. 60
3. Haarr, p. 115
4. Koht, pp. 218–20
5. C. J. Hambro, *I Saw it Happen in Norway*, pp. 11–14
6. Robert Pearson, *Gold Run*, Casemate, Oxford, 2015, p.57; Haarr, p. 179
7. Hambro, p. 22; Koht, p. 74
8. Koht, p. 74
9. Haarr, p. 184
10. Hambro, p. 22
11. François Kersaudy, *Norway 1940*, St Martins, New York, 1990, p. 78
12. Hambro, p. 50
13. Koht, pp. 78–9
14. Kersaudy, pp. 75–7
15. Ibid., p. 107
16. Ibid., p. 112
17. Koht, p. 85

18. Jon Rustung Hegland, *Nortraships Flåte, 1940–1941*, Vol 1, Dreyers Forlag, Oslo, 1976, p. 14; Thowsen, *Nortraship: Profit og Patriotisme*, pp. 102–3
19. Thowsen, *Nortraship: Profit og Patriotisme*, p.104
20. Ibid., pp. 107–13
21. Kollveit, *Trade Winds – A History of Norwegian Shipping*, p. 297
22. Thowsen, *Nortraship: Profit og Patriotisme*, p. 104; Kersaudy, p. 118
23. Thowsen, *Nortraship: Profit og Patriotisme*, pp. 115–20
24. Koht, p. 105
25. Thowsen, *Nortraship: Profit og Patriotisme*, pp. 150–1
26. Kersaudy, p. 121; Pearson, p. 114
27. Hambro, p. 83
28. Henry O Lunde, *Hitler's Preemptive War – The Battle of Norway, 1940*, Casemate, Drexel Hill, 2009, p. 369
29. Kersaudy, p. 219
30. Lunde, p. 525
31. Greene and Massignani, *Hitler Strikes North*, p. 417

Chapter 4: Nortraship Starts Operating in London
1. Thowsen, *Nortraship: Profitt og Patriotism*, p. 45
2. Ibid., pp. 114–20
3. Ibid., pp. 121–5
4. Ibid., pp. 131–5
5. Hegland, *Nortraships Flåte, 1940–1941*, Vol 1, p. 35
6. Ibid., p. 45
7. Lise Lindbaek, *Norway's New Saga of the Sea*, pp. 24–7
8. Ibid., p. 25
9. Ibid., pp. 24–5
10. Ibid., p. 26
11. Hegland, Vol 1, pp. 255–62
12. Thowsen, pp. 150–1
13. Ibid., p. 294
14. Ibid., p. 117
15. United States Maritime Commission Report to Congress for the Period Ending 25 October 1941, p. 2
16. Thowsen, p. 207
17. Roskill, *The War at Sea 1939–1945*, Vol I, The Defense, Naval and Military Press, 2004 Kindle, Appendix R, Table 1, p. 904
18. Hegland, Vol 1, p. 43

Chapter 5: A Shipping Crisis Develops for Britain
1. Dan Van der Vat, *The Atlantic Campaign*, New York, Harper & Row, 1988, p. 123
2. D. J. Payton-Smith, *Oil: A Study of War-Time Policy and Administration*, HMSO, 1971, Celsius eBook, p. 99
3. Ibid., p.161
4. Ibid, p. 688
5. Ibid., pp. 128–9
6. Ibid., p. 91

7. Behrens, *Merchant Shipping and the Demands of War*, HMSO, London, 1955, Celsius eBook, Chapter II
8. Ibid., Chapter III
9. Ibid.
10. Ibid., Chapter V
11. Roskill, *The War at Sea 1939–1945*, Vol I, p. 403
12. Ibid., p. 154
13. Behrens, Chapter XVII
14. Hegland, *Nortraships Flåte, 1940–1941*, Vol 1, p. 71
15. Behrens, Chapter IV
16. Van der Vat, p. 148
17. Roskill, *The War at Sea 1939–1945*, Vol I, pp. 169, 480
18. Payton-Smith, p.234
19. Van der Vat, p. 124
20. Hegland, Vol 1, p. 205
21. Behrens, Chapter II
22. Ibid., Chapter VI
23. Winston Churchill, *The Second World War: Their Finest Hour*, pp. 512–13
24. Behrens, Chapter VI
25. Payton-Smith, p. 232
26. Van der Vat, pp. 140–1

Chapter 6: Nortraship Expands to New York as the Crisis Deepens
1. Hegland, *Nortraships Flåte, 1940–1941*, Vol 1, pp. 255–9
2. Thowsen, *Nortraship: Profitt og Patriotisme*, p. 201
3. Ibid., p. 202
4. Ibid., pp. 230–1
5. Kaare Petersen, *The Saga of Norwegian Shipping*, pp. 175–6
6. Guri Hjeltnes, *Sjømann: Lang Vakt*, Vol 3, *Handlesflåten I Krig 1939–1945*, Grøndahl Dreyer, 1995, p. 70
7. Thowsen, p. 206; Bjørn Tore Rosendahl, 'Seafarers or War Sailors?', Doctoral Dissertation, University of Agder, 2017, p. 170
8. Guri Hjeltnes, p. 74
9. Rosendahl, 'Seafarers or War Sailors?', p. 41
10. Børn Tore Rosendahl, *Foreign Seafarers Remembered*, Stiftelsen Arkivet, Kristiansand, 2015, p. 7
11. Petersen, pp. 176–8; Stig Tenold, *Norwegian Shipping in the 20th Century*, p. 147
12. Roskill, S. W., *The War at Sea 1939–1945*, Vol I, Appendix R, Table I, pp. 904–5
13. Van der Vat, *The Atlantic Campaign*, pp. 81–2, 119; Roskill, Vol I, Appendix R, Table I, p. 904
14. Roskill, Vol I, Appendix R, Table I, p. 904
15. D. J. Payton-Smith, *Oil: A Study of War-Time Policy and Administration*, p. 234
16. Ibid., Table 51, p. 572; Table 48, pp. 668–9
17. Ibid., Table 58, p. 685
18. Behrens, *Merchant Shipping and the Demands of War*, Chapter VI
19. Ibid.
20. Van der Vat, p. 178
21. Thowsen, p. 202

Notes   187

22. Ibid.
23. Ibid., p. 230
24. Ibid., p. 218
25. Lewis Johnman and Hugh Murphy, 'The British Merchant Shipping Mission in the United States and British Shipbuilding in the Second World War,' *The Northern Mariner*, XII, No 3, July 2012, p. 4
26. Roskill, Vol I, Appendix R, Table 1, p. 904; Payton-Smith, p. 232
27. Hegland, Vol 1, p. 122
28. Winston Churchill, *Their Finest Hour*, p. 480

Chapter 7: Britain Looks for More Help as Nortraship Priorities Differ
1. Roskill, *The War at Sea 1939–1945*, Vol I, p. 657
2. Ibid., p. 700
3. Ibid., Tables I and II, pp. 904–5
4. Behrens, *Merchant Shipping and the Demands of War*, Chapter IX
5. Thowsen, *Nortraship: Profitt og Patriotisme*, pp. 299–300
6. Ibid., p. 303
7. Ibid., p. 307
8. Ibid., pp. 308–10, 315
9. Ibid., p. 361
10. Ibid., pp. 355–6
11. Ibid., p. 316
12. Ibid., p. 321
13. Ibid, p. 226
14. Emory Scott Land, *Winning the War with Ships*, McBride, New York, 1958, p. 21
15. United States Maritime Commission Report to Congress for the Period Ending 25 October 1941, pp. 2, 11–12
16. Payton-Smith, *Oil: A Study of War-Time Policy and Administration*, Table 7 p. 234 and Table 8 p. 294
17. Ibid., p. 285; Thowsen, p. 341
18. United States Maritime Commission Report to Congress for the Period Ending 25 October 1941, p. 7
19. *News of Norway*, 27 September 1941, Vol 1, No 36, pp. 1–2
20. Land, pp. 30–1
21. Thowsen, *Nortraship: Profitt og Patriotisme*, pp. 348–58
22. Thowsen in 'Business Goes to War' in *Britain & Norway in the Second World War*, p. 60
23. Thowsen, *Nortraship: Profitt og Patriotisme*, p. 380
24. Van der Vat, Dan, *The Pacific Campaign*, Touchstone, New York, 1991, p. 65
25. Land, p. 162
26. Ibid., p. 163
27. Hegland, *Nortraships Flåte, 1940–1941*, Vol 1, pp. 259–75
28. Roskill, Vol I, Tables I and II, pp. 903–5
29. Hegland, Vol 1, p. 253
30. Roskill, Vol I, Table II, pp. 904–5

Chapter 8: Global War Leads to Cooperation and More Ships
1. Thowsen, *Nortraship: Profitt og Patriotisme*, pp. 210, 249–50
2. 'Norway's Floating Empire', p. 42
3. Ibid., p. 43
4. Thowsen, p. 367
5. S. W. Roskill, *The War at Sea 1939–1945*, Vol II, The Period in Balance, Naval and Military Press, 2004, Kindle, p. 346
6. Roskill, Vol II, pp. 164–74
7. Dan Van der Vat, *The Atlantic Campaign*, p. 287; Thowsen, p. 373; Hegland, *Nortraships Flåte, 1942–1945*, Vol 2, pp. 34, 40, 99, 126
8. Payton-Smith, *Oil: A Study of War-Time Policy and Administration*, pp. 355–7
9. Van der Vat, p. 270
10. United States Maritime Commission Report to Congress for the Period Ending 30 June 1943, p. 8
11. Van der Vat, p. 240
12. United States Maritime Commission Report to Congress for the Period Ending 30 June 1942, p.5
13. Thowsen, pp. 387–90
14. Ibid., pp. 396–99
15. Behrens, *Merchant Shipping and the Demands of War*, Chapter XVII
16. Thowsen, p. 400
17. Ibid., pp. 404–5
18. Ibid.
19. Ibid., pp. 405–7
20. Ibid., pp. 412–14
21. Ibid., p. 415
22. Ibid., p. 416–17
23. Ibid., p. 421
24. Roskill, Vol II, p. 345
25. Ibid., p. 345
26. Hegland, Jon Rustung, *Nortraships Flåte, 1942–1945*, Vol 2, p. 189; Kolltveit, p. 296
27. Lauritz Pettersen, *Hjemmeflåten: Mellom Venn og Fiende*, Vol 5, *Handlesflåten I Krig 1939–1945*, Grøndahl Dreyer, 1992, p.347

Chapter 9: The War Ends but Nortraship Work Continues
1. Richard M. Leighton, 'U.S. Merchant Shipping and the British Import Crisis', in Kent Robert Greenfield, Editor, *Command Decisions*, Center of Military History, Washington, DC, 1987, pp. 202–3
2. Ibid., p. 205
3. Roskill, *The War at Sea 1939–1945*, Vol II, Appendix O, p. 744
4. Leighton, pp. 220–2
5. Hegland, *Nortraships Flåte, 1942–1945*, Vol 2, p. 376.
6. Basberg, Bjørn L, *Nortraship: Alliert og Konkurrent*, Vol 2, *Handlesflåten I Krig 1939–1945*, Grøndahl Dreyer, 1993, pp. 70–1
7. Ibid., pp. 81–3
8. Ibid., pp. 103–4
9. Ibid., pp. 109–15
10. Petersen, *The Saga of Norwegian Shipping*, pp. 172–4; Basberg, pp. 156–7

11. Petersen, p.173; Basberg, pp. 176–7
12. Basberg, pp. 206–7
13. Message from Roosevelt dispatched by Chiefs of Staff, 9 December 1944, included in Behrens, *Merchant Shipping and the Demands of War*, Appendix LXIX
14. Petersen, pp. 151–3
15. Basberg, pp. 288–95
16. Ibid., pp. 151–3
17. Petersen, p. 189; Basberg, pp. 302–18
18. Petersen, p. 189
19. Lauritz Pettersen, *Hjemmeflåten: Mellom Venn og Fiende* pp. 309–10; Basberg, pp. 319–21
20. Basberg, pp. 328–9
21. Kollveit, *Trade Winds – A History of Norwegian Shipping*, pp. 300–10; Basberg, 250–1
22. Basberg, p. 249
23. Basberg, pp. 262–3
24. Kollveit, pp. 310–11
25. Basberg, pp. 269–70

Chapter 10: The Struggle of Seafarers Tarnishes the Legacy of Nortraship
1. Guri Hjeltnes, *Krigsseiler: Krig, Hjemkomst, Oppgjor*, Vol 4, *Handlesflåten I Krig 1939–1945*, Grøndahl Dreyer, 1997, pp. 478, 486
2. Ibid., p. 482
3. Ibid., p. 479
4. Tenold, *Norwegian Shipping in the 20th Century*, p. 185
5. Hjeltnes, p. 494
6. Ibid., p. 461
7. Ibid., p. 533
8. Ibid., p. 508
9. Hegland, *Nortraships Flåte, 1942–1945*, Vol 2, p. 396
10. Petersen, *The Saga of Norwegian Shipping*, p. 117
11. Hjeltnes, p. 458
12. Ibid., p.462
13. Ibid., pp. 459–60, 462, 546
14. Ibid., pp. 520–2
15. Ibid., p. 526
16. Ibid., pp. 523–6
17. Rosendahl, *Foreign Seafarers Remembered*, p. 165
18. Speech by Anne-Grete Strøm-Erichsen, 3 August 2013, Norwegian Historical Archive
19. Rosendahl, p. 87
20. Basberg, *Nortraship: Alliert og Konkurrent*, Vol 2, *Handlesflåten I Krig 1939–1945*, pp. 115–20
21. Hegland, Vol 2, p. 395

Bibliography

Books

Ahlund, Claes (ed.), *Scandinavia in the First World War: Studies in the War Experience of the Northern Neutrals*, Nordic Academic Press, Lund, 2012.

Andenæs, Johs, Riste, O., and Skodvin, M., *Norway and the Second World War*, Johan Grundt Yanum Forlag, Oslo, 1966.

Basberg, Bjørn L., *Nortraship: Alliert og Konkurrent*, Vol 2, *Handlesflåten I Krig 1939–1945*, Grøndahl Dreyer, 1993.

Behrens, C. B. A., *Merchant Shipping and the Demands of War*, HMSO, London, 1955, Celsius eBook.

Burton, Anthony, *The Rise & Fall of British Shipbuilding*, History Press, Gloucestershire, 2013, Kindle.

Carruthers, Bob, (ed.), *Hitler's Forgotten Armies: Combat in Norway and Finland*, Coda Books, Henley in Arden, 2012, eBook.

Churchill, Winston S., *The Second World War: The Gathering Storm*, Vol 1, Bantam, New York, 1961.

Churchill, Winston S., *The Second World War: Their Finest Hour*, Vol 2, Bantam, New York, 1962.

Doughty, Martin, *Merchant Shipping in War*, Royal Historical Society, London, 1982.

Dunn, Steve R., *Southern Thunder: The Royal Navy and the Scandinavian Trade in World War One*, Seaforth, Barnsley, 2019, Kindle.

Edward, Bernard, *The Fighting Tramps*, Robert Hale, London, 1989.

Greene, Jack and Massignani, Alessandro, *Hitler Strikes North*, Frontline, 2013, Kindle.

Greenfield, Kent Roberts (ed.), *Command Decisions*, Center of Military History, Washington DC, 1987.

Haarr, Geirr H., *The German Invasion of Norway*, Naval Institute Press, Annapolis, 2009.

Hambro, C. J., *I Saw it Happen in Norway*, Appleton-Century, London, 1940.

Hegland, Jon Rustung, *Nortraships Flåte, 1940–1941*, Vol 1, Dreyers Forlag, Oslo, 1976.

Hegland, Jon Rustung, *Nortraships Flåte, 1942–1945*, Vol 2, Dreyers Forlag, Oslo, 1976.

Hjeltnes, Guri, *Krigssseiler: Krig, Hjemkomst, Oppgjor*, Vol 4, *Handlesflåten I Krig 1939–1945*, Grøndahl Dreyer, 1997.

Hjeltnes, Guri, *Sjømann: Lang Vakt*, Vol 3, *Handlesflåten I Krig 1939–1945*, Grøndahl Dreyer, 1995.

Howarth, Stephen and Law, Derek, (eds), *The Battle of the Atlantic 1939–1945*, Greenhill Books, London, 1994.

Joshi, Rajesh, *Norwegian Shipping – The Past, the Present and the Future*, Horn Forlag, Oslo, 2000.

Kersaudy, François, *Norway 1940*, St Martins, New York, 1990.

Koht, Halvdan, *Norway Neutral and Invaded*, Macmillan, New York, 1941.

Bibliography 191

Kollveit, Bård, *Trade Winds – A History of Norwegian Shipping*, Dreyers Forlag, Oslo, 1990.
Kynock, Joseph, *Norway 1940 – The Forgotten Fiasco*, Airlife, Shrewsbury, 2002.
Land, Emory Scott, *Winning the War with Ships*, McBride, New York, 1958.
Lane, Tony, *The Merchant Seamen's War*, Manchester University Press, Manchester, 1990.
Larson, Erik, *The Splendid and the Vile*, Crown, New York, 2020.
Leighton, Richard M. and Coakley, Robert W., *Global Logistics and Strategy, 1940–1943*, Center of Military History, Washington DC, 1995, Kindle.
Lindbaek, Lise, *Norway's New Saga of the Sea*, Transl. by Nora Solum, Exposition Press, New York, 1969.
Lukacs, John, *Five Days in London, May 1940*, Yale University Press, New Haven, 1990.
Lunde, Henrik O., *Hitler's Preemptive War – The Battle of Norway, 1940*, Casemate, Drexel Hill, 2009.
Olson, Lynne, *Last Hope Island*, Random House, New York, 1917.
Payton-Smith, D. J., *Oil: A Study of War-Time Policy and Administration*, HMSO, 1971, Celsius eBook.
Pearson, Robert, *Gold Run*, Casemate, Oxford, 2015.
Petersen, Kaare, *The Saga of Norwegian Shipping*, Dreyers Forlag, Oslo, 1955.
Pettersen, Lauritz, *Hjemmeflåten: Mellom Venn og Fiende*, Vol 5, *Handlesflåten I Krig 1939–1945*, Grøndahl Dreyer, 1992.
Rhys-Jones, Graham, *Churchill and the Norway Campaign*, Pen & Sword, Barnsley, 2008.
Rosendahl, Bjørn Tore, *Foreign Seafarers Remembered*, Stiftelsen Arkivet, Kristiansand, 2015.
Roskill, S. W., *A Merchant Fleet in War*, Collins, London, 1962.
Roskill, S. W., *The War at Sea 1939–1945*, Vol I, *The Defensive*, Naval and Military Press, 2004, Kindle.
Roskill, S. W., *The War at Sea 1939–1945*, Vol II, *The Period in Balance*, Naval and Military Press, 2004, Kindle.
Royal Norwegian Government's Information Office, *All for Norway!*, Augsberg Publishing House, Minneapolis, 1942.
Salmon, Patrick, (ed.), *Britain & Norway in the Second World War*, HMSO, London, 1995.
Slader, John, *The Fourth Service – Merchantmen at War 1939–45*, Robert Hale, London, 1994.
Slader, John, *The Red Duster at War*, William Kimber, London, 1988.
Stille, Mark E., *The Imperial Japanese Navy in the Pacific War*, Osprey, Oxford, 2014, Kindle.
Suhone, Lambert, Timpledon, Miriam, Marseken, Susan, (eds), *Nortraship*, Betascript Publishing, Beau Bassin, 2010.
Tenold, Stig, *Norwegian Shipping in the 20th Century*, Palgrave Macmillan, 2018, Open Access Publication.
Thowsen, Atle, *Nortraship: Profitt og Patriotisme*, Vol 1, *Handlesflåten I Krig 1939–1945*, Grøndahl Dreyer, 1992.
Van der Vat, Dan, *The Atlantic Campaign*, Harper & Row, New York, 1988.
Van der Vat, Dan, *The Pacific Campaign*, Touchstone, New York, 1991.
Woodman, Richard, *The Real Cruel Sea*, Pen & Sword, Barnsley, 2011, Kindle.

Official Reports

United States Maritime Commission Report to Congress for the Period Ending 25 October 1941.

United States Maritime Commission Report to Congress for the Period Ending 30 June 1942.

United States Maritime Commission Report to Congress for the Period Ending 30 June 1943.

United States Maritime Commission Report to Congress for the Period Ending 30 June 1944.

United States Maritime Commission Report to Congress for the Period Ending 30 June 1945.

Other

Johnman, Lewis and Murphy, Hugh, 'The British Merchant Shipping Mission in the United States and British Shipbuilding in the Second World War', *The Northern Mariner*, XII, No 3, July 2012, pp. 1–15.

Miller, Michael B., 'Sea Transport and Supply', *International Encyclopedia of the First World War, 1914–1918* OnLine.

News of Norway, 27 September 1941, Vol 1, No 36.

'Norway's Floating Empire,' Royal Norwegian Government's Information Center, Montreal, 1942.

Rosendahl, Bjørn Tore, 'Seafarers or War Sailors?', Doctoral Dissertation, University of Agder, 2017.

Siemianowski, Jordan, 'Behind the Scenes in Norway's Role in the Second World War: The Norwegian-British Tonnage Agreement from 11 November 1939', *Folia Scandinavica*, Vol 11, 2010, pp. 44–58.

Speech by Anne-Grete Strøm-Erichsen, 3 August 2013, Norwegian Historical Archive.

Stutthofdiaries.com

Warsailors.com

Index

Admiral Graf Spee, 24–5
Admiral Hipper, 28, 30
Admiralty, 23, 77, 83, 85, 98, 137
Africa, 8, 79, 95, 102,
   war in, 99, 105, 125–6, 138, 147
Air Ministry, 75, 77
Allied War Powers Act, 95
Altmark, 24–5
America, *see also* North America, United
   States, 29, 96, 167
   and Nortraship, 94, 101, 103, 117, 128,
     131, 136–7, 145
   during the war, 118–19, 124–5, 130,
     140, 147–8, 154
   oil, 20, 75, 113, 116
   shipbuilding, 112, 127, 138, 141, 144
   shipping and trades, 80, 87–8, 99–100,
     107–9, 111, 113–15, 123, 129, 132–5,
     152, 154

Åndalsnes, 50, 52–3
Anderssen, Andréas, 34
Angary, principle of, 11
Anglo-French Shipping Committee, 21
Anglo-Iranian/Persian Oil Company, 76
Archangel, 118
Arctic Circle, 2, 22, 29
Arctic Ocean, 2, 118
Arendal, 31–2
Arming merchant ships, 82–3
Asia, 8, 69, 96, 118–19, 152
Assembly of League of Nations, 40
Association of Industrialists, 42
Athenia, SS, 18
Atlantic Ocean, *see also* convoys, 22, 24,
   29, 54, 69–71, 80, 90–2, 94, 101, 108,
   113, 125–6, 128–9, 147
   attacks on shipping, 18, 68, 73, 96, 105,
     117, 121, 123–4, 134, 140
Australia and Australasia, 12, 79, 100, 105,
   119, 120, 125, 128, 167

BAM 100, 75–6, 97
BBC, 47
Baltic Sea, 22, 39, 78, 99, 117, 119
Bank of England, 64–5
Bank of Norway, 40, 52
Battle of Britain and Blitz, 97–9
Battle of Midway, 138
Belgium, 66, 106
Bergen, 26, 48, 91
   attack on, 28, 30, 44–5
Bergens Privatbank, 52
Black Sea, 117
Blockades, 9, 19, 21
Blücher, 33–4, 39, 41
Boots and Hammer Plans, 50
Bräuer, Curt, 33, 38–9, 40, 42–3, 45
Brazil, 92, 129
Britain, *see also* British Government,
   British military, British merchant fleet,
   Churchill, Royal Air Force, Royal
   Navy, tonnage agreements, tonnage
   discussions and negotiations, 2, 5, 11,
   17, 20–1, 26, 37
   and Nortraship, 58–73, 85, 88–93,
     99 100, 107 8, 112, 120, 114, 117,
     128–32, 135, 149, 152, 154
   imports, 8, 78, 83, 105, 137–9, 147
   in First World War, 9–12, 75
   oil supply and resupply, 75–7, 137–8
   shipbuilding and shipyards, 6, 102
   shipping crisis, 75–86
British Empire, 4, 18, 48, 96, 98, 105,
   118
   effects on shipping, 8–9, 77–9
British Government, *see also* Britain,
   Churchill
   Ministry of Shipping, 48, 59, 60, 64–6,
     78, 89, 92, 101, 107
   Ministry of War Transport, 108, 122–3,
     128, 130, 132, 135–7, 146, 149

pressuring Norwegians for ships, 21, 45–9, 58–62, 66–7, 69, 76, 91, 107, 128
rationing, 78, 98, 125, 138
shipping forecasts, 19
British Isles, 4, 12, 20, 81, 105
British merchant fleet:
  controlled fleet, 66, 75, 97, 102, 106
  losses, 20, 70, 81–2, 102, 105, 121, 139
  post war, 153
  ship shortages, 20, 22, 75–9, 112–13, 115–18
  size and comparisons, 6–8, 14, 75–6, 102
British Merchant Shipbuilding Mission, 101
British military, *see also* Battle of Britain and Blitz, Dunkirk, Royal Air Force, Royal Navy
  actions in Norway, 23, 28, 49–56
  other actions in war, 78, 99, 105, 125–6, 138, 147
British Petroleum, 8
British Shipping Mission, 115, 130
British Tanker Company, 76
British War Cabinet/Office, 44, 46, 49, 55
British War Risk Insurance Office, 60
Bunkering, 11, 13–14, 77, 98, 106, 137, 161
Burma, 119, 140, 147

Canada, 1, 49, 88, 94, 123, 153
Cape Horn, 4
Cape of Good Hope, 4
Caribbean, 20, 75–6, 90, 113, 123–5, 128–9, 138
Casablanca Conference, 139–40, 148
Casualties, *see* merchant fleets or militaries by country
Chile, 116
China, 111, 118, 140
Churchill, Winston, 94, 97, 114–15
  and Roosevelt, 85, 102, 110, 117, 119–20, 125, 139–40, 148
  as First Lord of Admiralty, 23, 25, 27–8, 85
  concerns about shipping, 84–5, 102–4, 105, 139
Clipper ships, 3

Coal, 21, 67, 80–1, 84, 100
  for ships, 1, 4, 6, 9–11, 14, 77
Colban, Erik, 46–8, 58–9, 60–1, 88, 155
Combined Shipping and Adjustment Board, 125–6, 128, 130–1, 133, 135–6, 138
Comintern Pact, 118
Committee of Imperial Defence, 83
Compensation Act, 151
Concentration Camps, 1
Convoys and escorts, 1–2, 80–1 102, 104–5, 118, 123
Council of Trade Unions, 42
Crimean War, 5
Cross, Ronald, 59, 108
Cross Trades, 105

Defensive Equipment Merchant Ship (DEMS), 83
Degaussing, 82, 85, 149
Denmark, 3, 9, 25, 85
  ships and shipping, 20, 49, 66
  surrender to Germany, 27, 41–2, 46
Det Norske Veritas, 15–16, 64
Devonshire, HMS, 56
Diesel–powered ships, 10, 14–16, 77, 99, 151, 154
Dietl, Eduard, 54–6
Dormer, Cecil, 41, 44, 46–7, 53, 55
Drøbok Sound, 34–5
Dry-cargo ships, *see also* Norwegian merchant fleet, 21, 77–8, 84, 102
Dumbarton, 83
Dunkirk, 55, 71, 73, 79, 170
Dutch ships, *see also* Netherlands, 11

E-boats, 96–7
Eden, Anthony, 123
Egersund, 31
Egypt, 79, 99, 105
Eidsvold, 26
Elverum, 43, 45–6
Employers Association, 42
England, 54, 56, 61, 63, 69, 80–1, 97, 116, 148, 177
English Channel, 74, 79–80, 84, 98, 140, 148
  threats to shipping, 81–2, 96–7, 117
Enterprise, HMS, 54
Erikson, Berge, 34

Index

Falkenhorst, Nikolaus von, 26, 38, 57
Federal Reserve Bank of New York, 54
Finland, 23, 99
Finnmark, 156
First World War, 9–14, 17–19, 83, 96, 100, 124
Fish and fishing, 2–4, 8, 10, 21, 23
Fishing vessels, 54, 56, 65
Fornebu airfield, 33, 35, 41
France, 1, 12–13, 17–18, 21–3, 25–6
  and Norwegian ships, 65, 67, 69, 99–100, 171
  invasion and occupation, 46, 55, 61, 67, 73, 79, 80, 84, 97, 104, 108, 117, 170
  military in Norway, 50, 54
  Normandy invasion, 140, 147–8
Fred Olsen Shipping, 72–3, 137
Frederick II, King, 3

Galathea, HMS, 52
Gällivare mine, 23
German merchant fleet, *see also* ship names, German military, 7, 23, 29, 96
German military, *see also* Luftwaffe, U-boats, 23
  attacks on merchant ships, 11–2, 24, 29, 96–7
  bombing of Britain, 97–9
  casualties and losses, 29–35, 57
  in North Africa, 138, 140, 147
  invasion of France and Low Countries, 55, 61, 79–80
  invasion of Norway, 26–57
  invasion of Russia, 117, 138
  strength of, 26–9, 30, 33, 44, 54
  warship groups, 28–36, 39, 41, 54
Germany, *see also* Hitler, 2, 18–19, 21–2, 29, 87–8, 152
  efforts to get Norwegian ships, 26, 58, 61–2, 67, 94
  in First World War, 9–12
Gibraltar, 105
Glasgow, HMS, 53–4
Glowworm, HMS, 28, 30
Gneisenau, 28
Gold, 5
  of Norway, 40–1, 53–4
Göring, Hermann, 80, 97
Gulf of Mexico, 113, 123–5

Haakon VII, King of Norway, *see also* Royal Decrees, 7, 9, 26–7, 88, 114, 143, 156, 172
  escape from Germans, 36–45, 47–57
  establishes Nortraship, 51–2
  in Britain, 85–6
  return to Norway, 154, 157
Haaland, Reidar, 157
Hague Convention, 11
Halifax, 105
Hamar, 40, 42
Hambro, Carl, 40, 48
Hambros Bank, 64
Harald V, King, 168
Harriman, Averell, 128
Hattedal, Rasmus, 37–8
Hestmanden, SS, 167
Hiroshima, 148
Hitler, Adolph, 19, 24–5, 32, 38, 44, 56, 96, 138
Hogmanay Agreement, 136–9, 141–3, 145
Horten Naval Base, 33–4
Horve, Thore, 164

Iceland, 104, 112, 118
India, 79, 105, 128
Indian Ocean, 73, 120–1, 125, 139, 147
Insurance, 10, 13, 17, 63–4, 91, 95, 120, 126, 163
  negotiations for, 20–1, 47–9, 58–60, 67, 107, 135, 137, 142
  settlements, 144, 149–50, 169
Ireland, 18, 82, 104
Italy, 46, 118, 140
  during the war, 73, 78, 87, 99, 105, 140, 147, 170

Jan Wellem, 29
Japan, 19, 118
  during the war, 119–21, 124, 131, 138, 140, 147–8, 152

Kasserine Pass, 140
Kattegat, 29
Kharkov, 147
King, Ernest, 124
Kirkenes, 156
Kiruna mine, 23
Kjeller airfield, 33, 41
Koht, Halvdan, 21, 38–40, 42–3, 47, 60

Kong Haakon VII, 144
Kriegsmarine, 19, 96
Krigsseilers, see Norwegian sailors/seafarers
Kristiansand, 26, 167
   attack on, 31–2, 39
Kristiansund, 53
Kummetz, Oskar, 33

Lægland, Johannes, 148
Laake, Kristian, 38, 43
Labour Party (Norway), 71
Land, Emory, 113, 115, 149
   and Roosevelt, 108, 110–11, 114, 116, 119
   and United States Maritime Commission, 101, 126
   and War Shipping Administration, 126, 128, 130, 134, 136
Lapland, 23
Leathers, Frederick, 108, 117, 128, 130, 132
Lend-Lease Act and Administration, 111–12, 117, 120, 128, 135–6, 145, 149
Leningrad, 146
Liberty Ships, 111, 127, 145, 152–3
Lie, Trygve, 41, 56, 61, 72, 89–93, 101, 109, 160, 169,
   settling strikes in New York, 94–5, 170
Lifeboats and lifesaving suits, 18, 163
Lillehammer, 40, 44–5, 51, 53
Liner ships and trades, 6, 16, 100–1, *see also* Norwegian merchant fleet
Liverpool 84, 99, 105
Ljungberg, Birger, 37, 55–6
Lloyds of London, 60, 64
London, *see also*, Battle of Britain and Blitz, Nortraship, 21, 41, 44–9, 52–3, 57, 81, 94, 98
Lorentzen, Øivind, *see also* Nortraship:
   appointment as Director Nortraship, 51–2, 61
   as head of London office, 57–8, 63–9, 67–81, 87–94
   as head of New York office, 100–1, 107–8, 110, 115, 120, 128–9, 131–4, 136, 150, 155, 161, 168–72
   disputes with Olsen, 65–6, 89–90, 93, 106–7, 143
   disputes with Reksten, 110, 122, 142–4
   disputes with Sunde, 101, 110, 122, 143
   resignation, 154

Lorentzen, Per, 89, 105
   allegations against, 93, 106,122, 144
Luftwaffe, 26–7, 30–1, 33, 35, 98
Lützow, 34

Märtha, Crown Princess, 44, 132–3
Maurice Plan, 50
Mediterranean, 68, 104, 112, 125, 147
   closure of, 73, 78–9, 92, 102, 105, 170
Merchant fleets, *see* fleets by country
Michelet, Jon, 165–6
Middle East, 6, 8, 20, 75–6, 102
Mines (anti-ship), *see also* English Channel, 27–9, 37–8, 81–2, 85
Molde, 53
Montreal, 6, 8, 20, 71
   Nortraship office in, 71, 88, 90
Mowinckel, Johan Ludwig, 122, 134
Murmansk, 118

Næss, Erling Dekke, 134, 154
   and Hogmanay Agreement, 136–9
   disputes with Sunde, 142–3
Nagasaki, 148
Namsos, 50
Napoleonic Wars, 3, 9
Narvik, 26–8, 39, 71, 78
   battle for, 29, 35, 54–6
   importance to Germany, 22–3, 45
Nasjonal Samling, 24, 157
National Health Insurance Programme, 95
National Maritime Board, 103
Netherlands, 9, 118–19
   shipping, 11, 20, 66, 106, 127, 132
Neutrality Acts, 111
New Guinea, 119, 140
New York, *see also* Nortraship, 1, 18, 54
Noel-Baker, Philip, 98, 123
Norge, 29
North America, *see also* America, United States, 2, 5, 8
   and Nortraship, 69, 71
   shipping and trades, 15–6, 80, 104
North Sea, 2, 12, 28, 54, 56, 79, 96, 99
Northern Pan-American Line (Nopal), 92–3
   audit of, 109–10
Nortraship, *see also* names of executives, Norwegian merchant fleet, Secret

Fund, tonnage agreements, tonnage discussions and negotiations, 58–9, 65–6, 75, 142–3
conflicts with shipowners, 72–3
disestablishment, 149–55
disputes with shipowners, 72–3
establishment and initial organization, 51–2, 57–62
legacy, 168–73
London office and operations, 58–73, 85, 88–93, 99–100, 107–8, 112, 120
New York office and operations, 85, 87–95, 99, 103, 126–7
organization, *see* Appendix IV
Oslo office, 154–5, 158–60
profits, 152
pursuit of new ships, 107, 109, 133, 144–5
relationship with British, 70–1, 132
relationship with Americans, 70, 115, 132
settlements, 149–53
Norway, *see also* Nortraship, Norwegian Government, Norwegian merchant fleet:
economy, 2, 7–8, 10
German invasion, 28–45, 49–57, 71
German occupation, 156–7
importance of shipping revenue, 7, 10, 51–2, 58, 106
neutrality, 5, 9, 13, 19, 22, 47–8
reconstruction and trials, 157
shipyards, 2, 4
Norway's National Insurance Administration, 163
Norwegian Chamber of Commerce, 59–60
Norwegian Constitution. 7, 26
Norwegian Consul in New York, 70
Norwegian Deposit and Accounting Office, 158–9
Norwegian Government, *see also* King Haakon, members of, tonnage agreements, tonnage discussions and negotiations, 15–16, 24, 32, 88
and Norwegian Shipowners Association, 10–1, 20–2
Directorate of Shipping, 18, 51
escape from Germans, 36–45, 47–57
exile in England, 85–6

Minister/Ministry of Foreign Affairs, 17, 109
Minister/Ministry of Provisioning/Supply, 18, 51, 61, 72, 94, 101, 106
Minister/Ministry of Shipping, 129, 131, 142–3, 160–2, 165, 169
return to Norway, 154, 156–7
Storting, 24, 36, 40–1, 47, 61, 161
transport of gold, 40–1, 53–4, 56
Norwegian Leads, 28
Norwegian merchant fleet, *see also* Nortraship, specific ships, tonnage agreements, tonnage discussions and negotiations, 21–2
evolution to modern fleet, 2–17, 14–16
fleet of Nortraship London, 90–1, 99–100, 123, 138
fleet of Nortraship New York, 90–1, 100, 103, 106, 108, 123, 138
German interest in, 26, 45–9
in First World War, 9–12
losses, 2, 12, 18, 26, 29, 70, 99, 102, 121, 123, 138, 148, *see* Appendix I
rebuilding after war, 152–4
ships captured by Germans, 61–2, 153
ships trapped, in Sweden, 99, 105
ship types,
dry-cargo, 22, 46, 61, 63, 66–7, 99, 109, 112, 116, 121, 137, 144
liners, 14, 16, 69, 72, 88, 91–2, 99–101, 103, 107–8, 116, 120, 123, 128–9, 131, 135, 137, 139, 142
refrigerated, 129, 142
tankers, 15, 19–20, 22, 37, 46, 61, 63, 66–7, 90–1, 97–100, 102–3, 107–8, 115–16, 121–3, 131, 137–8, 144, 148–9, 151–3
tramps, 4, 14, 18, 72, 99–100, 108, 116, 123, 151
whale processors and whalers, 65–7, 116, 137, 151
Norwegian military:
casualties and losses, 29–30
mobilization, 23, 25, 38, 41, 44
strength, 25–6, 44
Norwegian Navy Shooting Department, 83
Norwegian Sea, 28
Norwegian seafarers/seamen, *see also* Secret Fund
apology to, 166–7

casualties, 12, 166–7
pensions, 162–5
recent recognition, 166–8
salaries and salary disputes, 22, 67–8, 93–5, 169
strikes, protests, and litigation, 94, 160–2
treatment after war, 157–60, 168–9
Norwegian Seamen's Churches, 95
Norwegian Seamen's Homes, 95
Norwegian Seamen's Organization, 148
Norwegian Seamen's Savings Office, 94
Norwegian ship captains, 3, 6–7, 16, 59, 72, 120, 159
    concerns for insurance, 10, 64
    confusion during and after invasion, 17, 47–9, 51, 62–4, 89, 120
Norwegian shipowners, *see also* names, 10, 72, 170
    allegations of profiteering, 13–14
    disputes with Nortraship, 72–3, 88–90, 92
    in occupied Norway, 58, 63
    on Nortraship staff, 63, 91–3
    replacement ships, 145–6, 152–4, 169
    settlements after war, 150–2
Norwegian Shipowners Association, 17, 42, 48, 58, 65, 150
    negotiating for Norwegian Government, 10–1, 20–2
Norwegian Shipping and Trade Mission, *see* Nortraship
Norwegian Shipping Committee in New York, 70, 73, 87–8
Norwegian Supreme Court, 162
Norwegian War Insurance Fund, 17, 47
Nova Scotia, 105
Nybergsund, 43, 44, 46
Nygaardsvold, Johan, 39, 109, 114, 142–3, 172

Oil and petroleum, 6, 8, 11, 14–15, 24–5, 41, 74, 100, 105, 115–16, 118–19, 137, 151, 164
    deliveries and routings, 75–6, 97–8, 102, 112, 125, 147
    shuttle programme, 113, 125
    sources of, 8, 19–20, 75, 105
Oil Board, 19, 75, 98

Oil companies and refineries, 14–15, 76, 98, 16
Olav, Crown Prince, 45, 51, 55, 87, 156
Olsen, Ingolf Hysing, 48, 58–9, 60–1, 63, 88–90
    as head of Nortraship, 154–5
    as head of Nortraship London, 90–3, 100–1, 106–9, 120, 128, 131, 150, 168
    disputes with Lorentzen, 65–6, 89–90, 93, 143
    disputes with Sunde, 143
Olsen, Thomas, 72–3, 88, 92, 134, 137
Operation Torch, 125
Operation *Weserübung*, 25
Ore, 22–3, 45, 78
Oslo, 24–6, 30–1, 51, 53
    capture of, 32–45
Oslofjord, 33–4, 38–9
Otta, 52

Pacific Ocean, 8, 69, 121, 140
Panama Canal, 119
Pearl Harbor, 118–20, 124, 126, 131
Persian Gulf, 117
Philippines, 118–19, 147
Plan Agreement (October 1941), 131, 135, 137
Poland, 17–18, 21, 26, 33
    military in Norway, 54
Port congestion and capacity, 83–4, 99, 147
Prisoners of war, 1, 24–5, 159
Public Law 173, 114
Pyrite, 10–1

Queen Victoria, 4
Quisling, Vidkun, 24, 32–3, 36, 42–3, 44–6, 157

R4 Plan, 28–9
Raeder, Erich, 24
Rail and railroads, 30, 40, 41
    to Narvik, 22–3, 54
    transport of Norway's gold, 40, 53
Ramsdalen Valley, 52
Refineries, 20, 75–6, 98, 124–5
Reims, 148
Reksten, Hilmar, 91–3, 109–10, 122, 129, 133, 143–4, 172
Ringulv, 1–2, 16
Rio de Janeiro, 37

River Clyde, 82
River Thames, 80, 82
Rommel, 138, 140, 147
Ronda, 18
Roosevelt, Franklin Delano, 44, 115–16, 118, 132, 142, 146
  and Churchill, 85, 119–20, 121, 139–40, 148
  focus on shipping, 108, 110–11, 113–14, 123, 126–7, 140, 145, 148
Rosenberg, Alfred, 24
Rosendahl, Bjorn Tore, 167
Royal Air Force, 97–9
Royal Decrees, *see also* Appendices II and III, 17, 57–8, 72–3
  of 22 April 1940, 52, 61, 87, 170
  of 18 May 1940, 65, 87–9, 171
  of 25 October 1940, 90
Royal Marines, 83
Royal Navy, *see also* specific ships, 42, 56, 75–6, 85, 96, 112, 138
  blockades, 9, 19, 21
  mining off Norway, 27–9, 37–8
  versus German ships, 25, 28–9, 35
Ruge, Otto, 43–4, 49–50, 52–3, 55, 57
Russia, *see also* Soviet Union, 2, 111, 117, 138, 140
Russo-Finnish War, 27
Rygg, Nicolai, 40–1

Salter, Arthur, 115–16, 128, 130
Scharnhorst, 28
Scheme Agreement, 20–2, 37, 47, 67–9, 75, 91, 100, 106
Scoll, David, 135–6
Scotland, 1, 18, 82
Seamen's Hall of Remembrance in Stavern, 166–7
Secret Fund, *see also* Nortraship, 69, 155, 160–1, 164–6, 168–9
Ship losses, *see* specific ships and merchant fleets by country
Ship repairs, 62–3, 84, 126, 149
Ship Requisitioning Act, 114
Ship Sales Act, 152
Ship Warrants Act, 114
Shipbuilding and shipyards, *see also* Liberty ships, 12, 152
  in Britain, 6–7, 76, 85, 107, 111, 144
  in Norway, 2, 4, 150, 154, 169

  in Sweden, 146, 153
  in United States, 70, 101, 112–13, 115, 126–7, 130, 141, 143, 145, 147
Shipping routes and transit times, 75, 79, 92, 95
  across Atlantic Ocean, 81, 90
  across Indian Ocean, 73, 139, 147
  across Pacific Ocean, 81, 90
  around British Isles, 81–2
  to Middle East, 102
Sicily, 140, 147
Sickle Plan, 50
Skagerrak, 29
Skagerrak Sea, 2
Sneland, 148
South America,
  shipping and trades, 15, 51, 69, 90,
Soviet Union, *see also* Russia, 23, 117, 139, 148
  Eastern Front, 139–40
Stalin, 117, 139, 147
Stalingrad, 147
Stavanger, 26, 28, 31
Steamships, 1, 3–7, 10–11, 14, 84, 100, 151
Stockholm, 48, 42, 146, 150
Stola airfield, 31–2
Storting, *see* Norwegian Government
Strategic Shipping Board, 119, 126
Strøm-Erichsen, Grethe, 166
Suez, 79
Sunde, Arne, 161, 170–2
  as banker, 52, 64, 101
  as Minister of Supply/Shipping, 106–10, 117, 122, 129, 131–3, 136, 142–3, 146, 154
Supreme Allied War Council, 55
Sweden, 3, 20, 25, 30, 35, 38, 40, 47, 50, 52, 61, 78, 169
  as source of ore, 22–3
  neutrality, 9, 48
  Norwegian ships trapped in, 61, 99, 105
  shipyards, 146, 153

Tanker ships, *see also* Norwegian merchant fleet, 6, 8, 14, 19, 21, 24, 114, 124, 134
  British need for, 67, 75, 85, 98, 102–3, 107, 112–13, 122
  during invasion of Norway, 27, 29

routings and deliveries, 75, 79, 82, 97–8, 102, 104, 118, 138
Timber, 2–4, 8, 78
Todd Shipyard Corporate, 101
Tonnage agreements, *see also* specific agreements, 10–11, 67, 85, 113, 117, 131
Tonnage discussions and negotiations, 10–11, 23, 85, 107
   with Americans, 109, 131
   with British, 20–2, 45–9, 58–61, 66–9, 107, 122
   with British and Americans, 113, 117
Torp, Oscar, 40–1
Tramp ships and trade, *see also* Norwegian merchant fleet, 4, 144
Tripartite Pact, 118
Tromsø, 53–4, 58
Trondheim, 26, 28, 44, 49
   capture of, 30
   fighting in and around, 50–4
Tysla, 12

U-boats, 1, 12, 24, 124, 134
   Arctic, 118
   around Britain, 20, 80, 104–5,
   in Caribbean, 124–5
   in Gulf of Mexico, 124–5
   in North Atlantic, 96, 104–5, 108, 113, 140, 147
   off east coast United States, 123–6
United Kingdom, 19, 53, 98, 121
United Nations Relief and Rehabilitation Administration, 146, 149, 152
United States, *see also* America, North America, Roosevelt, government agencies, Lend-Lease, tonnage agreements, tonnage discussions and negotiations, 2, 5, 7–8, 10–12, 14–15, 40, 45, 51, 54, 149
   and Nortraship, 61, 89–90, 94–6, 108, 117, 129, 132, 137, 154
   and Norwegian ships/shipping, 49, 69, 88, 92, 100, 142, 145, 152, 163, 167, 171, 173
   as neutral country, 10, 49, 57, 70–1, 85, 113, 117–19

assistance to Britain, 85, 75–6, 78–9, 101, 103, 110–11, 115–16, 128–31, 140
Congress, 111–12, 114–15, 152
during the war, 123–5, 138, 147
entrance into the war, 118–20
State Department, 115, 129, 132–3, 135–6
United States Maritime Commission, *see also* Emory Land, 108, 112, 114–15, 119, 134–5, 149
shipbuilding, 101–2, 111, 120, 130, 141, 145
shipyards, 101, 111–13
United States merchant fleet, *see also* Liberty Ships, 127, 153
post war, 153, 169
ship shortages, 70, 126–7
size and comparisons, 7–8, 12, 14–15
United States Navy, 125
Uruguay, 116

Værnes, 30
Verdens Gang newspaper poll, 167
Vogt, Benjamin, 52–3, 63, 90

War Cabinet, 78, 99
War Cross, 34
War Damages Committee, 163
War Risk Insurance Office, 135, 154
War Sailor Monument, 166
War Shipping Administration, 126–7, 130, 132, 135–7, 140, 142, 145–6, 149
Washington Monument, 116
Washington Navy Yard, 132
Wehrmacht, 26
Weston, William, 135–6
Whale processors and whalers, *see also* Norwegian merchant fleet, 11, 22, 33, 63, 134
Wilfred Plan, 27–9
Wilson, Woodrow, 110
Wood, Kingsley, 108